CASING

Public Relations

son S. Wrench

an Schuman

onna Flayhan

Kendall Hunt
publishing company

Book Team

Chairman and Chief Executive Officer Mark C. Falb
President and Chief Operating Officer Chad M. Chandlee
Vice President, Higher Education David L. Tart
Director of Publishing Partnerships Paul B. Carty
Senior Editor Angela Willenbring
Vice President, Operations Timothy J. Beitzel
Senior Production Editor Mary Melloy
Cover Designer Mallory Blondin

Cover image © Shutterstock, Inc.

www.kendallhunt.com
Send all inquiries to:
4050 Westmark Drive
Dubuque, IA 52004-1840

Printed in the United States of America
10 9 8 7 6 5 4 3 2 1

Contents

PART I. PUBLIC RELATIONS ETHICS

PART II. SOCIAL RESPONSIBILITY

PART III. PUBLIC RELATIONS AND THE MEDIA

PART IV. WORKING WITH STAKEHOLDERS

PART V. REPUTATION AND BRAND MANAGEMENT

PART VI. RISK AND CRISIS COMMUNICATION

Preface

WHY CASES?

Casing Public Relations is a book written with fictional scenarios dealing with real issues developed in the cases. The cases represent a variety of scenarios, scenarios facing all levels of decision makers in pressing matters in public relations in our media and social media saturated world.

The book is edited to include cases that are written for undergraduate and entry level graduate courses in public relations and communication whether those courses are taught in liberal arts, business, or humanities. Because of the enormity and diversity of work done by those in the broad and global field of public relations, from corporate to consumer, to nonprofit, to business-to-business and business, to non-governmental organizations, and social justice campaigns, this book and these cases can be used in many ways within the classroom or online instructional settings.

For each case presented here, there are defining moments in the situations that create defining problems for the project management public relations team under discussion. Cases are written and created by diverse scholars and practitioners from across North America, yet all follow a similar style and structure of writing so that students reading the cases are able to distill the defining questions or problems into several sentences, no matter the background of the author or authors. There are never more than five problems in any one case. This limited scope of problems and style of writing, from diverse authors, is crafted intentionally because in real world public relations situations, members of teams must be able to distill a handful of key problems to tackle at any given moment. This is also done so that readers do not become confused and unable to focus on the important problems the writer intended to address.

A case study with more than five problems is difficult to discuss in a practical amount of time (a class period, for example) and apt to require many hours of rambling discussion. There are often multiple approaches to solving problems and several answers to a single case. Case writers do not indicate potential solutions or best solutions, enabling a class to apply the concepts of a PR course to the case itself and come up with a decision on their own. It is in the case analyses that students will decide upon the best solution, and most importantly learn the reasoning process that leads to good decision making in the fast-paced world of public relations.

Each case is written to end with a protagonist needing to make some decision that relates to a major public relations issue, or issues, at hand. This open-ended approach allows professor and students to grapple with the scenario presented, with an intentional approach, and come to conclusions, rather than having the author come to the conclusions and do the thinking for everyone else. Students engaged in case analysis learn to think, analyze, react, and evaluate so that they develop transferable critical, analytical, problem focused skills that they can transfer to other situations in workplace settings and in life in general.

This is a book that allows students to take apart the scenarios, imagine themselves in those scenarios (but at the safe distance of students rather than as entry level managers and employees whose divisions, jobs, reputations, and causes are on the line). This approach to teaching and learning was most notably developed in the legendary Harvard Law School over a century ago, and later adopted by *Harvard Business Review*.

Within each case, a situation is displayed and explored, using dialogue, setting, and internal thoughts of the protagonist, to create dilemmas that give readers a clear delineation of the problems and point the way to a discussion about possible solutions. Because the most effective way to depict a problem is to write situations or scenes that have conflict in them, many of the scenes have characters represent opposite points of view, enter into disagreements, and offer different solutions.

In the literary world, we call this drama. In the work world we call this the safe distance Case Method of study, so that decisions made in the work world are not based upon drama, but upon reasoning through the drama for information and ideas that bring the best decision-making abilities of the team and its members to the fore. This book is made up of good cases, and what is meant by a "good case" is that it first and foremost is a good story written in narrative fashion. As such, each situation or scene in every case study carries the narrative forward, relates directly to one of the major problems in the case, or provides insight into the personality, motives, and /or communicative behaviors and public relations strategies of one or more of the characters. The authors of the cases outline ideal situations that the writer knows will elicit conflicting opinions about potential solutions.

The authors of all of the cases are scholars of public relations or public relations practitioners, and while the backgrounds of the authors and writing styles are diverse, all authors have written the cases for students and discussants who may not be familiar with the background, details, and terminology of the situations in the different types of businesses or organizations under discussion. Jargon is kept to a minimum and information is kept in laypersons' terms. An actual public relations practitioner or project manager would, in actual situations, be expected to understand the business and its goals, policies, practices, and expectations.

Each and every author, or group of authors, uses short story writing techniques with flesh and blood characters, characters who are intriguing throughout the case. This style of writing helps to maximize retention, and is used in the cases for that purpose. Contextual memory is often overlooked in academic study, but it is the way human beings are naturally gifted in great memory recall, and it is the way we remember in everyday life. Each story element moves the narrative forward and authors do not "tell" the reader what happened but rather "show" the reader within the story itself, with the words, thoughts, and actions of the characters within the cases. While some exposition is at times necessary, the authors have kept in mind that this is a short story and the writing is void of academic jargon, references, and digressions into too much detail.

In each case, the authors grab the attention of readers with a character facing his or her biggest public relations problem ever. Whether the problem has to do with internal stakeholders, external stakeholders, traditional media, or social media, the scene is set for the confrontations, frustrations, concerns, ethical and economic dilemmas, conflict, and deliberation to allow the readers to analyze the situation from multiple perspectives, but to come to their own conclusions.

Authors present situations and scenes without any attempt at analysis: Scenes follow a logical order and illustrate a point, concept, or issue that relates to the problems to be analyzed. Readers should know that no signals are intended so that no one solution is implicitly preferred. The solutions and conclusions are left up to the students who read, discuss, and analyze the cases.

Our authors provide relevant details after presenting an opening that sets up the situation, details related to goals, strategies, dilemmas, issues, conflicts, roadblocks, appropriate research, relevant financial information, people, and relationships. Authors are intentionally stingy with numbers in these cases, using them only to help to solve the problems. This is done to avoid confusing readers or sending them off on unproductive analytical tangents. After analyzing these cases, students will know how to reason through arguments and ideas, come to a decision, and then implement a plan of action.

Each case uses as much dialogue as possible to bring the characters and the stories to life and to show the readers what is happening, rather than tell them what is happening. Thoughts of characters are also used at times, appearing in italics. So in these dialogues, external and internal, students can reason, feel, and react alongside each character.

Why Case Methods for Public Relations?

The Case Method approach to understanding public relations phenomena has been widely used in law and business schools around the world for over 100 years. The process enables students to apply theories and concepts that they are learning in an immediately applicable fashion. This maximizes retention. While there are a handful of public relations case studies books currently on the market, none of them contain the clear scope of what is currently taught in public relations courses and presented throughout this book. This *Casing Public Relations* collection mirrors the content currently being published in the major textbooks in the history and field of public relations. As such, *Casing Public Relations* is not a public relations textbook, but rather could be used as a supplement to traditional texts and utilized across public relations courses.

A major gap within current public relations case studies books is filled by the cases contained within this *Casing Public Relations* book. The other case books in print do not teach students how to utilize and prepare for case studies and real world scenarios with multiple elements to weigh; instead they examine non-fictional case studies of "what went wrong" or "what went right" in high profile cases. Those cases provide useful historical knowledge, but do not tend to develop critically engaged students who can think through new situations. While there are numerous books designed to help students learn how to prepare for a case (Ellet, 2007; Heath, 2006; Mauffette-Leenders, Erskine, & Leenders, 2007; Randrup, 2007), none of the public relations case studies books include the actual case content.

The first part of this *Casing Public Relations* book consists of two chapters, the first chapter gives a history of the case study as developed in Harvard Law School by an extraordinarily gifted professor over a century ago. The second chapter gives students and discussants the tools to use to prepare for case based class writing, discussion, and participation. Chapter Two includes a mini case to analyze regarding crisis communication, social media, and viral videos. Finally, Chapter Two provides specific instructions on how to write a case analysis. This intentionally simple instruction saves instructors time, so that class assignments and discussions can focus on the case at hand, rather than on "how to analyze the case" since that is covered in Chapter Two.

REFERENCES

Keyton, J., & Shockley-Zalabak, P. (2010). *Case studies for organizational communication: Understanding communication processes* (3rd ed.). New York, NY: Oxford.

Ellet, W. (2007). *The case study handbook: How to read, discuss, and write persuasively about cases.* Boston, Massachusetts: Harvard Business School Press.

Heath, J. (2006). *Teaching and writing case studies: A practical guide* (3rd ed.). Wharley End, United Kingdom: European Case Clearing House.

Mauffette-Leenders, L. A., Erskine, J. A., & Leenders, M. R. (2007). *Learning with cases* (4th ed.). London, Ontario, Canada: Richard Ivey School of Business.

Randrup, N. (2007). *The case method: Road map for how best to study, analyze and present cases.* Rodovre, Denmark: International Management Press.

About the Editors of this Collection

JASON S. WRENCH (Ed.D., West Virginia University) is an associate professor in the Communication and Media Department at the State University of New York at New Paltz. Dr. Wrench specializes in workplace learning and performance, or the intersection of instructional communication and organizational communication. His varied research interests include workplace learning and human performance improvement, computer-mediated communication, empirical research methods, humor, risk/crisis communication, and supervisor-subordinate interactions. Dr. Wrench regularly consults with individuals and organizations on workplace communication and as a professional speech coach for senior executives.

Dr. Wrench has published numerous books including: *Intercultural Communication: Power in Context, Communication, Affect, and Learning in the Classroom* (2000, Tapestry Press), *Principles of Public Speaking* (2003, The College Network), *Human Communication in Everyday Life: Explanations and Applications* (2008, Allyn & Bacon), *Quantitative Research Methods for Communication: A Hands-On Approach* (2008/2013, Oxford University Press), *The Directory of Communication Related Mental Measures* (2010, National Communication Association), *Stand Up, Speak Out: The Practice and Ethics of Public Speaking* (2011, Flat World Knowledge), and *Communication Apprehension, Avoidance, and Effectiveness* (2013, Allyn & Bacon). Dr. Wrench is also the editor of three books on the subject of organizational communication: *Casing Organizational Communication* (2011, Kendall Hunt), *Workplace Communication for the 21st Century: Tools and Strategies that Impact the Bottom Line: Vol. 1. Internal Workplace Communication*, and *Vol. 2. External Workplace Communication* (2013, both with Praeger). He is currently working on texts for organizational communication, interpersonal communication, and training and development. Dr. Wrench was the editor of the *Ohio Communication Journal* from 2005–2007, served as an associate editor for *Communication Research Reports* from 2007–2010, and been on the editorial board for numerous academic journals. Furthermore, Dr. Wrench has published over 30 research articles that have appeared in various journals: *Communication Quarterly, Communication Research Reports, Education, Human Communication, Journal of Homosexuality, Journal of Intercultural Communication, Southern Communication Journal, The Source: A Journal of Education*, and *The NACADA Journal* (National Association of Campus Advising).

JOAN SCHUMAN (M.A., SUNY Empire) has worked for decades in the field of public relations. Joan Schuman has owned a public relations/advertising/web search engine optimization agency for over 25 years in historic uptown Kingston, New York with clients and contacts from Hudson Valley and New York City to Montreal, Los Angeles, Baltimore, London, and Berlin. Ms. Shuman has experience with integrated marketing, advertising, public relations, and search engine optimization (SEO) for national and global corporations, single entrepreneurs, and small businesses. Her breadth of clients' needs have been met whether they are in financial, tourism, health care, business-to-business, e-commerce, fashion, manu-facturing, or not-for-profit sectors. Joan Schuman Public Relations has represented business clients as they go public, for NASDAQ trading, and clients who operate on shoestring budgets as not-for-profits. Joan Schuman also teaches undergraduate public relations students and graduate students through the International Institute of Business at SUNY New Paltz. Joan has authored over a hundred articles for clients on health care and science topics, and manages the content for several dozen websites. She has worked with a major investor relations firm to take a health care agency public; and has worked with the I Love New York tourism program to promote cities, regions, and resorts throughout the state of New York. Schuman sits on the boards of several non-profit agencies, and has handled the PR for fundraising campaigns. Ms. Schuman brings the diversity of her public relations experience to co-editing this public relations collection.

DONNA FLAYHAN (Ph.D., University of Iowa) brings both an academic and a professional background to her work in the area of public relations. With an academic background and decades of work in public health campaigns, along with decades of research and publications in media ecology and toxic synergy and public health campaigns, Dr. Flayhan brings a unique perspective to this collection. Dr. Flayhan is currently an associate professor of communication and media at the State University of New York at New Paltz where she directs the Concentration in Public Relations and teaches introductory and advanced public relations courses as well as courses in social media and strategic communication. In 2004 Dr. Flayhan founded and has since directed The Lower Manhattan Public Health Project to help the sick rescue, recovery, and clean-up workers from 9/11 receive the answers, benefits, and treatments that they deserve. Before moving to New York, Dr. Flayhan was a tenured professor and department chair at Goucher College, a small liberal arts college in Baltimore, Maryland. During her decade of public health and public relations work in Baltimore, she developed a service-learning curriculum for Goucher that integrated public relations courses into the Baltimore community, putting her students "in the field" while still in the classroom. During that time Dr. Flayhan led an inter-institutional grant that funded public health campaigns with scholars from the University of Maryland and Johns Hopkins University. That campaign included educating citizens through advertisements on the signs, symptoms, and sources of low level carbon monoxide poisoning, as well as educating emergency room medical staff on recognizing the signs and symptoms and implementing best treatment practices for low level chronic carbon monoxide exposures.

Dr. Flayhan has also worked collaboratively on public health campaigns for Gulf War Syndrome with Tobacco Use and Prevention for over 20 years, with peer reviewed national and international journal publications (from *Annals of Behavioral Medicine* to *International Archives of Environmental Health*). Dr. Flayhan was trained in media studies and public health campaigns at while working on a National Institutes of Health Grant at the University of Iowa and later used that knowledge of media, flow of information, and toxins and public health to inform her work on Gulf War Syndrome collaborating with scholars, and carbon monoxide awareness of sources, sign, and symptoms. When in 2004 Dr. Flayhan moved from Baltimore to New York she began directing what became The Lower Manhattan Public Health Project to work on the public health needs and consequences of the toxic aftermath of 9/11. Based upon that work, Flayhan was invited by the Council of Europe to conduct workshops in Warsaw, Poland on social justice campaign techniques for their All Different, All Equal Campaign. For The Lower Manhattan Public Health Project work Flayhan also received *The Jacques Ellul Award* for engaged and meaningful public health work in Mexico City in 2007. Dr. Flayhan's work on The Lower Manhattan Public Health Project was highlighted in the A&E Documentary *9/11's Toxic Dust*.

The editors of this collection, Jason Wrench, Donna Flayhan, and Joan Schuman, whose accomplishments are described above, bring a wealth of experience in enacting, teaching, studying, and writing about communication and public relations to their selection of cases to include in this book. Now let us take a moment to explain what exactly the fictional Case Method is and why we are using it here.

CHAPTER 1

Why Cases?

When covering any current material related to public relations in the 21st century, all forms of communication, from internal, to external, to traditional media, to social media must be addressed. In college level classroom discussions, students who had all grown up using the internet, chat features, texting, and social media simply can't believe that many businesses and organizations are led by people who have little to no understanding of current media and social media systems, how they work, and how information spreads—virally and at lightning speed.

Students of public relations are often shocked to find that many team leaders and project managers do not fully understand or appreciate the power of internal and external communications and how traditional media and social media have completely transformed the practices of decision making in everyday public relations. The idea that the new media landscapes, ushered in by the internet and then social media, RSS feeds, and the ability for information to spread virally, demand on the spot decisions that must be made within hours (sometimes minutes) of the spread of information is not new. Yet, the necessity for speed is often not understood by executives and whole departments until after major blunders have been made. Viral spreading strategies are sometimes intentional—like the BBC's *Britain's Got Talent* Susan Boyle debut performance in April 2009, where the work of viral video seeding company Unruly Media helped to capture and spread just the right information about an authentic and jaw dropping surprise performance. While some labels looked at that as some internet fluke, the label that signed Susan Boyle within weeks of the video going viral was pretty happy in November 2009 when Boyle's CD *I Dreamed a Dream* broke all UK chart history day one sales. Boyle's debut cd sold more copies on that day than any musical or group of musicians in UK chart history, including The Beatles and The Rolling Stones.

Information gone viral is often unintentional too, which often leads to the need for crisis communication responses. For example, the smoking gun internal British Petroleum (BP) email dated April 14, 2010 from an engineer working for BP calling the Deep Horizon rig that exploded on April 20, 2010 a "nightmare well" that should be shut down went viral in May 2010 as the oil continued to gush into the Gulf of Mexico. It used to take years of investigations for such memos to be revealed; it took hours for that memo to go around the world in April 2010. Even BP's own "spill cam," in place to watch the well at work, became the source of viral video footage that was analyzed by independent experts. When a single professor from

Purdue University called into CNN's Anderson Cooper show and said innocently that his calculations of the liquid flow rates put the number of gallons per day not at 500 (what BP had stated publicly), but 5,000 barrels a day, suddenly traditional and social media opinion leaders said, "hey, that's like an Exxon Valdez every four to five days." The enormity of the catastrophe was revealed. When BP tried to turn the "spill cam" off, the U.S. Congress stepped in to bar that from happening. Thus BP's own camera became the source of the enormity of the leak (all puns intended). That is the reality of public relations today.

Of course, as professors of public relations and communication, we can discuss the nonfiction cases and processes, and we should. But how do we teach students to react in real world situations in this new media landscape? Thankfully, over the last hundred years, a method has been devised in schools of business around the globe to help students see the applicability and utility of course content. This method is called the Case Method. The book you currently hold in your hands represents the culmination of a century of understanding about how students learn and apply concepts, skills, and theory to actual life events.

The Case Method is a fun and active way to learn about a wide range of different topics, but is a method of teaching that definitely takes preparation on the part of both the instructor and the student. In the next few pages, we are going to introduce you to the Case Method, including its history, types of cases, and benefits. In the next chapter, we will walk you through a process we recommend for analyzing a case that is based on a wealth of research written by a range of business related scholars from accounting, industrial psychology, management, organizational behavior, organizational communication, and so on.

HISTORY OF THE CASE METHOD

In 1870 Christopher Columbus Langdell was asked to take over as the dean of the Harvard Law School.[1] Prior to his taking the helm at Harvard Law School, the primary method for teaching law students was a practice called the Dwight method, which required students to memorize information about the current status of law and regurgitate this information in front of their peers. Langdell believed that this method was not the best possible method for teaching students, so he set out to develop a method based on his own personal learning experience. As a law student, Langdell read every legal precedent that was handed down by the various state and federal courses. These legal precedents, known as case law, generally included the facts of the case and a judge's decision and application of law to the specific case. Instead of having students memorize and regurgitate facts, Langdell believed that it was important for students not only to know the basic concepts of law, but also to be able to apply those concepts in a meaningful manner. Langdell put together a set of diverse legal cases into a single volume, which students would read and analyze prior to coming to class. During class, Langdell would pose questions related to a case and then randomly choose a student to answer the question, which ultimately became known as the Socratic method.

In 1908 the Harvard Business School was founded, and the original dean, Edwin F. Gay, tried to implement a similar method to that of the Harvard Law School, which he deemed the problem method. Unfortunately, the problem method wasn't really developed, so faculty ended up spending more time lecturing than actually discussing problems. In 1919 a former lawyer who had gone to Harvard Law School and had been teaching corporate finance at Harvard, Wallace P. Donham, was appointed the dean of the Harvard Business School. As a former student of the Socratic method, Donham saw the immediate benefit in learning by legal cases. However, businesses provided a fundamental difference from law—there are not business precedents written in the form of case law for students to digest. To help fill this gap, Donham created the Bureau for Business Research and encouraged faculty to spend time creating case studies about specific businesses and business leaders as a form of scholarly research.[2] These early cases were transcriptions of interactions between the professors and business leaders related to a specific decision or a set of decisions the individual had made. Ultimately, this form of teaching practice became known as the Case Method, and quickly became one of the primary tools for teaching business students at all major business schools.

Today, the Case Method is taught around the world in a variety of different educational contexts. Every field from graphic design to surgery has employed some version of the Case Method crystallized by the Harvard Business School. However, the Case Method is still mostly widely used in those fields related to various aspects of organizations: business, industrial psychological, management, organizational communication, organizational sociology, public relations, and so on.

TYPES OF CASES

Before we can delve into the various types of cases that exist, we really need to examine what we mean by the word "case" in the organizational context. Obviously, we do not have case law as lawyers have in the legal profession. As such, our use of the word "case" in the organizational context refers to a "description of an actual [or fictional] situation, commonly involving a decision, a challenge, an opportunity, or a problem or an issue faced by a person (or persons) in an organization. A case allows you to step figuratively into the position of a particular decision-maker."[3] In essence, a case is a story about a real business situation and how people could theoretically act and communicate within that situation. Most importantly, cases do not arrive at a specific decision for the reader. As Wallace Donham wrote when he first popularized the Case Method, a business case "contains no statement of the decision reached by the businessman [or business woman] … and generally business cases admit of more than one solution … [business cases] include both relevant and irrelevant material, in order that the student may obtain practice in selecting the facts that apply."[4]

Ultimately, cases have three basic characteristics: significance, sufficient information, and no conclusions.[5] First, a case must contain some kind of significant issue or a series of significant issues in the business world. For our purposes, a good organizational communication case must take on some facet of organizational communication that is relevant in the modern world. While examining how an organization uses the telegraph would not be significant in today's world, seeing the trials and tribulations of how corporate America is communicating with people via Twitter would be significant. Second, a case needs to provide the reader with sufficient information to draw possible outcomes. While all cases will provide sufficient information, not all possible relevant information is presented in every case. As often happens in the real world, people must make decisions based on limited information. Lastly, cases will not clearly spell out what the most appropriate decisions should be for a specific case. One of the goals of the Case Method is to enable readers to examine the facts, in light of their own knowledge and research, and arrive at a possible decision. Could your decision be wrong? Yes. Could your decision be right? Maybe. Obviously, the Case Method is ultimately dealing in the world of hypotheticals, so you will not know the ultimate ramifications of making the decision. The results, while important to consider, are secondary to the Case Method. The goal of the method is the learning experience and the application of course content to the case. One of the more fascinating parts of using the Case Method as a teacher is how different groups of students can arrive at radically different decisions for equally valid reasons.

There are often many possible decisions that could be arrived at when analyzing a case, so some students often become frustrated because they want to know the "best" way to solve the case. If you ask 100 different scholars for an answer to a case, you're likely to get 100 different answers. While not every possible outcome is equally valid, every outcome can be examined and discussed (I'll discuss more on this in the next chapter). Ultimately, there are two types of cases that you may encounter if you're a student of organizational communication: profile cases and fictional cases.

What we refer to as "profile cases" are cases that profile actual organizational phenomena and show how various real people handled those situations in real life. These cases tend to be lengthy because they must provide a great deal of detail about real organizational occurrences. For example, let's say we were going to write a case about the public relations strategies British Petroleum (BP) engaged in after the Deepwater Horizon explosion off the coast of Louisiana in 2010. In such a case, you'd have a few pages about deep water drilling, then you'd explain in detail the actual accident and the resulting crisis, then you would have a section on the initial response from BP, then you would have a section on independent experts and the use of social media, and then you would have a detailed retelling of the various communication strategies utilized by BP and by social media activists and independent experts. As you can well imagine, covering all of this information could result in a book if you really get into the detail. Yet students need information and scenarios that they can read, digest, and analyze each week in class. The non-fiction cases require an enormous amount of background knowledge, and each case could be an entire semester. Such non-fiction case approaches most resemble the original form of the case created by Harvard Business School in the 1920s.

Fictional cases, on the other hand, are shorter cases that are based in actual communication and public relations problems but have been fictionalized in an effort to make the case more succinct. This method of case writing was popularized in the *Harvard Business Review*, which concludes each issue with a short fictional case and then asks a handful of notable experts to weigh in on the case itself. For the text you have in your hand, we have chosen to utilize fictional cases because they are great for undergraduates or lower graduate student engagement. Furthermore, because these cases are more focused on a specific communication issue, readers can more easily apply organizational communication content, skills, and theory to the cases when determining possible courses of action.

BENEFITS OF THE CASE METHOD

By this point, you may be wondering why anyone would want to use the Case Method. And you'd be remiss if you didn't question the utility of this teaching technique. Besides the fact that the Case Method has been shown to be a highly flexible and meaningful learning experience for both undergraduate and graduate students, there are five basic reasons that the Case Method is beneficial.[6-7]

Cases Lend Reality to Indirect Experience

While the best form of learning is to learn something directly yourself, there is definitely reason to learn from the insights, strategies, and mistakes of others. As such, we can learn from others and the experiences they have had in the real world, which will ultimately make us all more prepared for handling situations. In terms of case studies, the case is an easy way to see what types of situations others have found themselves in, and then think through how we would behave in that same situation.

Cases Focus on Concrete Problems

One of the biggest obstacles that many undergraduates face when learning business related concepts is that they have no frame of reference. What I mean by "no frame of reference" is that your average undergraduates (and many graduate students) have limited or no corporate experience. As such, when we talk about theoretical ideas or how some corporate offices function, the only frame of reference many have is what they've seen through their parents or on television. These viewpoints may be slightly skewed, if not completely inaccurate. By delving into a specific case, you have the opportunity to engage a story based on real occurrences that happen in modern organizations. While the cases have been fictionalized in this book, the cases are based on a range of real-world problems that organizations have faced. Fictionalizing the cases helps the authors make them more concrete and easily understood.

Cases Develop Skill in Decision Making

Decision making is one of the most useful skills you will learn in the Case Method. In the next chapter, I'm going to walk you through a highly formalized way of analyzing an organizational communication case. The tips and strategies we employ for analyzing a case can be applied to any type of decision-making enterprise, so this skill will be very useful in all parts of your life.

Cases Broaden Student Insight

The fourth reason that the Case Method is useful for students is that it helps you broaden your own insight into a complex decision. While the decision you arrive at on your own may seem very logical, when you start to examine the decision in great detail you start to see that there are a wide range of possibilities inherent within a decision. For example, when you think about a simple decision like purchasing a hamburger from one restaurant over another, you may think that you're just purchasing a hamburger. The Case Method asks you to go further than just your taste buds and really delve into the ramifications of your decision. How does purchasing a hamburger from one fast-food restaurant over another one impact the world around you? If one restaurant uses Styrofoam to place its burger in and the other uses paper, the second burger joint is actually going to have a smaller negative impact on the environment. Often when we make decisions, we fail to take into account all of the possible risks and long-term outcomes associated with them. The Case Method is designed to help you more thoroughly think through how decisions are made and evaluated.

Cases Help Students See Varying Points-of-View

When you read a case study, you'll undoubtedly come to some kind of decision that you believe is the best one. One of the fascinating parts of the Case Method is the interaction that occurs during a class that uses the Case Method. When you have the opportunity to discuss a case with your peers, you'll quickly see a broader range of possible decisions that you didn't even think about while reading the case. Furthermore, you'll be asked to defend your own perspective and find the flaws in others' perspectives as well. While the Case Method is not a formalized debate, there are definitely parts of the Case Method that rely on an individual to think logically and systematically when arguing for a specific decision alternative. One of the goals of the Case Method is to help you see a wide variety of points-of-view. However, do not just assume that because your ideas and someone else's differ that the other person is always right. Instead, think logically and really analyze both your argument(s) and the other person's argument(s). While examining all sides of a case can help you see and understand varying points-of-view, the process can also help you sharpen your own argumentative skills.

CONCLUSION

In the past few pages, we have briefly presented the history of the Case Method, explained what a case is and the types of cases, and lastly explained how the Case Method can help you become a better student and a more functional member of an organization. In the next chapter, we are going to examine the Case Method process put forth in this book.

REFERENCES

1 Garvin, D. A. (2003). Making the case: Professional education for the world of practice. *Harvard Magazine, 106*(1), 56–107.

2 Donham, W. B. (1922). Business teaching by the case system. *The American Economic Review, 12*(1), 53–65.

3 Mauffette-Leenders, L. A., Erskine, J. A., & Leenders, M. R. (2007). *Learning with cases* (4th ed.). London, Ontario: Richard Ivey School of Business.

4 Donham, 1922, pp. 61–62.

5 Ellet, W. (2007). *The case study handbook: How to read, discuss, and write persuasively about cases*. Cambridge, MA: Harvard Business School Press.

6 Graham, P. T., & Cline, P. C. (1980). The case method: A basic teaching approach. *Theory Into Practice*, 19, 112–116.

7 Ford, L. (1969). *Using the case study in teaching and training*. Nashville, TN: Broadman Press.

CHAPTER 2

Analyzing Case Studies

The types of cases you are going to read in this book are what we call decision-based cases, or cases that require the reader to come to some kind of decision. Every case is essentially laid out in a very similar pattern. First, you will be introduced to the main character of the case. Second, you will be introduced to other individuals involved within the case. Third, you will be introduced to the main communication problem, or a number of communication problems that either the main character or her or his organization currently face. Lastly, you will be left with a character not sure which direction he or she should proceed. In essence, you, as the reader, will need to come up with the decision the main character should make.

DECISION MAKING AND CASE STUDIES

To help you work your way through the decision-making process, we have created a worksheet (Appendix A) that will help guide you through the decision-making process. Please understand that this is a formalized decision-making process based on the work of communication scholars Dennis Gouran and Randy Hirokawa.[1] The functional approach created by Gouran and Hirokawa involves five basic steps.

Step One—Understand the Problem

First, and foremost, someone making a decision needs to make sure that he or she completely understands the issue at hand. If you look at the worksheet provided in Appendix A, you'll notice that the first few questions all involve making sure you understand the decision that needs to be made. First, you're asked, "Who are the important characters within the case?" In some cases you'll only have two or three characters who are important, but in other cases you could have ten different characters, and you'll need to know how each character is important to the case. Second, you'll be asked about the main communication problem within the case. One of the hardest parts of making a decision is understanding what needs to be solved. As such, clearly articulating the communication problem very early in your analysis is essential. Lastly, you'll be asked to look for any causes that you see within the case that have led to the communication problem. No communication problem exists within a vacuum, so clearly articulating what the problems are will help you ultimately select decisions that are useful within the confines of the specific case.

In addition to a basic understanding of the problems and causes of the case, we also think it's important to start thinking about how the relevant organizational communication literature applies to the case at this point. One mistake that we can make is to come up with a decision and then to try to find relevant research to support the decision we've already made. However, when we look at research in retrospect, we often miss out on more logical choices.

Step Two—Select Criteria

The word "criterion" refers to a standard by which we can judge something (FYI—"criterion" is singular and "criteria" is plural). Of course, in the case of a decision, we are searching for standards by which we can judge our decisions. Previous research in the area of case study analysis has identified both quantitative and qualitative criteria that may help individuals and organizations judge their decisions.[2] Quantitative criteria are called such because they can be easily numerically measured and computed as having an impact on business functioning. Qualitative criteria, on the other hand, are criteria that are not easily numerically measured or computed. Table 2.1 shows a list of both quantitative and qualitative criteria for organizational communication cases. Please understand that these criteria are not exhaustive, so other criteria could definitely be added to the list. Furthermore, there are some instances where quantitative criteria are qualitatively applied and vice-versa, so this list is intended as a general list of possible criteria to be applied in a decision-making situation. While some of these criteria may be familiar to you, others may not be, so let's briefly explain what each of the criteria mean.

Quantitative Criteria

Profit. The money a business makes after accounting for all the expenses is its profit. At the end of the day, all organizations must be profitable or they will disappear. As such, whether an organization is a for-profit or a non-profit organization, the organization must be concerned with profit.

Cost. If profit is the right hand of an organization, then cost is the left hand of the organization. Cost can be defined as the price paid or required for acquiring, producing, or maintaining a product or service. All organizations have costs. The obvious goal is to ensure that the costs of your organization are less than the profits. However, the old adage that sometimes you have to spend money to make money is also true, but the goal is to ensure that your profits outweigh your costs.

Return on Investment. One concept that isn't overly discussed in many communication textbooks is an organization's return on investment (ROI). According to Patricia and Jack Phillips of the ROI Institute, an ROI is the "ultimate measure of accountability that answers the question: Is there a financial return for investing in a program, process, initiative, or performance improvement solution."[3] The ROI focuses on the benefits and costs gained from a specific endeavor. While the idea of conducting a cost-benefit analysis dates back to an article written by a French engineer named Jules Dupuit in 1848, the process of conducting a cost-benefit analysis was practically developed by the United States Corp of Engineers during the 1930s. A basic cost-benefit analysis is simple to calculate:

TABLE 2.1 *Decision Criteria*

Quantitative	Qualitative
Profit	Customer Satisfaction
Cost	Competitive Advantage
Return on Investment	Corporate Image
Cash Flow	Goodwill
Inventory Turn	Cultural Sensitivity
Productivity	Employee Motivation
Efficiency	Job Satisfaction

Capacity	Employee Health
	  - Physical
	  - Psychological
	  - Spiritual

Delivery Time	Safety
Quality	Synergy

Quantity	Ethics
	  - Business
	  - Communication

Errors	Innovation
Growth Rate	Obsolescence
Market Share	Flexibility

Risk
  - Physical
  - Organizational
	Pragmatism

Staff Turnover	Ease of Implementation

$$\text{Benefit Cost Ratio} \quad = \quad \frac{\text{Benefits}}{\text{Costs}}$$

The ROI is an extension of the cost-benefit analysis that was developed in the 1970s and 80s, and really became a hallmark of business measurement in the 1990s. Where a simple cost-benefit ratio examines whether the costs outweigh the benefits, the ROI wants to know how beneficial something was once the costs are balanced out of the equation. For example, imagine you invest $1 in a lemonade stand. At the end of the day, the lemonade entrepreneur hands you back $2. Because your initial investment was $1, we automatically subtract that from our profit, which leaves us with a net benefit of $1. Here is how we would calculate the ROI:

ROI (%) = (Net Benefits / Costs) * 100

ROI (%) = (1 / 1) * 100

ROI (%) = (1) * 100

ROI (%) = 100

What this says is that for every $1 we invested in the lemonade stand, we got back $1 after the costs were covered. Obviously, in the business world, the goal is to have much higher returns on investments than an ROI of 100%. Often ROIs less than 300% are considered losses in some organizations.

Cash Flow. Another important concept related to the amount of money an organization is taking in and spending is cash flow. Cash flow is the amount of cash a company generates and uses during a period. Cash inflow is money an organization has entering an organization from profits or investments. Cash outflow then is money that an organization has to spend because of expenses or investments. An organization must have enough inflow to balance its outflow. Having enough cash on hand ensures that an organization can meet its basic obligations in terms of expenses. If an organization's money is tied up in various investments and it does not have cash on hand, then the organization may become insolvent because the organization cannot meet its basic financial obligations.

Inventory Turn. Inventory turn is very important for organizations that produce any kind of product. Inventory turn can be defined as the number of times inventory is sold or used in a time period (e.g., a month, six months, one year, etc.). Obviously, if inventory is sitting on your shelves, then you're not making money off that inventory. Ultimately, the goal of any production-oriented organization is to turn the inventory as often as possible.

Productivity. Productivity examines the relationship between the amount of input into a system and the resulting output. Let's say you run a cleaning service and you know that if you hire three workers (input into the system), then you can clean nine office (resulting output). Ultimately, the amount of input into your system should positively affect your productivity.

Efficiency. From a business perspective, efficiency examines the relationship between means and ends, and is closely related to productivity. If a business process is efficient, then the right amount of input is in place to achieve a desired output. If an organization is inefficient, then the organization could either 1) use fewer inputs to produce the same output (lay people off and expect the same amount of work to be accomplished), or 2) the current inputs should produce a greater end result (keep the same number of workers, but expect them to do more). The goal of efficiency is to streamline a process without reaching the point of diminished returns, when the new input level is no longer able to reach the desired output level.

Capacity. Capacity is a concept closely related to productivity, and refers to the maximum amount or number that can be received or contained. Imagine you own a warehouse and supply coffee-related products to the West Coast. At some point, your warehouse will reach a point where you can no longer physically put any more material within the warehouse; this is capacity.

Delivery Time. Organizations that deal with products or services must be concerned with their delivery times, or the length of time it takes to deliver a product or service once a customer has ordered the product or service. If you're building a skyscraper, then your delivery time may be seen in years, but if you're delivering a textbook ordered on the internet, your delivery time should be in days. Different products and services will require different delivery times. One way to make your organization stand out is to ensure that you deliver a quality product or service as quickly as possible.

Quality. Quality refers to producing or providing products or services that meet the expressed and/or implied requirements of an organization's customers. While all organizations should strive for a specified level of quality, perfection may not be a realistic ultimate goal.

Quantity. Quantity is one of the easiest criteria to understand because it's a base count of some product or service. More formally, quantity is defined as the extent, size, or sum of countable or measurable discrete events, objects, or phenomena, expressed as a numerical value.

Errors. Whether we like them or not, eventually errors happen. In this sense, any product or service may lead to a mistake or a deviation from the intended output. The public often doesn't complain about some errors but becomes enraged at other errors when they occur. Obviously, errors that lead to harm are considerably more important than errors that do not cause harm to people. An error that causes a production line to slow down may lose revenue for the corporation, but an error on a production line that causes someone to lose an arm could be detrimental both to the corporation's profit and to its public image. Furthermore, there is a strong negative relationship between delivery time and quality. Depending on the product or service, you may side on either delivery time or quality. The faster you try to produce a product or deliver a service, the more likely you will have errors. If, on the other hand, you desire a high quality product or service, then delivery time will be slower as quality inspection is built into the system to prevent errors. There is also a negative relationship that exists between quality and quantity. The higher the quantity, the more likely you will have errors along the way. The higher your desired quality, the lower your quantity should be, which will lead to fewer errors.

Growth Rate. In an ideal economic environment, an organization will continue to increase its ability to provide products and services at a desired pace. As such, growth rate is the increase in the demand for a particular product or service over time. For growth rate to be effective, the organization needs to balance the requirements for new raw materials, employees, and so on into the organization (input), and the processing of those inputs in the creation of products and services (throughput), with its customer needs and desires (output). If an organization has too many new inputs and no outputs, the organization will become insolvent over time. If an organization doesn't have enough inputs or the throughput process is too slow, then the organization will not meet its obligations to its customers, which could lead to insolvency as well. Ultimately, an organization wants to ensure that it is able to increase the amounts of input and increase the throughput process in direct relationship to the demand from customers.

Market Share. Market share refers to the percentage of total industry sales that are made up by a particular company's individual sales. If you're in a very niche industry (e.g., canine acupuncture or knitted pencil cozies), you may have 100% of the market share. On the other hand, if you're a fast food restaurant specializing in hamburgers, then you may be competing with a large number of other organizations for the same market share.

Risk. For our purposes, risk can be defined as the chance that something negative will occur. We can break risk down into two categories: physical risk and organizational risk.

Physical risk. Physical risk is the likelihood that an individual will suffer loss of life or be injured in some fashion. As mandated by federal law, all organizations must be somewhat aware of the types of physical risks to which their employees are exposed. Some organizations innately have more physical risks associated with their business sector (e.g., the fishing industry, timber industry, etc.), and so considering the importance of risk becomes very important when making all kinds of decisions.

Organizational risk. Organizational risk, on the other hand, examines an organization's return on investment. Whether the investment is in a new employee, product, service, or financial investment, all organizations take risks when they invest. Often these investments do not turn out in favor of the organization. While having some risk will definitely help an organization grow, too much risk can end up sinking an organization if all of the returns on investment are lower than originally anticipated.

Employee Turnover and Downsizing. The final quantitative criterion is staff turnover, or the rate at which an organization gains and loses employees (includes both voluntary and involuntary turnover). Voluntary turnover occurs when an employee quits her or his job, whereas involuntary turnover is when an employer must ask an employee to quit (either in a firing or downsizing context). If you have too much staff turnover, the costs of hiring and training new employees may go through the roof. If you don't have any staff turnover, you may end up with a stagnant employee base that doesn't innovate. Most organizations attempt to hire and cultivate a working environment that keeps employees satisfied and engaged in their work, to avoid voluntary turnover while ensuring that "new blood" is regularly integrated into the organization.

Qualitative Criteria

The word "qualitative" refers to the relating to, or the measurement of or by, the quality of something rather than its quantity. In this respect, the word "quality" then is an examination of a degree or standard of excellence related to something. When we discuss qualitative criteria we are examining how organizations can excel within a specific category, but these categories are innately more arbitrary and not immediately numerically measurable. For example, the first criterion we'll examine is customer satisfaction. While most people can intrinsically understand what is meant by "customer satisfaction," there is no clear quantity immediately associated with the idea of customer satisfaction. While there are metrics that have been designed to attempt to measure all of the qualitative criteria discussed below, the qualitative criteria are innately nonnumerical. Let's look at all of the qualitative criteria discussed in Table 2.1.

Customer Satisfaction. Most organizations understand that making sure you have customers who are satisfied with the product or service is extremely important for ensuring that current customers become repeat customers. As a criterion, one must always question whether a decision being made is likely to increase customer satisfaction, maintain current satisfaction levels, or possibly decrease customer satisfaction.

Competitive Advantage. Competitive advantage is the superiority gained by an organization when the organization compares itself with products and services of other organizations within its target market. There are two ways an organization can make itself competitive. First, the organization can provide the same value as its competitors but at a lower price. In this case, the organization is figuring out how to manufacture a product or deliver a service in a fashion that is cheaper than its competitors. Another way an organization can compete is to set itself up as a luxury option and then charge more for the base product but sell less of the actual product. In essence, you're creating the myth that your product is a luxury product to be desired. While you may not sell as many products or services, the increased price offsets any value you lose and makes you competitive within your target market.

Corporate Image. Corporate image refers to the representation that an organization creates about itself for various stakeholders (employees, stockholders, customers, etc.). While an organization's ultimate image is based on the perceptions of various stakeholders, organizations can help foster a specific image through both internal communication and external communication. Common thematic areas involved in corporate image include the prestige of the organization, quality of its products and services, reputation of organizational leadership, perception of the organization in terms of its relationship to the environment, and so on.

Goodwill. Goodwill, as an organizational criterion, relates to an accounting concept that has been around for many years. In this respect, goodwill is seen as the intangible value of the organization that goes beyond the physical and non-physical assets of the organization (e.g., people, property, finances, etc.) and is generally based on stakeholder perceptions of the firm's reputation. From a communication perspective, goodwill refers to an individual's perception of another's perceived caring.[4] In this case, do you, as an organizational stakeholder, believe that an organization cares about you as an individual both as a stakeholder and as a person? Ultimately, the accounting and communication perspectives on goodwill are not mutually exclusive. While the accounting perspective tries to determine how organizations can quantify goodwill and make it an asset that can have clear value, the communication perspective lends itself to understanding how an organization actually develops goodwill. Organizations can build perceptions of goodwill, but these perceptions are built over a lengthy period of time. Ultimately goodwill is built through four basic functions: 1) expenditures on public relations and marketing; 2) products and services that meet and exceed customer expectations; 3) investment in the creation of long-lasting customer-provider relationships; and 4) organizational leadership that is perceived as ethical. Once an organization has built goodwill, generally the only way to negate that goodwill is through some kind of indiscretion by organizational leadership.

Cultural Sensitivity. Cultural sensitivity is the degree to which an organization is aware of the differences and similarities of different cultures and how culture impacts individual attitudes, values, beliefs, and behaviors. In the United States, there are a ton of different cultures represented, and organizations should be sensitive to their employees' needs and their customers' needs with respect to those cultures. Often organizations must balance various cultural needs that conflict, so organizational decision makers should tread thoughtfully when making decisions that relate to cultural issues.

Employee Motivation. Motivation, generally speaking, is the force that drives an individual to achieve her or his goals.[5] For organizational purposes, employee motivation then is the force that drives individual employees to achieve both the employee's goals at work and the organization's goals. Generally speaking, we break employee motivations into two basic categories: internal and external. Internal motivators are those forces that exist within an individual and drive her or him to achieve a goal. An example of an internal motivator could be work ethic. If someone believes in a strong work ethic, he or she may be more motivated to help achieve an organization's goals. If another person has a weak work ethic, he or she may be unmotivated to achieve an organization's goals. The second category of motivators is external, or factors outside an individual that can influence the individual to strive toward achieving a goal. One of the most common external motivators is monetary reward. If you're told that you'll receive a bonus if a product is produced on time, you'll be more motivated to achieve the organization's goal because you see a direct personal benefit.

Job Satisfaction. Job satisfaction, like employee motivation, is a concept that is very intangible and ambiguous. Job satisfaction is the emotional reaction that an individual has about her or his job. If people have positive emotional reactions to their jobs, they will be satisfied and content, whereas individuals who have negative emotional reactions will be unsatisfied. Ultimately, an individual's job satisfaction will impact her or his attitudes, values, beliefs, and behaviors on the job.

Employee Health. Employee health looks at the totality of an individual employee's physical, psychological, and spiritual well-being. In an ideal world, people would be able to disassociate their work life from other parts of their lives, but that is not realistic. As such, there has been an increased focus in considering employee health.

Physical health. Physical health refers to the physical well-being of an individual. When individuals are sick and unhealthy, they miss more work and are not as productive as when they are healthy. As such, many organizations are now investing a great deal of money to ensure that employees maintain their physical health, because it is actually a very good return on investment.[6]

Psychological health. Psychological health is the extent to which an individual is cognitively and emotionally well. Not only can a decrease in someone's psychological health be problematic for the individual, but her or his work performance can also be greatly negatively impacted as well. While there are some characteristics that can negatively impact an individual's psychological health that are outside the organization's control (e.g., divorce, ailing parent, mental disorder, etc.), there are others that are clearly based within the organization and can be curtailed by a vigilant organization (e.g., excessive stress, bullying, charlatanism, incivility, etc.).

Spiritual health. The notion of spiritual health is a fairly recent one for many organizational academics. As such, many organizational communication textbooks do not really broach the subject. Spiritual health can be defined as the "the enhancement of spiritual oneness with whatever a person considers to be more than oneself as an individual with reason, experience, and intuition; the ongoing development of an adherence to a responsible ethical system."[7] As with both physical and psychological health, when individuals do not feel spiritually healthy, their work performance can be negatively impacted to the organization's detriment.

Safety. One of the basic needs anyone has in a modern workplace is the feeling of safety. Whether this is safety from being unduly exposed to an organizational hazard (e.g., chemicals, heavy machinery, etc.) or safety from being exposed to workplace aggression and violence, people have an inherent need to be safe. You will never get people to work at their optimum levels within an organization if they don't feel safe.

Synergy. The notion of synergy stems from systems theory and basically states that the sum of the whole is greater than the sum of its parts. Practically speaking, synergy is the idea that individual actors, dynamics, materials, objects, processes, or systems will not help an organization as much as all of those parts working harmoniously with one another. For organizational optimization, all parts within an organization need to be working together to produce an optimal organizational outcome.

Ethics. Ethics, at its most basic level, is the discussion of whether a set of means justifies the desired ends. Ethics can be further explained, as a "critical analysis of cultural values to determine the validity of their vigorous rightness or wrongness in terms of two major criteria: truth and justice. Ethics is examining the relation of an individual to society, to nature, and/or to God. How do people make ethical decisions? They are influenced by how they perceive themselves in relation to goodness and/or excellence."[8] For our purposes, we divide ethics into two basic categories: business and communication.

Business ethics. Business ethics is defined as the determination of various business practices, processes, and outcomes as right or wrong. Owen and David Cherrington[9] discuss twelve common ethical lapses that happen in modern organizations:

- Taking things that do not belong to you (stealing);
- Saying things that you know are not true (lying);
- False impressions (fraud and deceit);
- Conflict of interest and influence buying (bribes, payoffs, and kickbacks);
- Hiding versus divulging information;
- Unfair advantage (cheating);
- Personal decadence;
- Interpersonal abuse (physical violence, sexual harassment, emotional abuse, abuse of one's position, racism, heterosexism, ageism, and sexism);
- Organizational abuse (inequity in compensation, performance appraisals that destroy self-esteem, transfers or time pressures that destroy family life, terminating people through no fault of their own, encouraging loyalty and not rewarding it, and creating the myth that the organization will benevolently protect or direct an employee's career are all examples of how organizations abuse employees);
- Rule violations;
- Accessory to unethical acts;
- and moral balance (ethical dilemmas).

Communication ethics. Communication ethics is defined as the determination of various organizational communication practices, processes, and outcomes as right or wrong. W. Charles Redding[10] created a typology of six different types of ethical problems commonly seen in organizational communication:

- Coercive (intolerance of dissent, restrictions of freedom of speech, refusal to listen, resorting to formal rules and regulations to stifle discussion or to squash complaints, etc.);
- Destructive (insults, put-downs, back-stabbing, character-assassination, using the untruth as a weapon, and not providing expected feedback);
- Deceptive (evasive or deliberately misleading messages, bureaucratic-style euphemisms designed to cover up problems, and "prettifying" unpleasant facts);
- Intrusive (hidden cameras, the tapping of telephones, and the application of computer technologies to the monitoring of employee behavior, etc.);
- Secretive (hoarding information and sweeping information under the rug);
- and Manipulative-exploitative (hiding one's true intentions and demagoguery).

Innovation. Innovation is the creating of something new. In the organizational realm, innovation can come in two distinct forms. First, innovation can be viewed as the extent to which an organization creates new and improved products and services. Second, innovation can also be an organization's ability to strategically streamline processes, increase its market share, increase its competitive advantage, and so on. Organizations that value innovation will be able to adapt more quickly to changing environments than organizations that do not value innovation.

Obsolescence. Obsolescence is what every organization should fear and is often the result of a lack of innovation. Obsolescence occurs when there is a significant decline in customer desire for an organization's products or services. Obsolescence occurs for a variety of different reasons: availability of alternatives that perform better or have new features; availability of alternatives that are of equal quality and cheaper; product or service is no longer viewed as necessary in the current market; and changes in customer preferences or requirements. Over the years many organizations die out because they sank all of their capital into creating one product or service that eventually became unnecessary or passé. Two classic examples (you may never heard of) are Generra Sportswear Company's Hypercolor clothing line (popular in the early 1990s, bankrupt in 1992) and the World POG Federation (popularity hit peak in 1993, bankrupt in 1995). While both of these organizations had numerous problems, one of the largest problems was that their income was based on a fad that quickly became obsolete.

Flexibility. The next qualitative criterion is flexibility, which refers to whether an organization, process, or decision can modify or adapt within a certain range and given timeframe. In environments that are highly chaotic, you need considerably more flexibility to adapt to changes than in environments that are highly stable. Ultimately, if you're in an organization where flexibility is very important, then a decision being made should be equally flexible.

Pragmatism. One of the hardest questions for some to answer is whether or not a given decision is actually pragmatic. Is the decision being advocated realistic or practical given the organization or the environment? When discussing some larger issues like innovation, sometimes decisions that are arrived at may be very lofty but not overly pragmatic. For example, if you're a small business, running a million dollar advertising campaign may be a great way to raise your market share, but it clearly wouldn't be pragmatic for most small businesses.

Ease of Implementation. The last qualitative criterion is ease of implementation, which refers to the speed and simplicity with which a decision alternative can be enacted. If an organization is making a decision in a highly chaotic environment, then having a decision that can be easily and quickly implemented becomes very important. If, however, your organization can take the time to implement a decision, then ease of implementation may not be a criterion with which your organization is overly concerned.

Using Criteria

In the previous sections we've discussed the quantitative and qualitative criteria that can be used for making decisions in public relations regardless of whether the organizations is a corporation, non-profit, governmental, or social justice agency. It is important to remember that criteria are tools that we use, as decision makers, to help us evaluate or judge potential decisions. As such, the selections of the criteria we view as the most important, given a specific decision, are very important. Figure 2.1 contains a short public relations and crisis communication case. After you have read it, we will walk through the dissection of the case.

Figure 2.1 *Sample Case*

FOOD, TUMORS, SOCIAL MEDIA, AND VIRAL VIDEOS

Crisis Communications for Comidamundo and for Whispers Worldwide Communications

Donna Flayhan SUNY New Paltz

It had been long understood at Comidamundo Food Worldwide Corporation—by every investor, member of the Board of Directors, CEO, scientist employed by the company, and public relations practitioner assigned to the account—that quarterly profits were the name of the game, and nothing else trumped that. So it went, on and on from the 1980s, throughout the 1990s, and into the 2000s. What happened back in 2010 would be a different story, but up until that point internal scientists

---

Figure 2.1 *Sample Case* continued

working for Comidamundo would try to bring warnings of dangers in their food products to the attention of their CEO and, if the CEO discussed the problems, even internally to the Board of Directors, he or she would be replaced. Many scientists resigned, but due to confidentiality oaths signed upon initial employment, they were legally barred from going to the public. Every once in a while over those three decades, class action suits would be initiated by parents claiming that their children had abnormal skin growths and strange tumors and that they were caused by the additives in Comidamundo's products. Public relations teams were told to deny the connections and warned by corporate lawyers that they, too, while not directly employed by Comidamundo, had signed confidentiality agreements when assigned to the account. Over the years, many public relations practitioners asked to be moved to other accounts. So many people had come and gone, and the potential crisis grew in numbers, but the sealed settlements in the class actions, with gag orders for all the parents who had agreed to the settlements, dealt with the risk from the lawsuits—as a straightforward financial question. The settlements and gags helped to keep the lid on the story of childhood epidermal diseases and distal tumors affecting fine and gross motor skills in hands and feet of children. The parents settled in order to get the necessary surgeries for their children, and in return were willing to sign agreements not to speak of the matter to anyone but doctors who specifically needed the information to treat the children. And so it went for 30 years, risk averted, crisis contained for Comidamundo.

For three decades, everyone understood that quarterly profits were the name of the game at Comidamundo, and all public relations frames were to be consistent with the ad campaign, "Quality Food Parents Count On," combined with the social responsibility campaigns around donations to after-school snack programs, discounts to the federal and state school lunch programs (on which the company made hundreds of millions of tax dollars, but still used to promote their generosity to the community), and at the annual, nationwide Thanksgiving Day donations to soup kitchens in rural areas.

But in 2010, there was a dramatic turn of events that the account team at Whisper Worldwide (WWW) Communications assigned to Comidamundo had been warning could happen over the past two years. The concerns from the Whisper Worldwide team fell on inattentive ears. Everyone on the Comidamundo account at Whisper Worldwide was top in their craft, and while some had ethical problems with the Comidamundo account, all had public relations strategy problems regarding the "say nothing, ever, about the skin conditions and tumors," approach to the floorspatime problem. The line to shareholders from the Board and CEO

Figure 2.1 *Sample Case* continued

would always be the same, "We would recommend removing flourspatime as a preservative if studies showed a connection to health problems, but they do not." Yet everyone knew the whole truth to that half-truth quote. It was true that there were no blind peer-reviewed studies of flourspatime, nor would there be, because no one was funding the independent scientists interested in studying the problem. There was a cozy relationship at the top of the FDA and Comidamundo (the Comidamundo CEO had worked at the FDA, and the current head of the FDA spent two decades at Comidamundo). So no such independent studies would ever be funded, and the status quo for dealing with the flourspatime risk remained intact. All members of the Whispers Worldwide account team knew that it was just a matter of time before the new era of social media and sharing could trigger a massive public relations crisis. In fact, two team members were sure that the crisis was just around the virtual corner.

In December of 2010, the emotionally compelling story broke of a little girl who had been a promising and beautiful dancer, but who could no longer dance due to unexplained tumor growths on her hands and feet. Her mom's friend, a filmmaker, had put together a little video to show the girl dancing, and then struggling to walk properly with the tumors, ending with the date and time of an upcoming fundraiser. The girl's name was Autumn Flame. Autumn Flame's parents had uploaded the video of ten-year-old Autumn dancing cut with eleven-year-old Autumn struggling to walk but still smiling to YouTube and then shared it on Facebook, so that friends and family could spread the word about the fundraiser. All proceeds would go toward the cost of the surgeries required to remove the rapidly growing, non-cancerous tumors. The video came to the attention of a cousin of one of the people originally invited to the fundraiser. When the cousin watched the video, she was moved to tears. Autumn's story was her daughter's story. Carol Stern saw her own child's story there in that video, and desperately wanted to tell her cousin to tell the mom about the preservative in Comidamundo food products, and so she violated the gag rule she had signed, and she wrote a status update about her own daughter's tumors, with a link to Comidamundo products containing flourspatime and encouraging all to avoid those products. Carol Stern also posted a comment below the video on YouTube, blaming Comidamundo, encouraging Autumn to avoid flourspatime, and asking if others had the same experience with an adolescent developing flourspatime-related tumors on the hands and feet. Over the next two days, a Facebook group was created, "Comidamundo Lies, Children Suffer," and with 404 page likes and many more shares, the video began to go viral beyond the initial fundraiser list of 73 invites.

Figure 2.1 *Sample Case* continued

The WWW public relations team assigned to the Comidamundo account had been arguing internally for almost a week about how to get Comidamundo to respond to this growing crisis; some did not see the growing power of social media and viral videos, others feared financial implications, but all were concerned. As Account Manager, Michael had a talented team. Together with Madeline, Nicole, Wendy, Liam, and Michael himself, the team of five had perfectly complementary skillsets that they brought to every account, and that Michael could always count on for sound input on creative ideas and strategies for implementation. As Account Manager, Michael had 20 years of experience at Whisper Worldwide. Under him were Account Executives Madeline and Nicole, each with over a decade of experience at WWW. Liam and Wendy were both entry level Assistants to Account Executives, but they were the clear experts on social media, images, and viral video seeding.

Liam and Wendy began discussing the coming social media tsunami facing Comidamundo just two days after the original upload of Autumn Flame's powerful story told with moving images in just under two minutes. Liam got a Google alert that a video was trending from hundreds to thousands of views and that Comidamundo had received references in the comments section with 43 likes, the most liked comment under the video. Comments included, "my son has big sunken holes on the palms of his hands and feet where the tumors were removed. It was when he stopped eating anything with flourspatime that no new tumors appeared. Good luck little Autumn, hang in there." Liam told Wendy about the video and comments. Wendy was not surprised; she had asked Michael to remove her from the Comidamundo account or to ask WWW to assign the account to another team. Michael had put in a request, he had been on the account long enough to know that Comidamundo was not interested in his suggestion of how to deal with the crisis *remove the unsafe preservative from the product slowly, while you settle the final cases.* The bean counters at Comidamundo (public relations slang for accountants and mathematically brilliant statisticians) calculated costs of future court settlements at $80,000 per case for group actions and $210,000 per case for individual litigants. They weighed these costs against the cost of buying new products and no longer purchasing the flourspatime from its own subsidiary. They calculated that dropping flourspatime would cost $3.3 million annually for a new preservative purchased by Comidamundo, and that the subsidiary—Forever Fresh—would fold for sure. They settled about 15 individual suits and 2 class action suits (total of 40 litigants) per year. The numbers always came back the same, and the norm would continue. There were no calculations for potential consumer boycotts

Figure 2.1 *Sample Case* continued

if the crisis became public, because there was an arrogant confidence in the numbers, and in the status quo by people at the top, many of whom did not even use email—never mind using and understand social media.

Everyone working for WWW on the Comidamundo account—Michael, Nicole, Madeline, Liam, and Wendy—knew that Comidamundo had a new CEO, but that was nothing new. Would the new CEO be willing to look at the bigger picture of cost-benefit ratios to include potential boycotts as a result of a flourspatime crisis? The team had also thought about going to their own CEO at Whisper Worldwide to ask to be removed from the account. But that would take a long time and Michael's team would be required to work side by side with the new team for at least six months, as was company policy for seamless transitioning of client accounts. Michael knew that dropping the client completely on grounds of potential Public Relations Society of America (PRSSA) and International Business (IB) ethics violations would mean that WWW would lose $60 million plus per year in contracts and fees with Comidamundo directly, and could lose another $33 million plus on the accounts of the 15 subsidiary corporations that Comidamundo would likely take with them to a new public relations firm. That's a $90 million plus loss for Whisper Worldwide on an $800 million per year intake from client contracts and fees. That's a big chunk. Yet, if WWW was found to be willfully withholding information on behalf of a client, then they could lose many of their new and high paying up and coming clients in areas of non-profit public relations, public health communication campaigns, and global non-governmental organization campaigns. Michael had the weight of the world on his shoulders, and although his two Account Executives did not seem to understand the enormity of the situation, at least their assistants Liam and Wendy were rightfully sounding the alarm about the emerging flourspatime Comidamundo crisis.

Michael walked into the office with a posture, facial expression, and measured speaking tone that indicated that he was holding himself back from expressing his true anger, but was not sure how much longer he could contain his brewing rage. He made no eye contact with anyone but stated slowly, forcibly, and in a deep tone that none had ever heard before, not in two years for Wendy and Liam, and not in over ten years for Nicole and Madeline, "Oh … Kay … Madeline … Nicole … Follow me … Follow me to my office." The dramatic pauses had their intended chilling impact on Nicole and Madeline.

The control with which Michael closed the door behind him demonstrated the same mood that was indicated by his speech; it looked as if it took everything Michael had in him not to slam the door. Nicole and Madeline exchanged puzzled

Figure 2.1   *Sample Case* continued

glances. Not only were Michael's tone, gait, and handling of the door something neither Account Executive had ever before witnessed in the boss that they had both enjoyed working for and with, but meetings were always scheduled in advance, by phone, email, text, even in crisis communication situations.

"Wendy and Liam have both been giving you the heads up on this viral video, I know, as you know," Since Michael instituted the "cc me policy" at the same time he brought on Liam and Wendy, both Nicole and Madeline had felt like he no longer trusted them to handle their jobs. Michael had explained that this was simply so that he, as the person ultimately responsible for every action or inaction taken on any account for which he is Account Manager, would always be working with full information and not require third person updates that can be unintentionally or intentionally inaccurate.

"It has been five days since you were alerted to the video trending on YouTube and the number one liked status blaming our client Comidamundo. What have you done?"

Silence.

Michael looked at Nicole, nodding, *nothing, you have done nothing.*

Michael then purposely turned his body away from Nicole and looked at Madeline directly, "Speak."

Madeline hesitated as Michael glared, "I, I researched the authenticity of the video … honest family too broke to pay for surgery, they live in a small town in Iowa." the increased intensity of the intense glare caused Madeline to drift off mid-sentence.

Nicole spoke up, more to help her fellow Account Executive and friend Madeline, than for any real knowledge on the viral video or the tumor problem, "perhaps we should put out some experts to discuss the role of pesticides and cancerous tumors—pitch to our favorite medical bloggers, do the traditional media morning show circuit, and then reference the case of children struck down with pesticide induced illness and tumors. We no longer have the Globanto Chemical accounts, so no risk to other clients—a public service to citizens really."

She's so talented at spinning a new web with existing information, but she has no moral compass. Ironic. She has no awareness at all that others may have an ethically driven approach that finds what she just said reprehensible—the very idea escapes her. If she were a lawyer, all the Casey Anthonys, OJ Simpsons, and others of the world would flock to her, thought Michael as he feigned deep thought on the case at hand.

Figure 2.1 *Sample Case* continued

"I am older than both of you," he blurted suddenly and then raised his voice, "practically older than both of you thirty-somethings combined, yet I know that 48 hours, not 5 days, is our timetable to response to an emerging social media crisis. Remember the Toyota and Domino's cases in our social media training? Do you? Two days, it has been five days, and not a word, not a strategy plan in place, never mind a plan of action to be implemented." He held his lips tightly as he ended the sentence with "for Christ's sake."

Nicole bristled, not only at the use of the Lord's name in vain, but because Michael, even as an atheist, had always respected her deep religious beliefs and made sure that others on the team respected them too.

That had to be intentional Nicole thought. She then glanced over at Madeline and show-smiled a small smile of support *at least Madeline is taking my side.* With Nicole, it was always about a side. That infuriated her assistant Wendy in many a strategy discussion. Wendy would fume internally, *take a goddam freaking position based on the ideas and arguments, not the source of the words.* In nearly every meeting over the two years since Wendy had joined the team, no matter the content, from crisis communication to mundane planning session, it was always about taking a side, forming an alliance, with Nicole. *I could handle her censorship of my once daily f-bomb and lords-name-in-vain way of speaking much easier if she'd be a thinker rather than a parrot* thought Wendy more times than she could ever care to count.

"Nicole, get a conference call set up with Comidamundo CEO what's his name, the new guy. He's in Rio out of the Brazil office, so we need our Portuguese interpreter. Set the conference call for 2:00 pm, it's 10 am now and we are in the same time zone, so it should work. From our end I want the entire team on the call and everyone to speak freely. Get that good interpreter who understands nuances ... Janet. Get Janet. Make it happen." Michael looked at neither at Nicole or Madeline as he sat down at his desk and turned his attention to the computer.

"He's so mad at us," Nicole said. "He's just freaking out, he's not mad at us. Don't take it so personally. I had an answer and strategy ready, we'll see what he thinks when he calms down," said Madeline. Nicole nodded and let out a deep breath. She could always count on Madeline—clear headed and loyal. Madeline thought, simultaneously, *I do love you Nicole, but you are about as deep as a mud puddle, loyal as a dog, but no sense that times have been a changing—never a social media plan thought of, only the implementation of my ideas, well, that is useful.* "Nicole, get that team of social media interns to start that interactive culture cultivating thing. Get the blog sphere busy with all of the great things that Comidamundo

Figure 2.1 *Sample Case* continued

does for children. Get that buzz buzzing about social responsibility as we used to say in word of mouth lobbying days my sister."

Madeline glanced back at Nicole as she sat down to her desk, "you need to do get them blogging before 11:00 am, that way we'll have a bunch of examples of this-is-what-we-have-done for the 2:00 pm conference call." Wendy looked over at Nicole as Madeline walked away, "your plan is to talk about the lovely donations of Comidamundo to the starving masses? Or is it to talk about the food in schools program? The one that every social media savvy person on the planet knows is complete bullshit? You are out of touch."

I'd fire her in a minute, but Michael loves her. He always says it one way or another "Wendy is of this generation and understand them and the new media, we need her. She has promised to stop swearing and offending you and your beliefs." "Whatever," Nicole realized she said it aloud only when Wendy said, "Whatever, what? What the effff …?" Nicole looked startled. "Don't worry Nicole I won't say the real F word, but what the efff are you talking about?"

"Nothing. Come up with some ideas, we might have a conference call at 2 with Comidamundo's new CEO." Just then, a Google calendar alert bell rang on all of the computers and devices in the team's office at once. *Meeting confirmed and angels getting wings* thought Wendy. "Lots of angels getting their wings," smiled Nicole, as if the whole unpleasant interaction never happened. *I've been working with her way too long*, thought Wendy as she smiled to herself. She may not be religious which seems uncaring to Nicole, but Wendy is a very ethical person and fancies herself as being a lot like the dad in *What a Wonderful Life*. Both worked in corporations but kept their hearts and souls and humanity intact.

On all those bell ringing calendars up popped, 2:00 pm video conference, via secure server, Janet will interpret, all will video from desktops. Both Liam and Wendy smiled, they loved talking into the computer screen and seeing the others in small screens, great way to brainstorm. Nicole and Madeline both groaned independently of one another … technology, a face to face with the CEO and no time to prepare or change clothes. Michael was glad to know the meeting would happen soon.

As Liam walked by he looked to Wendy. She grinned, "we have a video conference with the Comidamundo CEO, our whole team—via secure video conference." Liam replied, "yes, I saw the note," and grinned as they made eye contact—secure video conference, *these people really don't understand anything about new technology.*

Figure 2.1 *Sample Case* continued

Liam continued to Madeline's office thinking, *thank the dear lord … oh that's kind of funny due to Nicole's Lordliness, but thank the dear lord I don't work under Nicole. Being Madeline's assistant is not bad at all. She may be naive in the world of social media, like Nicole, but she's very smart, creative, and a detailed researcher. She gets her facts straight every time.*

The video chat made Liam and Wendy feel like they were in a Google hangout, comfortable. Whereas Madeline leaned over the top of her computer just before all were connected to say, "this is like what I watch my son do on OoVoo right?" "Yes," replied Liam and Wendy in unison. "What's OoVoo?" asked Nicole before all went silent."

Janet was a gifted interpreter, and at the end of the two-hour-long session, it was clear that the new CEO at Comidamundo represented the same old story. "Just keep saying how good we are for kids and communities. Nicole, we like your idea of diluting the argument by introducing another possible cause with the pesticides and fungicides. We modify our foods, so no need for pesticide and fungicide applications, we dumped that relationship years ago. Madeline, that family, that woman … Carol Stern, research her and see if she is in violation of the gag order, if so we'll get a judge to shut her up and we'll give a takedown notice for her YouTube comments and that Facebook page."

Liam and Wendy spoke at the same time, then Wendy stopped to allow Liam to speak, "Mr. Riccarro, I respectfully disagree. The social good campaigns get mocked and parodied in social media and that spreads virally."

After the conference Michael said, as if trying to convince himself, "The new CEO seems smart. Maybe he will make his bean counters finally count the boycott beans that will follow as this crisis continues to spread, the more victims who upload videos, the further the boycott will reach." Nicole and Madeline nodded in vigorous agreement. Michael felt worried when Nicole and Madeline agreed so quickly and Liam and Wendy remained silent.

Et tu Michael? thought Wendy. Then she said, "He didn't hear a word we said. He nodded but his plan was to have Nicole and Madeline do what they have already done and nothing else. He doesn't plan to change a thing, and you are in wishful thinking land that he is going to have his bean counters put boycotts into the equation. I think we need to break ties with Comidamundo, before our own bean counters start telling us about how bad WWW looks and how our cutting-edge health, non-profit, and non-governmental organization clients are fleeing for Braveheart. Combined they make up $288 million of our contracts and fees, let's not forget about our reputation and our other, growing, client base." Wendy wanted to argue

Figure 2.1 *Sample Case* continued

on ethical grounds, but money talks and she wanted WWW to do the right thing even if not for the right reasons.

Michael nodded in agreement, "If we can't convince Comidamundo that the costs of the boycott need to be part of their statistical analyses, knowing that with social media we will not be able to control the frame with social responsibility alone. Then we might need to advise WWW to drop the account to save our growing accounts." Michael continued, "Didn't Liam say there's a parody video of our 'Comidamundo feeds the hungry clip' where the homeless man says something like 'I may not have shoes, but I have food thanks to Comidamundo, and these cool foot tumors are like the shoes I can't afford!?'"

Liam looked down at his iPad, "There are 412, make that 413, spoof videos, and someone is encouraging a contest on the anti-Comidamundo Facebook page."

Wendy turned to Madeline, "You are not going to turn in that poor mother, Carol Stern, who was just trying to help others not suffer, are you?" Guilt and shame work sometimes, but not with Madeline and Nicole, they spin everything.

Madeline acted appalled that Wendy couldn't see the reality of Ms. Stern's ethics breach, "If Carol Stern signed a confidentiality agreement, then she broke a contract that she willingly signed and took money for, she is in the wrong."

Wendy shot back, "Took the money for her child's surgery. Her child who has lifelong disabilities related to the actions of Comidamundo."

"Not the point," said Madeline.

"Whatever the ethics, Comidamundo's new CEO does not understand social media. Go after Carol Stern, take down her accounts, and the social media movement will have a field day, they have mirror images of everything, they will pop up again under new names, and Carol Stern will be a name that the anti-Comidamundo groups rally around and support."

"Well, it is now 5:13 pm, we need a decision and plan of action by 5:30, let's get to work," said Michael. He was so stressed he didn't hear Wendy whisper to Liam, "If they slander that poor woman, Carol, I'm sending out the recording of the conference call to some bloggers." Liam looked shocked, "You taped it?" Wendy smiled and nodded a clear yes.

Madeline and Nicole were worried that a plan to disconnect from Comidamundo would mean immediate downsizing at WWW, and they realized that their positions were vulnerable in this new age of social media. They argued to keep the account and try to convince Comidamundo to count the costs of a boycott.

Liam, who loved Wendy, felt that he must let Michael know to weigh that information in his decision. Wendy said she'd just keep it to herself and hope Michael

Figure 2.1 *Sample Case* continued

chose the right path, which in her opinion was to break with Comidamundo and its subsidiaries, clean house at WWW based on ethics and social media savvy, and take it from there.

Michael thought through all the implications of each decision. This was a tough one in so many ways.

In any public relations decision, the types of criteria can vary. In some cases, all of the criteria could be theoretically applicable. For this reason, we recommend limiting the number of criteria you select to three (total—not three from quantitative and three from qualitative). Depending on the criteria that you select, you may end up with radically different types of decisions.

From the case, find two possible strategies to use as a member of the WWW account team assigned to the Comidamundo account. Let's evaluate each of these decisions through a few different criteria.

The first criterion you could select could be costs for Comidamundo. Your team, using Comidamundo's numbers and those from WWW, could put several scenarios in chart form. The first scenario would be the one used for decades, with the cost of replacing the preservative and the cost of paying out settlements. The second cost scenario could bring in the boycott numbers, with the cost in the first scenario combined with the anticipated potential losses caused by consumer boycotts. The third cost scenario could add a sudden drop in stock prices for Comidamundo to the first two scenarios.

Another possible criterion you could examine is the cost to Michael and Whispers World-wide if the scandal continues to break, WWW does not drop the Comidamundo Account, and Comidamundo decides to continue with the status quo. If Wendy decides to leak the taped conference call, then everyone will know that WWW has violated the golden rule of public relations, and all of its lucrative and constant cash flow from government, non-profit, and non-governmental organizations will run to that new social media startup out of Scotland, Braveheart Communications, the one that says—"Whispering is for Secrets: We Help You to Shout the Truth."

In addition to cost-benefit analyses for Comidamundo and for WWW, there are many social and ethical implications of this case. Let's examine the case using a third criterion, communication ethics. One of W. Charles Redding's six types of organizational communication ethical lapses involves deceptive communication. Under this classification, we can argue that picking the first option, while monetarily beneficial, actually doesn't fit the situation and is therefore just "greenwashing" of the current problem. Is Comidamundo an unethical company that WWW should sever ties with based on ethical criteria alone? Ethical criteria in combination with the potential loss of clients to Braveheart? Ethical criteria that include discussions of downsizing staff at WWW to include just Account Managers and Account Assistants, but no Account Executives?

Hopefully, you can see how, depending on which criteria you select, you can end up with very different conclusions. Ultimately, the criteria that you select for evaluating possible decision alternatives will guide the decision-making process.

Once you've selected your three decision criteria, you also need to think about your criteria in terms of how you will measure these criteria. One of the goals of any decision criteria is to help guide the decision making, but you need to have the ability to think through how these criteria will be achieved through the decision. For example, if one of your criteria is customer satisfaction, you need to ask yourself how a decision alternative will improve customer satisfaction. But you also need to take this a step further and think about how you will know if customer satisfaction has increased because of enacting your decision alternative. In other words, how are you going to measure customer satisfaction?

Obviously, the quantitative criteria have pre-built-in measurement tools; that's why they are quantitative criteria. Qualitative criteria, on the other hand, still must be measured, but you, as the decision maker, need to really think through how you will measure the specific criteria. In the case discussed in Figure 2.1, how would you measure whether or not a specific decision is communicatively ethical? While using Redding's six criteria for ethical organizational communication is one tool you could use to measure the ethicality of a decision, it's not the only way of evaluating communication ethics.

Overall, when it comes to selecting and using decision criteria, you really need to think through the selection, use, and measurement of the criteria you select. The last part of the worksheet discussed in Appendix A asks you to then rank the three criteria you've selected. We ask you to do this because often we have to make a determination of which criterion is the most important. If we had selected the criteria cost, staff turnover, and ethics as our three criteria for the case in Figure 2.1, we clearly need to know which criterion is more important to our decision-making process.

Step Three—Identifying Solutions

The third of Gouran and Hirokawa's[11] five basic steps of decision making is identifying possible solutions. Some cases will come with pre-determined decision alternatives, but most cases will require you, the reader, to come up with possible decision alternatives. For the purposes of the Case Method, most scholars generally agree that you should develop at least three well-articulated decision alternatives. Nils Randrup[12] recommends four possible tools for determining possible solutions: visualization, experience, knowledge of other solutions, and academic discipline/theory/models.

Visualization. The first way to come to a possible decision is to put yourself in the position of the main decision-making character within the case. Really try to see the different issues and possible decisions from the main character's position within the story. Often, when we put ourselves into the shoes of the main character, decisions become very apparent.

Experience. A second way of generating possible alternatives comes from our own experiences in life. Maybe an organization you've worked in faced a similar dilemma. If so, how did your organization proceed? Maybe your organization made a good decision or maybe your organization made a horrible decision. Either way, using your own experience in various organizations can help you think of possible decision alternatives.

Knowledge of Other Solutions. We often hear about how organizations handle various situations through the modern press. Maybe you heard about a specific decision on the nightly news, or read about a decision in a business magazine like *BusinessWeek*. In either case, we can use the decisions we hear or read about and apply them to the cases in this book.

Academic Discipline/Theory/Models. The last way you can arrive at various decisions is through the application of academic content. Whatever textbook your professor uses in your organizational communication course, the book is filled with all kinds of theories and models that can lead to actual decision alternatives. One of the great things about the Case Method is the ability to take the course content you are learning and clearly apply that content to the decision-making process. I would recommend trying to find at least one decision alternative that clearly stems from your course readings. However, your professor may have other guidelines, so make sure you always follow your professor's guidelines.

Once you've created a list of possible alternatives, you really need to filter them into a list of practical and realistic guidelines based on the context of the case. Here are some helpful hints when creating and selecting decision alternatives:

- Be Realistic! First, and foremost, the decisions that you arrive at should be realistic given the context of a given case. While it may be fun to ship all of your annoying coworkers to the moon, there are no cases where that would be a realistic alternative. Instead, really think through what types of decisions you think the main character could make in a given case.

- Avoid Overlap! One problem that many new case analysts have is a problem with overlap. In other words, their decisions tend to overlap one another, making each decision fairly indistinguishable from the next. The goal of writing three different possible alternatives is to have three different alternatives. So try to make sure that all of your alternatives are mutually exclusive.

- Decisions Mandatory! One copout that some people will try to use is just not to make a decision. Not making a decision is not allowable in a case-based class. You need to take a stand and really make a decision. While there are definitely some decisions that are better than others, not making a decision is generally going to get you nowhere in life.

- Status Quo! While not making a decision is not a viable decision-making option, keeping the status quo can be a viable decision alternative. There are some cases where not changing one's behavior or course of action can be appropriate. While I recommend you use this method of decision making sparingly, you can definitely argue that the status quo is better than other possible decision alternatives in some cases.

- Don't Sandwich! When I use the word "sandwich" here, I'm talking about taking two really weak decisions and then placing the one decision you like between the two weak ones. All three of the decision alternatives that you create for a given case should be strong and viable. While different decision alternatives may prove problematic when you evaluate them using your criteria, all of the decisions you create should be viable given the context of the case.
- Think Implementation! At some point the actors within a case will have to implement the decision you have selected. Think through any possible risks or obstacles that could interfere with selected decisions. If a decision is ultimately not pragmatic given the confines of the case, then it's probably not a viable decision.

While these six strategies will help you think through the alternatives you come up with, there is no single best way to arrive at your three decision alternatives.

Step Four—Reviewing Decision Alternatives

Once you have created your list of decision alternatives, it's time to start evaluating those decision alternatives. First and foremost, we evaluate all of our decision alternatives using the decision criteria we selected prior to creating them. One reason why it is important to select your criteria first is because it prevents you from selecting criteria that specifically lead to one decision alternative. Think logically as you apply your criteria and really think through how each possible criterion either supports or doesn't support a given decision alternative. If you examine the Case Study Worksheet provided in Appendix A, you'll see that the various parts of analyzing the decision alternatives are broken down to help you take each criterion and see how it either supports or doesn't support each decision alternative.

Step Five—Selecting the Best Decision Alternative

Ultimately, you will select the decision alternative that you believe best supports the context of the case and is most supported by the decision criteria that you have selected. Once you've selected the criteria, then you need to start thinking about how the decision will actually play out as it is implemented. For our purposes, I broke down this section into two basic areas: goals and action steps.

Goals. The first step in the post-decision selection process is to think through the ultimate goals of the decision. What are the basic goals or outcomes that you hope to achieve by implementing your decision alternative? Additionally, based on how you decided to measure your criteria, think about how you will determine if your goal is being met.

Action Steps. Most decisions do not happen in a vacuum and often require a series of short-term and long-term action steps to fully implement the decision. Ask yourself, "What short-term and long-term steps are necessary to completely implement my chosen decision alternative?" Most decisions involve some level of long-term monitoring to ensure the overall effectiveness of the decision made.

CONCLUSION

In this chapter we have introduced you to the basics of the Case Method. At first, the Case Method may seem a little clunky and hard to manage as you start evaluating cases and discussing the cases in your organizational communication course. As with any new skill, learning how to evaluate and discuss cases takes time and effort. However, if you really work through the Case Method before, during, and after class, you will quickly see how important a formalized decision-making process is for the business world and in your own life.

REFERENCES

1 Gouran, D. S., & Hirokawa, R. Y. (1983). The role of communication in decision-making groups: A functional perspective. In M. S. Mander (Ed.), *Communication in transition: Issues and debate in current research* (pp. 168–185). New York: Praeger.

Gouran, D. S., & Hirokawa, R. Y. (1996). Functional theory and communication in decision-making and problem solving groups: An expanded view. In R. Y. Hirokawa & M. S. Poole (Eds.), *Communication and group decision-making* (2nd ed., pp. 55–80). Thousand Oaks, CA: Sage.

2 Mauffette-Leenders, L. A., Erskine, J. A., & Leenders, M. R. (2007). *Learning with cases* (4th ed.). London, Ontario, Canada: Richard Ivey School of Business.

3 Phillips, P. P., & Phillips, J. (2005). *Return on investment (ROI) basics*. Alexandria, VA: ASTD Press, p. 1.

4 McCroskey, J. C., & Teven, J. J. (1999). Goodwill: A reexamination of the construct and its measurement. *Communication Monographs, 66*(1), 90–103.

5 Latham, G. P. (2007). *Work motivation: History, theory, research, and practice*. Thousand Oaks, CA: Sage.

6 Berry, L. L., Mirabito, A. M., & Baun, W. B. (2010). What's the hard return on employee wellness programs? *Harvard Business Review, 88*(12), 104–112.

7 Giacalone, R. A., & Jurkiewicz, C. L. (2003). Toward a science of workplace spirituality. In R. A. Giacalone & C. L. Jurkiewicz (Eds.), *Handbook of workplace spirituality and organizational performance* (pp. 3–28). Armonk, New York: M.E. Sharpe. (p. 8).

8 Parhizgar, K. D., & Parhizgar, R. (2006). *Multicultural business ethics and global managerial moral reasoning*. Lanham, MD: University Press of America. (p. 77)

9 Cherrington, J. O., & Cherrington, D. J. (1992). A menu of moral issues: One week in the life of the Wall Street Journal. *Journal of Business Ethics, 11*, 255–265

10 Redding, W. C. (1996). Ethics and the study of organizational communication: When will we wake up? In J. A. Jaksa & M. S. Pritchard (Eds.), *Responsible communication: Ethical issues in business, industry, and the professions* (pp. 17–40). Cresskill, NJ: Hampton Press.

11 Gouran & Hirokawa (1983, 1996)

12 Randrup, N. (2007). *The case method: Roadmap for how best to study, analyze and present cases.* Rodovre: Denmark: International Management Press.

This chapter is a revised version of "Analyzing Case Studies" that first appeared in Jason Wrench's (2012) publication *Casing Organizational Communication* published by Kendall Hunt.

Public Relations Ethics

CHAPTER 3

Photo Op: Natural Disasters and Public Relations

Thomas Wagner, Tyler Raible, Sarah Jolly, and Maria Butauski
Xavier University

ABSTRACT

Rhythm Peterson is interim director of social media for a national campaign and faced with the dilemma of how to accurately represent Governor Morgan Reynolds who is running for vice president. Rhythm is conflicted between the pressure to provide a favorable representation of Governor Reynolds and an internal belief that impression management should accurately reflect reality.

"And in conclusion, we have pulled ahead by three points!" Governor Morgan Reynolds exclaims as she triumphantly finishes her presentation to a round of thunderous applause. "And I could not have done it without Harold, our very own campaign manager."

Harold Crowley stood and hugged Governor Reynolds. "Congratulations everyone! Our hard work is paying off! Governor Morgan Reynolds will take the vice presidency this fall!" The office broke into another swell of applause.

Governor Reynolds was running for vice president of the United States with her running mate Hillary Ferrara, a wildly popular moderate conservative governor from Texas. Although the overall campaign was run out of Governor Ferrara's headquarters in Texas, Governor Reynolds' part of the campaign was housed in Boston where she had served as governor for two terms before leaving to run for national office. The combination of Ferrara and Reynolds had been unique in many ways. It was the first all-female ticket for the U.S. presidency and the first ticket containing members from opposite parties; Ferrara was a moderate conservative and Morgan a moderate progressive. Governor Reynolds' campaign team, headed by Harold, was exhausted after months of the grueling election process. Yet their close-knit group helped maintain enthusiasm about the election.

"Before everyone leaves, I have one more order of business." Harold announced as everyone packed up to head home after a successful day. "As we all know, Patricia is now on maternity leave. I would like to introduce our new interim director of social media, Rhythm Peterson!" Everyone greeted Rhythm with polite clapping.

"Thank you everyone." Rhythm addressed his new coworkers. "I know that you all want to get home, so I just want to say I look forward to working with you, and go Ferrara-Reynolds!"

"Hey Rhythm, ready for lunch?" Carol smiled sweetly, stopping by Rhythm's desk.

Rhythm groaned and looked at his watch. "My stomach is definitely ready for lunch, but I haven't even gotten through half of these photos from New Orleans yet."

"That's okay." Carol sighed. "Campaign season is intense! I will grab you a sandwich."

Rhythm nodded in acquiescence and turned back to his computer. Governor Reynolds was currently canvassing in New Orleans, donating money and helping to rebuild a homeless shelter still in shambles after the latest hurricane struck the area. Just that morning, Rhythm had received dozens of photos of the vice presidential candidate at fundraisers, laying bricks, and breaking ground. Rhythm ran his fingers through his brown hair, which he imagined now had considerably more grey in it after just a few weeks of campaign work.

Carol returned with his turkey sandwich. "How hard is it to pick a photo anyway?" Carol teased. Carol was a finance intern for the team, and did not understand the nuances behind social media.

"It shouldn't be this difficult" Rhythm exclaimed. "I cannot decide on a single picture to post to Morgan's official Twitter account, there is just something weird about them." Carol shrugged and returned to her desk.

Finally, Rhythm settled on a photo of Morgan, grinning widely, proudly serving the first pot of soup to the New Orleans homeless under the makeshift shelter with the caption, "Proud to be in New Orleans with the New Hope Homeless Shelter! #hurricanerelief #ReynoldsVP."

A few days later, Rhythm was out for a drink at Alynn's Bar with his long-time friend Jermaine. Rhythm and Jermaine Hays played in the same punk band in college and were roommates for two semesters. It was only a matter of time before Jermaine, a journalist from a national progressive television news network, started to grill Rhythm about the Reynolds campaign.

"Did you just bring me out here to get dirt on Governor Reynolds?" questioned Rhythm.

"Listen Rhy, we've been friends for years. We're tight, right? You can tell me about the campaign, you know it won't get anywhere." Jermaine smiled slyly as he sipped his Grey Goose martini.

"We both know that's a lie," retorted Rhythm. "You've never been able to keep a secret. But why the sudden interest in Morgan? What's your angle?"

Jermaine started to play with his phone as he exhaled slowly. "Listen, we've been friends for years. That's why I wanted to check with you before I said anything serious."

"Alright, what are you going on about now?" Rhythm's nostrils flared with frustration as his friend danced around the subject.

"OK. I'll lay it on the table. I have on good authority that the governor's pictures at the hurricane relief camp were staged. I heard that it was all a set-up to amp up the campaign. So, I gotta ask man. Are the photos for real or what? What's the real story?"

Jermaine's question was met with stunned silence from Rhythm as he stared intently at his drink, hoping to find the answers somewhere in the foam of his beer.

"I don't know, man," Rhythm started," I thought they were real. I mean, I was there when they took the picture. I don't really know if they ended up working at the relief center or not. Tell ya what. I'll look into it. I'll check back with Harold and see what's going on. Do me a favor though?"

"You got it. Whatcha need?"

Rhythm glanced sideways at his drinking partner and grinned slightly. "Try not to say anything until we know the truth. If they are staged, then we may have a problem. But if they are legit, we don't wanna lampoon an innocent person, right?"

A smirk crept across Jermaine's lips as he looked up to say "Lampoon an innocent candidate? You know we're dealing with politicians, right? No one is innocent."

Rhythm had a difficult time getting ready to go to work the next morning, Jermaine's accusation had kept him up for most of the night. He was already having a difficult time trying to break into his coworkers' inner circle. Since he was hired halfway through the election process, he had not been able to form strong friendships.

As soon as he arrived at the office, Rhythm sent an email to Morgan asking for details on the work that the vice president was doing, ostensibly for a press release in the works. After a few minutes, Rhythm decided to call George Moody, his colleague from his previous job at a PR firm.

"Hey George, you have a minute?" Rhythm asked when George answered the phone.

"Sure, but just a minute!" George exclaimed, sounding typically frazzled because of an upcoming deadline. "I need to finish writing up this media advisory about my client's benefit dinner. What's up?"

"Well …" Rhythm paused, not quite decided on what he was going to ask. "As a PR specialist, have you ever gotten information from your client that turned out to, uh, not be true?"

"Sure, plenty of times!" George casually proclaimed.

"Really?" Rhythm was shocked. He had never been in this predicament before, and it was reassuring that his friend might have some advice.

"It is actually more common than you might think. My clients constantly want to make them look better so they do not think that a little bit of fibbing will be a problem. Plus, they figure that if they are ever found out they can blame it on us, the PR middle men."

Rhythm's heart sank. He did not like to hear that he could be culpable if it turned out that Morgan really was lying about volunteering. "So what did you do?"

"I usually just refer to the PRSA's code of ethics," George replied. "The code says that we should be honest, but at the same time, we should be honest while advancing the interests of our clients. Loyalty is also a main tenet; we should be loyal to our clients, but also to the greater society."

Rhythm knew he should have paid more attention during his ethics course while in school, but he never thought a situation like this would apply to him. It always seemed so cut and dried during class.

"I usually just use my best judgment," George explained. "If I feel that the situation is small enough not to impact the greater society, then I need to be loyal to who is paying my bills. Hope that helps buddy, but I really have to finish this advisory."

"I understand, George. Thanks so much for your help." Rhythm hung up the phone, feeling even worse. His client was running for the vice presidency of the United States, how much more impact on society could a person have?

To make matters worse, when Rhythm checked his email, he had a terse reply from Harold stating, "You should have all the information needed" and "please do not directly email the candidate."

So, Rhythm attempted to do some follow-up. He first decided to try and call Governor Reynolds' publicist.

"I promise that every picture we send you is valid, Mr. Peterson. Thank you for calling," and the publicist's phone went dead with a click.

"Well that didn't tell me much," Rhythm muttered under his breath as he dialed the number of the director of the shelter at which Governor Reynolds was recorded volunteering.

"Hi, my name is Rhythm Peterson. I work for vice presidential candidate Morgan Reynolds. I was hoping to ask you a few questions."

"Oh, hello Mr. Peterson. We so appreciate everything that Candidate Reynolds does for us, but if you please we are very busy. Thank you for calling." Once again, the line went dead almost immediately.

Rhythm groaned. The woman sounded sincere in thanking Morgan, but at the same time such an abrupt dismissal could mean that she was annoyed that Morgan was only pretending to help in the wake of these disasters. "This is not my job!" Rhythm exclaimed. "I am not a journalist!"

As if on cue, Rhythm's phone rang. It was Rhythm's contact from a national conservative news network, Fred Applebaum.

"Hi Fred, how's it going?"

"Doing great Rhythm, thanks! Fantastic really. I was just working on this story about Governor Reynolds, love those pictures you sent over, just love them. I just needed a few details filled in though, can you give me the number of hours that Morgan has put into the shelter?"

"Well, actually, I'm not really sure ..." Rhythm stuttered.

"Oh that's just fine, I'll write 'countless hours.' And when exactly did Morgan start these philanthropic efforts?"

"Unfortunately I can't tell you that either," Rhythm paused. "I do remember hearing something about Morgan participating in service in high school."

"That's cool. I can write that Morgan has been involved in philanthropy since long before the candidacy! Fabulous. If you could just send me a few more pictures of Morgan getting really down and dirty at the shelter, which would be great!"

Rhythm hung up the phone feeling exhausted. Fred talked so fast.

Fred's story had barely run the next day when Rhythm got a call from Jermaine. "Did you see the news story this morning? 'Lauded as a hero'? Morgan is a 'philanthropic genius'? Are you kidding me with this? We don't even know if Morgan has done more than lift a finger for a few photo ops! Did you have something to do with this?"

"Don't get angry at me, Jermaine, we don't want a repeat of senior year," Rhythm could feel his blood boiling. "I tried to follow up on the legitimacy of some of these claims, but all I got were dead ends. Researching is your job, not mine."

Over the next few weeks, it was all Rhythm could do to mediate between the conservative network's overblown claims and the liberal network's villainizing of his boss as an insincere fraud. The entire time, a bigger, and very real, storm was brewing on the horizon. A mere three months before the elections, Hurricane Halle hit the East Coast with an unprecedented ferocity.

"The cameras! Do we have proper waterproofing equipment for the cameras?" Harold was frantic as he tried to organize Morgan's trip to North Carolina in light of the new storm. "Did we hire that extra photographer?"

Rhythm was typing up press releases and media advisories as fast as he could as the office descended into organized chaos. "When will Morgan touchdown in Wilmington?" he shouted.

Rhythm's phone was ringing off the hook, and he could not help but notice several missed calls from both Jermaine and Fred. He shook his head and ignored them as he prepared to update the proper social media channels.

"How many hotel rooms did we book?" Harold was yelling at someone. "Do we have enough for the extra personnel?"

"Shouldn't you be asking if someone has arranged for the right emergency materials for Morgan to give to the victims?" Rhythm dared to ask.

"This is an election campaign, not the Red Cross," Harold snapped. "Make sure you get those releases out to the local media before Morgan arrives in North Carolina."

The crew landed in North Carolina only a couple hours after Rhythm had turned in the last of the releases. He could feel a momentary sense of relief pass over him as he leaned back in his chair. With his hands behind his head, his mind began to wander. He thought about the dismissals from Harold, the topic avoidance from everyone else, and the hero and villain displays of the vice presidential candidate. He needed answers. And he wasn't about to be the person who could be dismissed so easily.

At some point during his inner monologue, there was a light tapping at his door.

"Can I come in?" sang Carol from his doorway. "I've been thinking about the campaign."

Rhythm responded with a nod and gestured toward the empty chair in his office.

"Ok," Carol began, "you were having trouble picking out a picture, right? They were all nice pictures or whatever, but is it true that they were fake? Shouldn't we tell someone if they were? I just don't get it … you PR people are always so confusing …"

With a sigh, Rhythm looked down at his desk. "It's not that easy. I know that we have an obligation to be honest with people, but we also have to look out for the client. I can't do something that'll hurt Morgan's chances. After all, it might just cost me my job."

"Well that's stupid!" Carol shouted. "You should tell the truth no matter what! I don't think you can cop out like that. At least talk to Harold about it or something."

"Fine. I'll give him a call tomorrow morning."

Rhythm was on his way to work when he received a call from Harold. After a few minutes of idle chit chat and a recap on the status of the office, Rhythm decided to voice his concerns about the pictures.

"I just want to know if the pictures were real," Rhythm finished, desperately.

Harold responded with a snort. "What does it matter? They're already all over the media. You're doing your job fine, just let it go already."

"But don't we have an obligation to uphold honesty in the way we present material? Our job isn't to deceive," Rhythm responded.

"Exactly. Your job isn't to deceive," Harold uttered. "Your job isn't to investigate. Your job is to manage the social media for Governor Reynolds. Listen, I need you to write another press release about the work the governor is doing in North Carolina right now. I'll send you a couple pictures and a fact sheet. Just make the candidate look good. Want to think about something? Think about how cool it is to have the governor as a client. Think about that."

DISCUSSION QUESTIONS

1. Who should Rhythm discuss these issues with?
2. Is it right for Morgan to use Rhythm as a PR professional to exploit natural disasters for political gain?
3. Should Rhythm confront Morgan directly?
4. What about Rhythm's contacts in the media? Should he try to work with them to get the real story out?
5. Should Rhythm tell the truth, even if it costs him the job?
6. What do you think of George's interpretation of the PRSA code of ethics? How is this different from your interpretation?
7. What would you do if you were Rhythm?

KEY TERMS

Natural Disasters, PR Ethics, Reputation Management, Social Networking Sites

CHAPTER 4

One, Two, Three Strikes You're Out

Alisa Agozzino, PhD
Ohio Northern University

ABSTRACT

Austin Tallman is all geared up for an outstanding senior season in college baseball. When his coach bans Twitter for the season, Austin decides to create a pseudo account to get around the ban. Things get tough when posts get noticed and spread like wildfire throughout social networking channels.

This was Austin Tallman's third year as a starter on his college's men's baseball team. As a senior, he was excited for the possibilities that lay ahead. Riding the bus to the game was always nerve-wracking. He grabbed a pillow and tried to fall asleep.

"Tallman!" Coach Elm exclaimed. "Can you come up here to chat?"

Austin jumped to his feet and slowly made his way to the front of the bus where the coaches sat. In the back of his mind he wondered what he had done that could warrant such an odd request.

"Tallman, the coaching staff need you and the guys on the team to implement some new rules this year as we start the season. As the senior co-captain, I need you to take the reins on implementing a Twitter ban during the entire season. This means even on the days we aren't playing."

"But coach … I'm a PR major, I have to tweet for my social media class," Austin tried to explain.

"It's too much of a risk," Coach Elm explained. "I've heard how detrimental this Twitter can be to a program and if we just ban it completely we won't have to worry about it."

"But what about my class?" asked Austin.

"You'll just need to drop the class for the semester. Pick it back up when you're out of season. Would you let the rest of the team know by the weekend? That cool?"

Austin nodded his head in agreement and made his way back to his seat. Slumping down and putting back in his iPod ear buds, he laid his head on the pillow and looked out the window. *This sucks*, he thought. Austin was super active in his social networking channels as he was a public relations major who thought highly of connecting with others quickly through Twitter, Facebook, and LinkedIn.

"I don't want to take that class in the Spring. At least I have until the weekend to get this all straightened out," thought Austin.

FRIDAY'S TEAM PRACTICE

"Bring it in!" shouted Coach Elm from across the field. Each player came running to huddle underneath the dugout.

The next five minutes of announcements from coach and staff consisted of instructions for Saturday's pre-game, bus travel schedule, and equipment packing lists.

"Finally," Coach Elm asked, "have your captains explained your Twitter ban for the season?"

Everyone blankly looked toward Austin and Isaac, the team captains.

"I take that as a no," said coach.

Coach Elm, frustrated, spent the next several minutes explaining how the ban would be in place for the remainder of the season. Coach handed out a social media policy for all to sign. Everyone knelt down around the dugout and signed the forms and handed them to Coach before leaving.

As the team was dismissed Blake, a sophomore, ran up to Austin. "Hey Austin," Blake whispered. "What are you going to do about your Twitter account? Just leave it dormant for the rest of the season?" Blake was the one of those student-athletes who was on the team, but would probably never take the field unless it was a guaranteed win. He also was the type who loved to stir up drama.

Uncomfortably Austin answered, "Uh, yeah. Sounds like I don't have a choice."

But as Blake walked away unhappy with the non-drama answer, Austin knew he had a better plan in mind. Austin quickly set up a pseudo Twitter account so he could remain active on Twitter. Austin felt confident in his decision since the chances of Coach Elm ever figuring it out were slim to none, as he wasn't very media savvy.

STOLEN BASE

Austin couldn't help but tweet about baseball on a regular basis. After all, it's all he knew outside the classroom in the spring. He had quite the following with over 500 after two weeks and over 1500 after six. Because of the nature of the tweets, people were intrigued. Austin had started tweeting about different members of the team and insider information of the locker room. Here were some of his latest tweets:

> *If I hear Joe complain one more time about coach I'm going to lose it. Dude, keep your trap shut!*

> *#tigerbaseball Baseball Party @ Sam & Luke's Saturday night after game. 34837 East Denton Street #tigerbaseball*

> *Feeling bad 4 JC. Confirmed ACL is torn. In hospital found out has diabetes & blood count is low. Man needs 2 catch a break. #tigerbaseball*

Because Austin was hashtagging #tigerbaseball some of the players started to pick up on the Twitter account. Most were checking the account and following the posts, but no one had said anything.

Coach Elm, on the other hand, slammed the door of the locker room after practice. Most thought it was in regard to their poor practice. Instead Coach threw several papers to the middle of the room.

"What is this?" he questioned. "What the hell is this?" he asked as he pointed to pages of tweets from Austin's pseudo account. Austin's heart sank. *Busted*, he thought. But no one said anything.

"Does anyone know who is tweeting from this account? Is it one of you?" Coach Elm asked as he scanned the room.

Again everyone sat staring, not saying a word. Austin thought about speaking up; after all, it was he. He didn't want the whole team to get yelled at for no reason. However, he just sat and stared with the rest of them.

Coach was infuriated, but without anyone claiming the Twitter account he assumed it was not a player. "This is exactly why we have a ban against this!" he shouted. "A: Joe what's your problem with me? Be man enough to own up! You got something wrong, don't complain, come talk to me. I'm a likable and reasonable guy. B: Party? There better be NO baseball party happening on my watch. C: Info on JC is now public knowledge … this kills our game plan against the Bears on Saturday. They know our best pitcher is now out for the season. They now plan for Joe to pitch. Does NO one think through these things? We have two weeks until conference. Inside information to your friends and family needs to be kept to a minimum. No one needs to know what's happening inside our locker room."

WILD PITCH

Since Austin had dodged a bullet, he laid low for a week or so. As conference season and NCAA playoffs drew near, Austin slowly forgot the sinking feeling in the locker room when asked about the Twitter account and was back at it. The biggest mistake happened after the big conference win one Saturday night.

Great win for #tigerbaseball. Toke it up! pic.twitter.com/9Fr83ldz

Austin posted a picture with the tweet of JC and left fielder, Martin, smoking joints. He had taken the picture across the room and no one had even noticed. Five minutes after posting the picture Austin glanced down at his phone. Realizing what he had done, he quickly removed the tweet from his account. *Oh man*, he thought, *that could have been bad.*

It was too late. Austin had too many followers who had retweeted the senior's pseudo account picture and tweet. Within an hour the photo was on Facebook and Austin got that sinking feeling again. *Good thing there are so many people at this party. They'll never trace it back to me.* By now others were starting to see the picture through all types of social networking sites. The picture even popped up when Googled under another conference school's newspaper with the headline "We may not be the best baseball team in the conference, but we're smarter than the Tigers." He knew it wouldn't be long until Coach caught wind of it and the entire team would be in trouble again.

RUN DOWN

Sunday morning each baseball player had a text and email waiting on them when they awoke. It read, "Team meeting 11:00 am locker room—Coach Elm."

As Austin read the message he knew what was going to be said. He felt really bad for JC and Martin as he knew they'd be kicked off the team for their actions. He grabbed his jacket and hat and headed toward the door. He didn't want to be late to the meeting. He grabbed his phone and did a quick glance at his Twitter account. He had so many postings on his Twitter wall he didn't know where to start. He read a few of the first ones and started to tear up. What had he done? The postings were from a variety of people. From parents of his teammates, from friends at school and some from people he didn't know. The one that hurt the most was from one of the freshmen's parents.

It read:

> #tigerbaseball had a nice run ... too bad it was all for nothing. Whoever runs this account is a faceless coward! Way to ruin everything!

FORCED OUT

As Austin arrived at the sports center locker room he was the first one. He sat down and looked around at the lockers. *Wow, seriously, how did this get so out of control?* he thought. Slowly teammates started to roll in, but no one said anything. Bob Dell, the athletic director, walked in with some other older gentleman whom no one recognized.

"Everyone here?" asked Dell.

Austin did a quick look around. "Yep," he responded.

"Good," responded Dell. "All of you know why you are here and what has happened, correct?"

Slowly all the guys nodded their heads.

"Boys, these gentleman are here from the NCAA and need to ask each of you some questions individually in order to get to the bottom of this predicament. Is anyone uncomfortable with speaking with them?" asked Dell.

No one responded. Austin glanced around the room. He knew this was going to be bad, but not this bad. NCAA was involved now? This wasn't good for JC or Martin, nor the team, let alone the university.

"Alright, good."

One by one the baseball players disappeared from the room and never returned. Austin couldn't take it anymore. He volunteered to go next. There was no use everyone going through this torture when he could just admit his guilt and be done with it.

It was Austin's turn to go in next. Dell walked through the door and Austin stood.

"Sit down son," he said. "Your teammates in the photo have admitted their guilt. There is no longer any need to move further with interviews. I will need you all to remain quiet about this situation until our 1:00 pm news conference. Understood?"

CLEAN UP HITTER

At 1:00 pm all the players met at Austin's off-campus apartment to watch Coach Elm and AD Dell conduct the press conference. Because the team was a large state school with national recognition, the story had garnered national attention. The first part of the press conference was very somber. The coach spoke of the players and their actions. Dell came to the podium and spoke of what the school was doing to comply with the NCAA. Austin felt sick to his stomach.

"If I ever find that idiot who posted that picture I'm going to punch them in the face," screamed one of Austin's teammates.

"They shouldn't have been doing drugs anyways," pointed out Blake. "Too bad for Martin … but now I'll finally see the field."

Doubt it, thought Austin.

Watching the entire press conference on television was surreal. Austin stared blankly at the screen. *How am I ever going to get out of this mess?*

DISCUSSION QUESTIONS

1. What are the PR ethical issues that are prevalent in the case?
2. As the university sports information officer, how are you going to monitor accounts like Austin's pseudo account and do you interact with these types of outside accounts? Why or why not?
3. Did Coach Elm help or hinder his program by implementing the Twitter ban? Explain.
4. As the head communications officer at the university, how do you prepare Coach Elm and AD Dell for the press conference? What are key points that must be covered?

KEY TERMS

Social Networking, PR Ethics, Press Conference

CHAPTER 5

Whose Press Release Is It, Anyway?

Thomas Wagner, Maria Butauski, Tyler Raible, and Sarah Jolly
Xavier University

ABSTRACT

As an intern at a public relations firm, Suzy Kelly is faced with an ethical dilemma when she is asked to put a more senior member of the firm's name on her press release. Seeking advice from co-workers and her professor, Suzy learns multiple perspectives on authorship and is left with a choice.

Megan Sanchez and Suzy Kelly are having their weekly meeting to go over what Suzy is learning while working with Metro, a large public transportation system in the Southeast. They discuss strengths and weaknesses in Suzy's work and Suzy discusses suggestions for Megan's social media calendar. Megan and Suzy have a very friendly mentor-mentee relationship and Suzy enjoys working for her.

"That's great, Suzy. It's hard for me to stay caught up with all of this social media stuff."

"Well, this calendar has been very helpful with keeping track of post schedules," Suzy explains.

"It definitely has. Speaking of schedules, have you set up an appointment to go over the new transit plan with Sam?" Megan asks.

"We just traded emails earlier this morning. We are going to meet later this afternoon."

"That's great. I just want to make sure you will be able to meet the deadline for Friday. Sam is a busy guy since the new transit maps were implemented." The concern in Megan's voice is clear.

Suzy reassures her, stating, "I know! I'll be sure to take good notes and get you the draft of my press release before Friday."

Megan smiles and exclaims, "Speaking of which, the readership for your press releases is dropping. We are having a hard time getting people to read them. I think your stories are great but we need something to get the readers to open the page and spend time on the release."

"Hmm ... Well, I brought a copy of this month's release. Would you like to read it now and let me know what you think?"

Megan reads over the release and begins making editing marks on the page. She states supportively, "It looks great! I'll finish the edits with a few minor changes. Also, I decided that Sam will have the byline for your next story because it's his program. Putting his name on it will bring a little star power."

Star power? Suzy thinks. The comment really catches her off guard as she mumbles "Oh, okay. I'll get the release to you shortly after I interview him."

"Great! Just set it on my desk when you're finished. Then we can edit and send it out to all of the local papers," Megan says with a directive tone.

Staring at her computer screen, Suzy thinks, *so that's it. Megan wants me to create the press release like I always do, but she wants me to put Sam's name on it when I'm done. I think it's a load of crap. I'm doing all the work and he's getting the credit.*

Suzy's colleague Ted tries to give advice. "Listen Suz, it's your work. I don't think you should give credit away that easily, ya know? Look at it this way. Would you put my name on it instead of yours?"

"Of course not. I wrote it!"

"So don't put his name on it. He shouldn't get to reap the benefits of your labor. I think you should run it with your name," Ted confidently espouses.

Suzy reflects and states, "But I'm just the intern. I don't have any real power here. Megan won't listen to me and she would probably be upset if I sent it out with my name. Besides, if we do put his name on it, it'll probably get read more frequently. I mean, he's done a lot of good around here, so maybe it'll be for the benefit of everyone if they think he did it. At least my release will get read."

"But Suz, what's the point if they don't know you wrote it? Who cares if the author is some big shot in the group or just a no-name intern?"

"Thanks Ted, that totally made me feel better," Suzy says sarcastically. "Glad to hear I'm just some lowly intern."

"That's not what I meant," Ted sighs into the phone. "Let me try again. I don't think that having his name on the press release will make it any more readable. I mean, it's still boring even if it has his name on it."

"You're not helping. Interns have feeling too."

"That's not what I meant. Just try to keep your journalistic integrity in check. If anyone has to suffer through the press release, it should be because they want to read YOUR work."

"Thanks, Ted. That helps."

That afternoon, Suzy had a pre-planned interview set up with Sam Washington, Metro's transit route planner, to get some information about the new transit lines. The interview goes off pretty much as planned, and Suzy ends up with a number of really good quotations to include in the story.

"Have I answered all of your questions?" Sam asks with an anxious grin.

"Yes, Sam. Thank you very much!" Suzy confidently states, then pauses to say, "Well, there is one more thing, but it is more of a personal matter."

"Sure, Suzy. I am pretty busy, but anything for my favorite intern!"

Suzy nervously explains, "Well, I do not want to go behind Megan's back, but did you know that she asked me to put your name on the byline for this press release that I am working on?"

"No, I had no idea. Using a known name for the press release is not unheard of in order to generate press. Does that make you uncomfortable?" Sam asks with concern.

"Well, a little. I know that I am just an intern, but isn't it dishonest to put your name on the press release?"

Sam reassures Suzy by stating, "It does not matter to me whose name is on the press release, I just want to make sure that the media knows about what we are accomplishing here."

"I do too."

"Did you talk to Megan about this, Suzy?"

"Not yet. I was a little surprised when she asked me, and since she is my supervisor I did not want to question her."

"I would suggest talking to Megan. If it makes you uncomfortable for ethical reasons, tell her that."

"Yeah, it just stinks that I can't put this article in my portfolio or anything because it's running with your name and it will probably get published in more papers than my previous releases have."

"Well, if you just want to see your own name in print, you might want to think about how much good this new bus route is doing the city. The more people know about it, the better it will be for everyone, and we need the press for that. Sometimes you have to make things about your organization and not yourself."

Suzy states a little abashedly, "Okay, you are right. Thank you again for making time for me out of your busy schedule."

"No problem. Let me know what you end up deciding, and keep your head up. This is a good work experience for you to carry on to your future endeavors, Suzy."

"Thanks, Sam. See ya around! Have a good weekend."

"You too, and like I said, let me know what you decide."

The next morning Suzy enters Megan's office and puts the story on her desk. "Here's my press release about the new bus routes, Megan."

"Awesome, Suz! Glad you got it done ahead of time. I'll look it over after lunch."

"Sounds good, just pass it on when you are finished looking it over."

Suzy turns to leave Megan's office, but quickly decides to turn around. Suzy asks, "Why are we running this article with Sam's name? That's being dishonest to the public, isn't it?"

Megan patiently but firmly explains, "It is very typical in the PR world to write a press release for someone else, especially if that someone else is higher up than you. For example, I write press releases in Brian's name all of the time because he is our CEO and simply doesn't have the time to write them himself."

"I see."

Megan sees that Suzy is still unsure of the situation and provides further explanation. "Think of it this way," Megan starts. "Let's say Brian is dealing with major press issues because one of our buses crashed and many people were hurt or influenced by the crash. He's busy handling phone calls and sitting in meetings to talk about the issue, while I'm writing a press release on his behalf about our efforts. When it hits the papers and people see that he personally wrote to inform the public, they will likely take more time to read it than if you or I had written it."

"I guess that makes sense. Thanks for taking the time to better explain it to me; I guess I'm still questioning the ethics of the situation here."

Megan, concerned, replies, "How so?"

"Well, our jobs are to be honest and truthful to all of our publics, right?"

"That is correct."

"The way I see it, putting his name on something I wrote is a lie. This would not be any different than lying about safety measures we take on the buses."

"Well, Suzy, those are two completely different issues. Lying about safety measures could put someone in danger. Placing Sam's name on the byline of your article isn't really threatening anyone's safety. In fact, because of public transportation's safety record as compared to individuals in automobiles, you could even say that it could save lives."

Frustrated, Suzy vents, "But on the subject of ethics, a lie is a lie. Our profession is mistrusted by so many people because of all of the lies that PR professionals tell or all of the truths that are withheld by them."

"I see where you are coming from, but you must understand that every company or organization uses the same practice I am using to gain readership. Sam's name is more recognizable than yours and that's just how it is. Remember, this is PR, not journalism. Ultimately, in this field, it's about your client's needs, not your own."

Suzy reluctantly says, "Guess this serves as a real world reality check, huh?"

Megan sighs and explains, "Of course it does. But listen, if you hadn't learned it here you would've learned it elsewhere. I promise you that."

Suzy still isn't convinced that this is the ethical thing to do, so she decides to seek out one of her professors from college who taught a public relations ethics class.

"Hi, Dr. Thomas!" Suzy exclaims.

"Hey, Suzy! Good to see you. I haven't seen you around since our ethics class last semester. How is everything going?"

"Things are going really well. Managing class and my internship is tough, but I enjoy it."

"Well, that is to be expected, but I'm glad to hear you're managing it all."

"Yeah, me too. I actually came to talk to you about dealing with something at my internship.

"Great, let's see if I can help. What's going on?" Dr. Thomas says, leaning forward and showing interest in helping.

"Well, Dr. Thomas, I write these press releases every month ..."

"Yes! I saw one of your articles in the local paper last week. Great stuff and it's fulfilling to be published, isn't it?"

"Of course, but that's what I came here to talk to you about. I am writing a story about the new bus routes and my supervisor wants me to put the transit route planner's name on the byline instead of mine."

"I'm guessing this is an ethical dilemma to you?"

"Yeah, it definitely is. Especially after taking your ethics class last semester. I don't think I should feel comfortable with lying about who wrote the story. I mean it's my hard work, I should be the one getting recognition for it."

"That is true, but the transit route planner deserves recognition as well, don't you think?" Dr. Thomas challenges.

"He's getting recognition! I interviewed him and he has quotes all over the article."

Dr. Thomas pauses, looks down, and then back into Suzy's eyes stating, "I know this is difficult, especially after you've put time and effort into getting this ready for the press, but this happens across the board in businesses and organizations."

"But it's unethical because it's a lie." Suzy firmly states.

"Yes, it can be considered lying. Remember all of our ethical debates in class?"

"Yes, of course," Suzy says quickly.

"Think back to the discussions after our debates. Sometimes we cannot change the standard although it may be considered unethical. Our discussion on product placement really sticks out to me. We all agreed it isn't fair to advertise to people when they don't realize they are getting advertised to, but we all came to the conclusion that there's nothing we can personally do to fix that."

"So it's just like, we can't personally make CEOs find the time to write a press release, so we write it for them?

"That's exactly what I am getting at." Dr. Thomas leans back to signify that the conversation has shifted. Dr. Thomas' teaching methods include getting students to draw the conclusion, even if it took leading questions and statements to get the students there.

"I guess that all makes sense," Suzy reluctantly states.

"Look, I know it's hard to run a story you wrote with someone else's name, especially when you are working on building your portfolio, but this is just one of those things that will probably never change. People have been doing this in our industry for a long time."

"That's true, but I wish I had the power to change it."

"In a sense, you do. You don't have to run the story, Suzy. If you're not comfortable with it, pull the story and have someone else re-write it. I don't think your supervisor would be happy with that though."

"She'd probably be even less happy if I sent it out with my name on it anyway."

"That may be true. Just remember, if it's something you are absolute uncomfortable with doing, then don't, but you must also remember how much power you actually have in this situation."

"Thanks for talking with me, Dr. Thomas. I really appreciate it."

"No problem, Suzy. Stop by any time."

DISCUSSION QUESTIONS

1. Explain each character in the story's differences in ethical perspectives on the issue of authorship.
2. Do you see any alternatives to the method Megan suggested that will still improve exposure and readership of the press release?
3. What are Suzy's options?
4. What would you do if you were Suzy? Why would you make this choice?
5. How does the PRSA inform a decision on this press release situation?

KEY TERMS

Press Release, PR Ethics

CHAPTER 6

Search for a Winning Solution

Pauline A. Howes
Kennesaw State University

ABSTRACT

An 83-year-old man working as a grocery store bagger to pay the medical bills of his late wife wins a contest prize, but is ineligible to receive it because he works for a customer of the contest-sponsoring company. The news media hear about the situation, the grocery store is unhappy, and positive publicity for the company is at risk.

"Well, what would you like to hear first: the good news or the bad news?" Mark Roberts said as he plopped down in the chair across from his boss's desk late Wednesday afternoon. He had just finished talking to a consumer watch reporter at a local television station in Des Moines, Iowa, and he knew potential trouble was brewing that could cast a dark shadow on the national consumer promotion for All Star candy.

Sharon Franklin, director of public relations for All Star Candy Co., let out a small sigh as she glanced at her phone to check the time. Yes, it was already close to 6 pm and she had promised her daughter that she would make it to her seventh-grade volleyball championship match that evening. *So what else is new*, she thought. *Problems always seem to pop up at the end of the day when you have some place to be and something to do.*

"Do I really have a choice?" Sharon said with a smile. Mark was one of three public relations managers on her team who supported the brand marketing department. He was a young PR professional, but learning fast. Every new experience helped him gain understanding about how to handle different situations, and she was pleased to see his professional development over the past year.

"The good news is that our publicity efforts for the Million-Dollar Cash Star promotion are starting to show results and the brand manager for All Star Candy is pleased with our efforts," he said. "The not-so-good news is that I just got off a call from a television reporter who wants a comment from us about what she says is our refusal to give a $25,000 prize to an 83-year-old man who says he has a winning game piece."

Mark went on to explain that the reporter told him the man said he bought a candy bar at Hanratty's Grocery, where he works part time as a bagger. When he opened the package he found a sealed packet that contained a game piece stating, "Congratulations, you are a Cash

Star Winner of $25,000!" He called the 800-number provided to claim his prize but was told he was ineligible to be a winner because he was an employee of an All Star Candy customer, Hanratty's Grocery.

"Rules are rules, and we have to follow them strictly for any promotional contest we run," Sharon said. "I know it's disappointing for this man, but it sounds pretty straightforward to me."

"There's more to this story, though," Mark added. "Apparently Mr. Martin, that's the man's name, is a real institution at Hanratty's. Everyone who works there loves him and all the shoppers think the world of him. He started working at Hanratty's two years ago to augment his pension. His wife had cancer and expenses related to her illness had wiped out their life savings. He needed the money just to make ends meet. His wife passed away a few months ago, and he still is paying off some of her medical bills."

"That does put things in bit different light. Still, we need to check out the situation before we make any comment," Sharon said. "We don't even know for sure that the man has a valid winning game piece. What's the reporter's deadline? Is she planning to air the story tonight?"

"She's eager to go with the story, but if I tell her we're checking into the matter and will get back to her in time for her deadline tomorrow, I think she'll hold the story until she hears our side of things," Mark said.

"That would give us a chance to find out what's going on and figure out the best way to handle this," Sharon said. "A story that makes All Star Candy look like the big, bad company denying a prize to an 83-year-old bagger in a grocery store is not the kind of attention we want for this promotion."

WHAT'S AT STAKE: THE MILLION-DOLLAR CASH STAR PROMOTION

Fortunately, the reporter agreed to hold off on the story, but said she definitely was going to air it the following day, whether All Star Candy had a comment or not. Mark knew that the next day would have to start early and involve key people from several departments. He left urgent email messages proposing an 8 am meeting for Joanie Mills, All Star Candy brand manager; Scott Davidson, marketing legal counsel; and Jim Craft, director of customer sales.

On the drive home, Mark thought about how important the Million-Dollar Cash Star promotion was to the business and recalled how much time and effort he and his colleagues in marketing and other departments had put into creating and implementing the program. The Million-Dollar Cash Star promotion was designed to bring fun and excitement to a candy brand that was well known and enjoyed by many, but its sales in recent years were sluggish.

The brand-marketing team for All Star Candy worked with an outside promotions agency, Archer, to create a consumer promotion that would connect with current consumers in a way that would encourage more frequent purchases while attracting new buyers to try the candy for the first time. Also important, the promotion fit well as part of the brand's overall advertising campaign which used the tag line, "Unwrap the Star in You."

The promotion was a national sweepstakes that would run for four months. Three grand prizes of $1 million were offered, along with five prizes of $50,000, 10 prizes of $25,000, and 1,000 prizes of $10 each. In addition, 5,000 Star Candy packages contained a coupon for a free candy bar. Consumers had to "unwrap" the candy bar to find out if they were a winner of a prize or a coupon. Inside the winning candy bar wrappers was a small sealed packet that held a printed game piece stating the prize and instructing consumers to call a toll-free number to verify their game pieces and claim their prizes.

Television and radio commercials and online ads were running to generate awareness of the sweepstakes. They featured celebrity "stars" who were promoting the candy bar as paid spokespersons for the brand. In stores, special point-of-sale displays helped draw attention to the promotion.

All Star Candy Co. valued its relationships with customers, the stores that sell its products. The company knew that higher sales of Star candy bars would also be good business for those stores. That's why the customer sales department was involved early in the planning phase of the promotion. Incorporating input from a customer perspective helped make the promotion more flexible to adapt to stores of varied sizes and needs. Being customer friendly helped All Star Candy's customer account representatives sell the promotion to store managers and secure good locations for the in-store displays.

From a public relations perspective, the promotion had multiple opportunities to gain awareness of the brand: from the kick-off announcement with a stack of real bills totaling a million dollars providing a photo opportunity, albeit with guards standing by, to plans to publicize the million-dollar winners by bringing them to All Star Candy's headquarters for a special event. Even announcements of winners of the smaller prizes could help promote the game and Star Candy. A bad-news story about the promotion could put these plans in jeopardy.

No question, the company had invested a substantial portion of its annual marketing budget in the Million-Dollar Cash Star promotion and was counting on its success to reinvigorate the product and boost sales. Working out this situation is going to put a whole new spin on the concept of "integrated marketing," Mark thought as he pulled into his driveway.

MEETING OF THE MINDS

Jim Craft just finished talking to his contact at Hanratty's Grocery as he hopped onto the elevator on his way to the fifth-floor conference room where he hoped to get some answers about what was happening with the Cash Star promotion. He was running a few minutes late because of a phone conversation with an anxious and unhappy customer.

As director of customer sales, Craft was responsible for being the liaison between All Star Candy and major customers, such as Hanratty's Grocery. Hanratty's was a growing chain in the Midwest and Craft and his account team had spent a considerable amount of time with the store's management group to cultivate a trusting, collaborative relationship. Hanratty's eagerly supported the in-store promotional activities of Star Candy and the result was a win-win for both. Last year, sales of All Star Candy products in Hanratty's stores rose nearly

8 percent, and the Cash Star promotion promised to extend that growth this year. But this morning, the folks at Hanratty's were not happy customers.

"My ears are burning," Craft said to the group of representatives from public relations, marketing, and legal, seated around the conference-room table. "I'm sorry that I'm a few minutes late, but I was talking—or maybe I should say listening—to my counterpart at Hanratty's, and they are not at all happy with us right now. What is going on with the promotion?"

"No problem. We're just getting started," Mark said. "I was explaining that I arranged this meeting because we received a media call late yesterday about a Hanratty's employee saying he was denied a $25,000 prize in our Cash Star promotion. It turns out the gentleman, Mr. Martin, is 83 years old and works as a bagger at a Hanratty's grocery store to supplement his retirement income and pay off his late wife's medical bills.

"If this is the case, the media and the general public are going to view All Star Candy, rightly or wrongly, as the 'bad guy.' It's the classic David versus Goliath story—big, rich corporation being mean to a senior citizen who is just barely making ends meet," Mark explained.

"This is not the kind of PR I want for our promotion," said Joanie Mills, Star Candy brand manager. "Can't you just explain to the reporter that we have rules and the rules say very specifically that employees of All Star Candy and its customers are not eligible to be winners in the Star Cash promotion? Mr. Martin works for one of our customers, Hanratty's, so we are on the side of right in this matter."

"I could give that response to the reporter, but I sincerely doubt whether it would make the story go away or result in a positive outcome for us," Mark said.

"To build on what Joanie is saying, from a legal perspective, all contests and sweepstakes such as ours, must follow strict guidelines to ensure fairness and to protect the consumer," added Scott Davidson, marketing legal counsel. "We have to establish and follow explicit rules or else we'll be in violation of legal regulations and open to lawsuits from people who feel the contest was unfairly administered."

"All I know is that I have an unhappy customer on my hands," Jim said. "We're not the only ones getting contacted by the media. Hanratty's also received a media call about this and wants to know what it should say. And, the folks there really like Mr. Martin—he's like family to them. They'll feel terribly bad if he doesn't get the prize money. Can't we just make an exception and give it to him? Wouldn't that solve the problem?"

"Unfortunately, that may address one issue, but it would create a really difficult legal situation for us," Jim said. "Let me try to explain without getting into too much legalese." He told the group that when a contest is created, the number of prizes to be awarded must be disclosed and all prizes must be made equally available to keep the game fair. The odds of winning must be stated publicly and if a prize is awarded to someone who is considered ineligible according to the rules, the odds of winning go down for everyone else.

"So, bottom line, if we take this prize out of the prize pool by giving it to Mr. Martin, we are altering the game odds as well as violating the published rules of the game," Jim concluded.

"A lot of times, we run a contest and prizes go unclaimed. I'll bet that happens this time around, too. Maybe we could consider giving Mr. Martin the money and have one less unclaimed prize at the end of the promotion," Joanie said.

"Sorry, no can do," Jim said. "Technically speaking, we would still be influencing the overall odds of winning, and, besides, we say in the rules that all unclaimed prizes will be awarded through a random second-chance drawing."

"It's frustrating because we make the rules known on packaging and our website," Joanie replied. "And the rule prohibiting employees of our company and customers from receiving a prize is done to help protect the integrity of the game. We don't want to create a situation or the illusion of a situation in which employees who have access to large quantities of our product could find product packages containing winning game pieces."

"Speaking of websites, we need to keep in mind that this story will spread like wildfire if it hits the internet. I'm a little surprised it hasn't already done so. But I can envision some pretty ugly tweets," Mark said. "We really need to resolve this as soon as we can today. The consumer watch reporter I talked to yesterday promised she would air the story today, no matter what, and I don't see any way I could ask her to give us more time. Besides, if not this TV station, another media outlet will catch wind of the situation and go with it."

"Why would the media even care about something like this? Don't they have more important things to cover?" Jim asked.

"You have to understand that media cover all types of news and they love to tell a story like this one that they believe tugs at the heartstrings. There's an element of conflict between Mr. Martin and our company, which media use to create a story. Plus, any time a big company is seen as stubbing its toe or making a misstep, it's perceived as news, even though we sure wouldn't agree," Mark said.

ANOTHER OPTION TO CONSIDER

"Okay, I get it," Jim said. "Then what can we do, what options do we have? All I know is that we have an unhappy customer who is looking to us to resolve this situation so the outcome is positive. And they want it done now."

Mark had a suggestion, but he wasn't sure how it would be received. "What about if we gave Mr. Martin the money, but as a gift, not a contest prize," he said. "We could put another $25,000-winning game piece into the prize pool to maintain the integrity of the contest."

"Who has money in their budget to do that?" Joanie responded. "We're running on empty."

"It sounds feasible from a legal perspective," Scott said, "though you may be opening a can of worms by setting a precedent for future prize claims."

"Hey, we may be able to turn this from a negative to a positive in the eyes of the customer if we did that," Jim said. "I could find some of the money in my budget and surely we can find the rest if we all looked hard enough. Why, we could even host a celebration to honor Mr. Martin at the store and present him the money as a gift from All Star Candy. Maybe that TV reporter would even cover it!"

Oh boy, everybody thinks they are a PR expert, Mark thought, but it actually was a good way to think about how the situation could be a winner for everyone.

"Based on all we've discussed, it appears we have two options," Mark said. First, we can stand by the rules of the contest and explain that to be fair to all participants, as well as to follow legal regulations, we cannot give Mr. Martin the prize. Or, we can make the presentation as a gift, explaining why he couldn't win the money, but under these special circumstances we decided to honor an employee of a valued customer in this way." *What should All Star Candy do?*

DISCUSSION QUESTIONS

1. What might Mark say to the reporter to persuade her not to run the story until the company can look into the matter and provide a comment?
2. Should a company always "stick to the rules" and accept potentially negative consequences?
3. If the money is given to Mr. Martin as a gift, how could All Star Candy handle possible copycats attempting to claim a contest prize?
4. Does this situation present an ethical consideration for All Star Candy, as well as a legal consideration?
5. What public relations ideas would you suggest to increase consumer awareness of the Million-Dollar Cash Star promotion?

KEY TERMS

Media Relations, Brand Management, PR Ethics, External Crisis Communication

CHAPTER 7

The Mysterious Case of Cosmo Sludge

Jason S. Wrench and Francesca Rogo
SUNY New Paltz

ABSTRACT

When one of her clients is involved in a hazardous waste spill, Karyn Kassing faces the dilemma of a lifetime. How should she encourage her client to proceed?

"Thanks, John. This is Keiko Kagome, reporting live from Yokohama, Japan." Keiko stared into the camera as she held the microphone so the viewers could hear her around the world. Keiko had dreamed of this type of story from the moment she became a broadcast journalist.

"Keiko, Lauren Redding here—"

"Hi Lauren," Keiko responded, staring into the camera. *Oh my god!!!* Keiko wanted to scream out loud. *I can't believe I'm talking live with John Cartwright and Lauren Redding, two of BCNN's legendary news anchors!*

Keiko had started working for BCNN (BroadCast News Network) in the fall as a translator on the Tokyo desk. She quickly worked her way through Tokyo because the higher-ups at BCNN had heard all about Keiko's work ethic. If someone needed to put in extra work, Keiko was the go-to person for the job. Before too long an opportunity opened at the Yokohama office, Japan's second largest city, so Keiko jumped at the opportunity. Raised in Osaka and educated in Cambridge, Keiko was hardly the typical fresh-faced broadcast graduate.

In fact, it was her late-night work ethic that led her to the position she was standing in right now. About 11:00 pm a story manager from BCNN called in asking if any of the on-air talent was available immediately. Unfortunately, Keiko and one of the camera operators were the only people in the office, so Keiko's supervisor grabbed a jacket out of her own office, throwing it on Keiko as the fresh-faced journalist sped off in the van with the cameraman, Nagaharu Wakahisa. Keiko was still on the phone with the BCNN newsroom trying to get a heads up on the unfolding story.

Keiko held on for dear life as Nagaharu sped through the city of 3.7 million. Thankfully, there was relatively little traffic at 11:30 pm on a Thursday evening. Of course, to the BCNN anchors in New York City, it was only 10:30 am. Keiko and Nagaharu's destination was an intersection nestled between the Intercontinental Hotel and Cosmo World, the largest indoor theme park in Asia. But tonight's news story had nothing to do with the theme park. No, tonight's story had to do with the intersection next to Cosmo World that blocks the bridge between Cosmo World and the Intercontinental Hotel on the other side.

"So, Keiko, what's happening on the ground there in Yokohama?" Lauren asked.

"Lauren and John, about an hour ago, a white, foaming sludge started appearing in the intersection. No one seems to know where the slime is coming from or what is causing the slime. If you look over my shoulder," the camera quickly zoomed past her to where a number of individuals wearing hazmat suits were gathered, "you can see that the government health officials are taking samples of the sludge."

"Does it smell?" John asked.

"I'm glad you asked John," Keiko responded, making a crinkled nose to further illustrate what she was about to say, "I can honestly say this is the worst thing I've ever smelled."

"Keiko, we're actually going to switch to a live feed one of our sister networks is showing from a helicopter in the air, can you please narrate what it is that we're looking at here?"

Keiko stared at a small display monitor that Nagaharu had set up so Keiko could see the live feed. As she stared at the video, she told the network personalities that it looked like the mass was about half the size of a football field. She also added that from her vantage point (before hazmat had shown up), she had measured the sludge at around 11 inches thick, and that the sludge had a consistency of a combination of tar and mud.

For the next two hours, Keiko and Nagaharu were on standby waiting for the BCNN anchors to come back for periodic reports. Almost immediately, BCNN had scientific experts in the fields of geology, chemistry, and environmental science, along with leading theorists in terrorism, environmental toxins, and environmental cleanups. The experts debated what the sludge could be while Keiko and Nagaharu were periodically called back to give live updates.

Sadly, the updates weren't that interesting because the sludge just kind of sat there for two hours not doing much of anything. Nagaharu kept feeding the B-reel for the studio, which was starting to get run on a loop as the various "experts" attempted to determine what the sludge was from half-a-world away.

At almost 1:30 am, Nagaharu motioned for Keiko to turn around and look. She stared in disbelief as the sludge was quickly retreating. Through her earpiece she heard two environmentalists discussing the possibility of toxic waste from the ocean coming ashore. She didn't want to be pushy, but she knew this was news.

"Excuse me."

"Did someone say something?" Keiko could see John checking his Earwig to see if it was working.

"John and Lauren—"

"Oh, Keiko," Lauren exclaimed. "What can we do for you?" As if Keiko were a small child who had just entered into an adult conversation.

"Actually, I have breaking news from here in Nagaharu, the sludge has actually started retreating."

"What!?" exclaimed John and Lauren almost simultaneously.

"If you go to our current film, you can see that in just the past five minutes the sludge has started seeping away from the barricades that were established by the police. In fact, the sludge appears to be disappearing at the same rate it appeared just a few short hours ago." Keiko could hear someone in her ear telling her to keep talking because the network was trying to get the helicopter pilot back to the area. Not quite sure what to say, Keiko just started in on a recap of the night's events. Just when she was afraid she didn't have anything else to say, the image from the helicopter was back on the screen.

"As you can see here, the sludge has already gone from almost half a football stadium to about the size of a small park. At this rate, the sludge will be all but gone in the next 30 minutes."

Keiko kept doing her check-ins with BCNN, but the excitement of the evening was starting to wear on her. By 2:00 am, the sludge had all but vanished. Now, a whole new panel of BCNN experts were talking about the sludge's departure. *Gotta love the 24-hour news cycle,* she thought to herself.

She rested her head against the passenger window as Nagaharu drove back to the station more slowly this time. She was almost surprised when Nagaharu shook her awake. She went into the building, collected her belongings, and walked home in the cool of the early morning. As she walked in the door of her apartment, she glanced at her watch and thought, *I have to be back at the station in five hours.* She didn't bother to undress; she just saw her bed and collapsed on top of it after double-checking to make sure her alarm clock was set.

YOU WIN SLUDGE, YOU LOSE SLUDGE

Karyn Kassing, CEO of The Kassing Group, was sitting in her office on the 25th floor of a Manhattan high rise when her secretary buzzed her.

"Ms. Kassing, Zubaydah Abdul from Wabâl Pharmaceuticals is on the line."

"Give me a minute to finish this email, and then patch her through." Karyn finished typing a press release for a Fortune 500 company and sent it to one of her copyeditors to ensure that the evening news would pick up the story by 5 pm. *Just in time for the 6 pm news,* she thought.

She hit send on her email right when the phone started buzzing. She placed her Bluetooth headset in her ear, gently tapping the side of the device, "Dr. Abdul, so nice to hear from you. It's got to be close to quitting time for you in Dubai?"

"That is correct, Ms. Kassing."

Karyn stared at the series of clocks on the opposite wall clearly indicating major time zones across the world. She saw 10 am on the New York clock and 18:00 (or 5 pm) on the Dubai clock.

"So, Dr. Abdul, what can the Kassing Group do for Wabâl Pharmaceuticals?"

"This is confidential?" Zubaydah questioned, wanting to ascertain if she could trust Karyn with dicey information.

"Dr. Abdul, I can guarantee that the Kassing Group and its employees are completely discrete when it comes to our clients' information. I don't discuss other clients' information with you and I don't discuss your information with other clients." Sensing that she could go on, she added, "So back to the reason you called today?"

"We've had a minor leak of some of our industrial byproduct that seeped out from our facility in Yokohama, Japan."

"OK, how bad is the leak?"

Dr. Abdul could sense from the question that Karyn was talking risk factors and not image factors at this point, so she said, "The waste is not harmful. In clinical testing, the waste did not increase morbidity or mortality rates in mice."

"So, the only outcome data you have on this substance is in mice?" Karyn questioned.

"I'm sorry, Ms. Kassing, we never had any reason to run any specific tests examining the substance because it's always been contained, stored in biohazard containers, and sealed in concrete bunkers in an industrial waste facility an hour south of the plant."

Karyn could sense that Zubaydah, did not like where this line of questioning was taking her. Although Karyn had no reason to think that Dr. Abdul was hiding anything from her, she still needed to get all of the facts.

"OK, so the first step is to get you to send us all of your corporate information about this byproduct. The more we know about the material, the more organized and targeted our management of this crisis can be."

"I trust you and the Kassing Group. You were a gift from Allah when we had that massive international recall two years ago. When I heard about the leak, I told the board president that we should contact our best external PR firm in Manhattan."

"Thank you for the compliment, Dr. Abdul. I'm just a fixer. I help introduce people in their times of need to those in various sectors who can help them get through the crisis."

With that Karyn promised to call Dr. Abdul back before nightly prayers in Dubai and hung up the phone. Immediately, she called one of her most trusted account reps, Devin Treadway.

Within 30 minutes, Devin and his small team of PR specialists were sitting in a small conference room a few doors down from Karyn's office. When she entered the room, the team quickly shot to attention. Devin, on the other hand, barely acknowledged her presence before saying, "Karyn, you do remember we have the Pop's Pizza crisis right now? We've already issued a press release informing the public that Pop's Pizza does not condone drinking and driving and that Pop's DUI is a clear stain on the family-friendly nature of Pop's Pizza."

"Trust me, Devin, I know what all of my teams are working on," she acknowledged with a simple lift of one of her eyebrows. "Speaking of Pop's, the local newspaper today got ahold of the mug shot."

Devin slammed his newspaper down, "Geez! How did none of you not know that this morning!?" he blurted out, staring at his team. "You're paid to make sure our client looks good. We can't do our work if we don't know all the facts. And one small, teensy-weensy fact would have been that his mug shot was released!"

"Anyways," Karyn continued, "I kind of need you on a more important case. We have a new client who had a biological spill in Japan. For now, I'm not going to talk about who the client is, but we should be getting some internal memos later this morning about the industrial waste that was spilled. I need to have this ready prior to 1:00 this afternoon. I need to call the client by 1:44."

The specificity of the time went over everyone but Devin's head in the room. He immediately knew which client he was dealing with because of the specificity of evening prayers at 8:44 pm in June.

Karyn was about to continue talking when one of Devin's minions raised her hand. Karyn looked at the young woman and responded, "Yes. And oh yeah, this isn't school. No need to raise your hand to ask a question or go to the bathroom," she informed the young woman sarcastically.

Devin rolled his eyes, shooting Karyn a sideways glance. The other young PR associates had looks of shock on their faces. In Devin's world, Karyn's sarcasm was legendary, but the younger associates never quite knew how to handle her.

"Ms. Kassing."

"Please, call me Karyn," she responded in an effort to soften her image.

"Karyn," the young woman started hesitantly. "You mentioned that this client is involved in a chemical spill of some kind in Japan. Is this by chance the spill occurring in Yokohama?"

The look of pause on Karyn's face indicated that the young woman had hit the nail on the head. Karyn took a second to collect her thoughts before asking, "What do you know about a chemical spill in Yokohama?"

"Well, it's currently all over social media and the news. Please, the sludge even has its own hashtag on Twitter already '#CosmoSludge.'"

Karyn let a short curse slip from between her lips before asking the young woman to continue.

"Well, from what I can tell, this white sludge started appearing next to a big amusement park in Yokohama. My fiancé is originally from Japan, and actually worked in that amusement park as a teenager. The sludge started appearing as the park was closing, so some of his old friends who still work there started snapping pictures and uploading them to Facebook, Twitter, Instagram, etc."

Karyn, paused letting all of this new information soak in. *Why didn't Dr. Abdul let me know about any of this?*

"Heck, I even received a video of the sludge from my fiancé earlier." The young woman pulled out her cell phone, her fingers gliding over its surface before turning the camera toward Karyn, showing her the video in question.

Karyn lowered herself into one of the conference chairs as she watched the sludge grow and grow. She watched as it took over the amusement park's parking lot. She processed the video knowing that it would go viral in hours if it hadn't already gone viral.

After watching the video, she turned to the group and informed them to call anyone they needed to call because it was about to be a very long day. "In fact," she warned them, "This is one of those days that tends to make or break a PR professional's career. The decisions we make in the next few hours will be some of the most crucial decisions you're faced with in this firm."

Looking at her watch, *11:45 already*, she thought to herself. Thinking about the massive scope of this crisis, she decided this was going to be an all-hands-on-deck situation. She called her secretary and asked her to call all of the account heads. She then checked her smartphone to see if Dr. Abdul had emailed her any of the files. *Still nothing!*

She walked back to her office to grab a few tools she'd need for the next few hours, and took a brief moment to dig up some research on what was happening in Japan. She quickly found BCNN's streaming news coverage. Everyone covering the event seemed to be jumping out of their chairs with glee at the crisis. *If we don't handle this situation correctly, those vultures will devour Wabâl Pharmaceuticals and us in the process.*

By 12:15, the entire office had convened in the largest conference room. There were more cell phones, tablets, and laptops at the ready than she'd seen in a long time. She briefed the company on what was transpiring, again concealing the identity of her client. The last thing she wanted was for anyone to accidentally leak Wabâl Pharmaceuticals' name before she was ready for it to happen.

The group immediately started discussing possible ways to help the client. They came up with message strategy ideas, a list of possible experts they could turn to, and how to ultimately help the client repair their reputation after the crisis subsided.

Around 12:40, there is a soft rap on the conference room door before Karyn's secretary poked her head into the room informing her that she had a phone call.

"Can it wait!?" Karyn questioned.

"Ms. Kassing, it's the same person you were talking with earlier this morning?"

For a second, Karyn tried to interpret her secretary's meaning before realizing that her secretary was alluding to Dr. Abdul. Karyn told the group she'd be back in a minute and walked back to her office.

This time, she didn't bother with the Bluetooth, she just picked up the receiver. "Dr. Abdul, what can I do for you? I still need a few more hours to complete a PR prospectus for you."

"Ms. Kassing, thank you for indulging me here. But apparently, our little mishap in Japan has gone away. The board has decided that it's not in our best interests to say anything at this point."

"I would agree about not speaking out too quickly, but we need to get on top of this and soon," Karyn interjected.

"I think you're missing my point. We won't be needing your services after all. Well, we may, just not today." With that, Dr. Abdul ended the conversation.

Karyn sat looking at her desk phone. *Zubaydah is making a seriously detrimental, calculated mistake.* She sat looking at her phone, deciding what would be in The Kassing Group's best interests at this point.

DISCUSSION QUESTIONS

1. What should Karyn tell Dr. Abdul to do?
2. Is Karyn ethically obligated to inform anyone about the culprit behind the leak in Japan?
3. How do you think the Kassing Group should handle preemptive reputation management for Wabâl Pharmaceuticals?

KEY TERMS

Crisis Communication, PR Ethics, Reputation Management

PART II Social Responsibility

CHAPTER 8

Being Clear at the Clear River Nuclear Power Plant: Risk Communication Goes Critical

William J. Kinsella
North Carolina State University

ABSTRACT

Mandy Middleman is working in her first job as a new public relations professional, at the Clear River Nuclear Power Plant. While the two other members of her public relations team are away, she is confronted with a sudden situation that requires a prompt and effective response. Risk communication, crisis communication, and questions of public trust are at play as Mandy struggles to respond effectively.

AN ORDINARY DAY

"Well, everyone, I want to thank you for visiting Universal Energy's Clear River Nuclear Power Plant and our Energy Universe Visitor Center today. I know you need to get back to school, but I think we have time for one last question."

Mandy Middleman was finishing the last of the day's school group tours, this one with a class of fifth graders from Peaceful Plains Elementary. After four tours and two project planning meetings, she was eager to get back to her office to catch up on answering email inquiries about the plant and its public outreach programs. As the junior member of a three-person public relations team, Mandy often thought there were more things to do each day than the day could possibly allow.

A mom who had volunteered to help with the class trip, and who had asked some skeptical questions throughout the tour, spoke up.

"When we drove in here on the school bus, we saw some men fishing in the river right outside the gate. Is it OK to do that?" Mandy had heard this question before, and replied as she had in the past.

"Well, they're outside the gate so we have no authority over what they choose to do. Local people enjoy fishing there because the water coming out of the plant's cooling system is warm, and fish like to congregate there. But there's nothing to be concerned about—it was called the

Clear River long before our plant was here, and we're proud to say it's still clear. The water is monitored closely, and is always well within state and federal guidelines. As we saw in the exhibit, you get more radiation when you fly across the country in an airplane."

A fifth-grader turned to his dad, who had also come along on the trip. "Dad, do we have to go on that plane Saturday to visit Grandma and Grandpa?" The adults with the group laughed, and Mandy couldn't help but smile, herself.

As the group made its way to the exit, Mandy gave out the customary souvenirs. "Thanks again for visiting, everyone. On your way out, please take one of our 'Tom Atomic' 3D laser pins or key chains—you get to choose which one." As usual, there was a scramble for the two boxes of souvenirs, and then a long time passed as the students made their choices. Then the group was gone.

"Whew," said Mandy, turning to Eddie the security guard. "Now back to those emails."

"I don't know why you let them choose," said Eddie. "It takes forever."

Mandy smiled again. "But it makes them feel like they're involved, you know—like they're in control."

Eddie didn't seem convinced. "Well, anyway," he continued, "Mr. Biggs wants you to get over to his office right away ... there's something going on ..."

"Really? What did he say is going on?"

"Darned if I know—it wasn't very clear ..."

TIME TO SHINE

Mandy quickly made her way from the Visitor Center, through the second security gate, and on to the plant's administration building. Mr. Biggs was on the phone in his office, talking urgently and in low tones, while two other men stood by engaged in a heated conversation. Mandy recognized them as Wayne Scott, the plant's chief engineer, and Reggie Layton, one of the two resident inspectors stationed there by the U.S. Nuclear Regulatory Commission (NRC). As she entered, Mr. Biggs hung up his phone and turned, with a troubled look on his face.

"OK, Mandy, we have a situation here," he said.

"What's going on, sir?"

"There's been a pipe break in one of the steam generators. It looks like two workers were exposed, and we've shut down both units. Reggie says we have an NRC-reportable incident, and more NRC folks are on their way here. Corporate is sending people, too."

She'd never experienced such an event, but Mandy knew these were standard organizational responses. The NRC has strict guidelines for being informed about these kinds of situations, although the responsibility for managing them remains with the plant's owner, her employer, Universal Energy. Although the problem involved only one of the plant's two reactors, Mandy assumed the incident response plan called for shutting both down as a safety measure. Corporate would obviously want to send people from the main office, and already Mandy could anticipate some interesting moments ahead. Like many managers and technical people in the nuclear field, including Scottie the chief engineer, Mr. Biggs was a former naval officer. Mandy had heard him speak of the Clear River plant as "my ship" on many occasions. She knew he didn't take kindly to outsiders, whether corporate officials or NRC inspectors, looking over his shoulder. But those issues were not her main concern. Mr. Biggs soon confirmed her larger worry.

"We need to have a press conference and make a statement in time for the evening news. Scottie has a lot on his plate right now, but we all need to take a few minutes to figure out what we should say. Then I need you to get on the horn with the media and let them know what time we can get this thing done and out of the way."

"Of course, sir, but you know Allie is away at a conference and Bob had to go out of town for a funeral. I'm the only PR person here right now."

"Then I guess we have to go with the C-team, and that's you. Let's get moving, Mandy—it's your time to shine."

A LEAK IN THE SYSTEM

Reggie left to join his NRC colleague in the reactor containment area—he had his own work to do and he knew Mr. Biggs wouldn't want him around for the discussion that was about to take place. The NRC would surely release its own statement about the situation, but the company's decisions about public communication were, at least for now, an internal matter.

"Have we alerted the county emergency management people?" asked Mandy.

"We're not required to do that—there's been no release off-site," replied Mr. Biggs. Mandy knew better than to question the wisdom of his decision.

"Can we take more time to organize this press conference?" she ventured. "Do we have to do this before the evening news?"

"NRC will have this out to the media in no time—we want to get out in front of it," responded Biggs. "And let's be clear about this: We need to get this plant back on line ASAP. It costs the company a million dollars a day when we're not operating. Corporate will be all over me for that. Let's handle the public relations thing quickly and effectively, while Scottie and his crew get the problem fixed so we can be back on line."

Again, Mandy was concerned but thought it best not to challenge her boss. Then the phone rang.

Mr. Biggs took the call, then hung up and turned to Mandy and Scottie. "Dammit," he said, "somebody leaked the news to the media already. And those people from CANT have heard—I don't know how they do it—they're better than military intelligence."

"Citizens Against Nuclear Technologies," muttered Scottie, "You gotta love the name. Those people are bound to make trouble for us, like they did when we had the tritium leak. They'll be down at the gate giving Eddie grief, even before the reporters get here. They mobilize faster than the Marine Corps."

"Well" said Mandy, "let's talk about our plan for the press conference, and if anyone gets here before then, I can go meet with them."

BEING CLEAR ABOUT NUCLEAR

Less than an hour later, Mandy was at the gate. About a dozen people from CANT had arrived, and Mandy recognized the woman from the day's final tour among them. *Well, that explains why she was asking all those questions*, thought Mandy. *She obviously has a point of view about nuclear energy.*

"Hello, everyone," began Mandy. "I'm Mandy Middleman, from the plant's public relations office. I'll be happy to give you an update on the situation."

"We'd like to speak with the plant manager, please," said a member of the group. "He hasn't returned our calls, and nothing has been said publicly about what happened here today. We want to know what's going on, and respectfully, we want to hear from someone in authority. We had enough public relations talk when you had the tritium leak last year."

"I wasn't working here then," Mandy replied. "So I don't know how that situation was handled." She didn't add that she was still in her last year of college at that time, finishing her degree in public relations. "But I'm afraid the manager can't meet with you right now—he's busy handling the technical problem that we're dealing with."

"So the problem is still underway," said the woman from the afternoon's tour. "My daughter and I were here today, and little did I know that there was a problem going on. You were our tour guide and you didn't say anything about it. How do we know we weren't exposed to radiation?"

"I didn't know about it at the time," said Mandy. "It only happened while our tour was underway. I heard about it afterward. I do remember you and your daughter from the tour."

"You don't seem to know much," said the man who had spoken first. "How much radiation has been released?"

"I'm sorry, I don't know the answer to that question. Our health physics team is still collecting data on that. But we're confident that no radiation was released beyond the immediate location where a pipe broke."

"We heard differently," replied the man from CANT. "We want to know the full story."

"I'll look into that and get back to you as soon as I have some information," Mandy responded.

"Has any radiation gotten into the river?" asked the woman from the tour. "My family operates a seafood restaurant, and we serve oysters from the bay. The river leads directly to the bay, and we can't have our oysters contaminated."

"I don't think there's any reason to believe there has been contamination beyond the plant's containment area," said Mandy. "We have defense-in-depth measures to prevent that from happening."

"Defense in depth," said another member of the group, ironically. "Sounds pretty fancy, but why should we trust you on that? Your company has a history of cutting costs and disregarding public health and safety—we saw that big time last year."

"This is a risky situation," declared another group member. "We heard there was a pipe break, and two workers got burned and had to go to the hospital. That's how we found out about this—not from your company, but from someone who works at the hospital."

"Those workers were burned by steam, not by radiation," Mandy replied. "And I'm happy to tell you they're doing fine now."

"Doing fine? They just went through a bad and painful accident, and how do we know they're out of the woods yet? We all know radiation can take a long time to do its thing. They could get sick years from now."

"Let me be clear about this," said Mandy, in the most authoritative tone she could muster. "Their radiation exposures were very low, and their level of risk for any further health effects is very low."

"How do you know that—you're not an expert on that stuff. You're not being clear with us at all about this situation. We want to talk with someone who's in charge."

Things quickly got worse. Mandy found herself taking question after question, and not having answers that would satisfy the group. The situation was getting out of control. Then Mandy saw the TV vans arriving, from two of the local network affiliate stations, with their big antennas that would broadcast the story far and wide. There were cars pulling up as well, and she recognized one of the drivers as a reporter for the local paper. He seemed especially interested in the people from CANT, and appeared to know some of them.

It was time for the press conference to begin.

DISCUSSION QUESTIONS

1. Did Mandy handle the conversation with the people from CANT as well as she might have? Are there other things she could have done or said?

2. What concerns did the people from CANT express? In your view, were these concerns realistic and appropriate?

3. Was Mandy properly prepared for this encounter with concerned members of the public? If not, was this a failure on her part?

4. What were the roles of Mandy's corporate employer, Universal Energy, and her plant manager, Mr. Biggs, in creating and responding to this public relations situation?

5. What public relations work could have been done in advance, before the episode described here, that might have made the situation go better?

KEY TERMS

Risk Communication, External Crisis Communication, Trust/Credibility Building, Social Responsibility

Health Care Disparities at Hope Hospital: Impotent Government Relations and Injured Communities

Anastacia Kurylo
Center for Intercultural New Media Research

ABSTRACT

A respected newspaper reports about racial disparities in health care provided by the local Hope Hospital. City council members, including Tom Farghes representing District 1, try to reach out to their constituents to alleviate concerns and quiet criticism. The election is coming soon. Between an impotent government attempt to assuage the situation and the injuries the attempt causes to affected communities, the outcome does not look good for the election. With various public relations strategies available, the council members need to make some tough choices about how to proceed.

Council Member Tom Farghes leaned back in his high-backed leather chair as his campaign director, Darlene Chaikin, pushed play on the DVD player. Immediately, images of voiceover of the work Tom had completed during his first term on the city council streamed across the screen creating a clear narrative of his dedication to Ashland City, the people who live there, and to building a stable economic environment for the future.

As the ubiquitous voiceover, "I'm Tom Farghes, and I approve this message," played, Darlene turned to Tom and asked, "So, what do you think?"

Tom pondered the ad for a few seconds before responding. "I generally think we've got a really strong, clear message in here. I'm pretty satisfied with what the PR guys are coming up with thus far."

Relieved, Darlene let out a quick breath and smiled. "I hoped you'd like this one. The PR firm we've hired has done some test marketing on this ad, and I can tell you that it was scoring off the charts with potential voters, so I really think we've got a winner on our hands."

Tom smiled and was glad to know that his campaign was in the hands of true professionals.

Ashland City is a thriving metropolitan area of about 250,000. The per capital income rose 5% during Tom's first three years on the city council, well above the national average which was at an all-time low. Unemployment rates for the city are the lowest in the country, making it no wonder that the population increased 10% in the last three years. City council members like Tom have prided themselves on the role they have played in maintaining and improving conditions in the city. Every commercial for an incumbent running in the upcoming election, including those paid for by Tom Farghes' campaign, speaks about that council member's role in creating the current positive economic state of the city.

Despite the hopeful prospects for Ashland City, an undercurrent of local residents who are not happy is emerging. Along with the economic boom for this city of 250,000 people came increased awareness of the disparities in the treatment of its residents. Communities are divided because public services have not kept pace with the local economic upturn, in part because of the economic downturn across the country.

A CRISIS IN HEALTH CARE

"Tom, we've got a problem," Darlene said on Tom's voicemail. "You need to call me as soon as you get this message."

Tom had turned off his cell phone during a council meeting, so he was just now getting out of a long meeting about the need to re-purpose some funds to fix some pressing infrastructure needs in the community.

As Tom made his way back to his office just off the council chambers, he dialed Darlene's number. After just one ring, Darlene answered.

"Tom, Jeremy at *The Herald* gave me a heads up on some breaking news in tomorrow's paper," Darlene spat out in a dizzying haze of words.

"Darlene, slow down, take a breath, and tell me what's going on." Tom then heard Darlene take a deep breath before starting again.

"OK, you know how the Ashland City College was conducting the study on health care in Ashland City?"

"Yes, of course I do. I was an early champion of the project and helped them secure funds from the National Institutes of Health grant."

"Well," Darlene started hesitantly, "the results are out and they are not pretty."

"What do you mean, 'not pretty'?"

"OK, so Jeremy at *The Herald* called me tonight for a comment from your office on the results."

"But we haven't even seen the results."

"That's exactly what I told him, which was when he gave me a brief rundown of what was going to be tomorrow's headline."

Tom could sense that Darlene was checking her notes on the other end of the phone to get the headline correct. *She always has everything so meticulously detailed when dealing with press issues*, Tom thought to himself.

"OK, so the headline for tomorrow reads, 'District 1—Clearly There's No Hope for Minorities.'"

Tom was the city council member from District 1, so he was clearly concerned about the implications of this headline.

"Apparently," Darlene continued, "There are huge health care disparities between minority and white patients at Hope Hospital."

"How bad is it?" Tom asked.

"From what little Jeremy would tell me, the data are pretty conclusive that District 1 constituents are not receiving the same level of medical care as people in the other districts."

As a white council member in the most diverse district in Ashland City, Tom knew what the repercussions of this information could be for not only his district but for his campaign as well. He paused for a moment trying to come up with a strategy for going forward. "At this point, we need to get our hands on the data and see what's going on for ourselves. Call Dr. Russell, the lead investigator at Ashland City College, and get the data as soon as possible."

"That may not be until tomorrow morning," Darlene warned.

"I understand that, but I think we need to see the full picture before we issue any comments. For now, I'm going to go home and get some shuteye while I can. I have a sneaking suspicion tomorrow is going to be a very long day."

Tom woke the next morning and immediately went outside to retrieve his copy of the *The Herald*. Sure enough, the headline of the day included racial disparities in health care. One of the more fascinating factors of the article involved a table that clearly illustrated some of the major problems related to health care disparity (Table 9.1).

TABLE 9.1	Health Care Disparities at Hope Hospital				
	District 1	**District 2**	**District 3**	**District 4**	**District 5**
Race					
Black	45%	12%	17%	15%	21%
Latino/a	26%	3%	5%	10%	37%
Asian/Pacific Islander	10%	7%	10%	15%	6%
White	19%	78%	68%	60%	36%
Health Disparity					
Hospital-Acquired Infections/1000	30	13	7	19	18
Length of Stay (in Days)	1	5	4	3	3
Mortality (Infant)/1000	13	1	3	9	8
Mortality (All Ages)/1000	21	4	5	15	12
Cost (per Patient)	32,524	72,361	91,422	64,907	54,062

Based on these results, his constituents were more likely to get infected while in the hospital, stayed less time than other districts, had higher infant mortality rates, higher mortality rates overall, and their medical costs were a fraction of that of some of the districts with higher rates of White residents. Basically, the hospital seemed to spend less time with his constituents, resulting a really skewed picture. After taking a second to digest the numbers, Tom picked up the phone and called Darlene.

"Tom, I was waiting for your phone call."

"I figured you would be," Tom responded. "So, what's your take on the article?"

"Well, I definitely think the picture is pretty clear here. There are clear disparities going on based on the numbers alone."

"OK?"

"However, I talked with Dr. Russell at Ashland City College and he definitely wanted to point out a few errors in *The Herald*'s interpretation of the facts."

"Do tell."

"Well," Darlene started. "First, some of the numbers may indicate differences, but the results don't indicate 'actual' differences based on the statistical analysis."

"What do you mean by actual?"

"Tom, I suffered through college statistics eons ago, so all I can say at this point is that the numbers may appear different, but they are not 'statistically' different … whatever that means."

"OK, well, let's not bother with the semantics at this point," Tom warned. "What about the cost per patient differential? Did Russell have anything to say on that one?"

"Actually, Dr. Russell said that one was probably the most damning. From what I've written down here, apparently the cost differential noted illustrates that patients from District 1 simply receive fewer medical services from Hope Hospital, which is why District 1 patients' numbers are as low as they are."

"So, there really is a clear difference in how my constituents are treated at Hope compared to constituents in other hospitals?"

"Apparently so."

OUTRAGE BEGINS

Almost immediately, the phone at Councilman Farghes' office and campaign headquarters began ringing. On one hand, he had a number of his constituents calling to find out what he was going to do about the clear incidents of racism at Hope Hospital. On the other hand, he heard almost immediately from Hope Hospital's PR department claiming that the study was flawed and that he should come out dismissing the report as biased and stand firm with Hope Hospital.

Over the next week, Councilman Farghes' office and campaign headquarters were inundated with phone calls, letters, and emails from his constituents voicing their concerns. In his official press release on the subject, Councilman Farghes commended the Ashland City College research team for clearly highlighting this issue of injustice. As the councilman for the district most clearly impacted by health care disparity at Hope Hospital, he promised to look into this issue further and ensure that the public's outrage was heard.

GOVERNMENT RELATIONS

After a week of constant reaction to the *The Herald* article, Ashland City's council decided to hold an open forum on the subject of the health care disparity article.

Although District 1 had the highest ratio of minority community members, all council members felt the pressure to respond. In an untimely turn for the worse, two-thirds of the seats in each of the five districts were up for re-election in November, only a couple of months away, so everyone was feeling pressure to do something.

When discussing whether public hearings were necessary, Tom told his fellow council members, "I strongly advocate that some action must be taken before the response heightens. Residents of the districts with mostly minority populations like my own District 1 are being vocal about expressing their outrage. Worse, they are starting to organize." "Not only is this a public relations problem for city council members," Tom reminded the council, "ultimately, there is legitimate reason to be concerned about the racial disparity in health care evidenced by these statistics."

Working in conjunction with administrators and physicians at Hope Hospital, city council members coordinated a public relations plan to provide residents of their districts a chance to voice their concerns in a public, controlled, and predictable forum.

In a passionate plea, Tom argued for the plan, saying, "Democratic processes are the foundation of American culture and give people an opportunity to have their voices heard."

Ultimately, Tom proposed a plan that would help the city council members build trust within their districts. The goal of the plan was to allow the city council members to foster trust and credibility within minority communities. Council members identified two ways to accomplish this goal. First, they intended for the event to be informative. Thus, hospital representatives would be present to address relevant issues. Additionally, scholars from local universities who study issues of health and race were also invited to speak. Second, they intended the event to give residents in the communities that were disproportionately affected a chance to voice their concerns to those in positions of power to effect change.

The plan for the event was solidified and disseminated to each district. The council members, representatives from Hope Hospital, and local scholars would be at the podium to speak and respond to questions. Residents were invited to attend. Because of the overwhelming interest from residents in speaking at the event, those who wished to do so were required to register in advance starting at 7am on the morning of the 9am event. The mayor was expected to attend as well.

PUBLIC FORUMS

Once the event began, Tom introduced himself and the four other council members. During the introductions each council member provided five to ten minutes of explanation about why the topic was important to them personally. The only interruption to this process was when the mayor arrived 20 minutes after the start of the event. She was introduced by the Tom and took her seat in the front row of the audience.

After the council members spoke, the panel of experts was introduced, including three hospital representatives and Dr. Russell and his two colleagues who worked on the project. Tom started by asking the panel a variety of relevant questions about the health disparities in the community. Panelists were instructed that they each had up to six minutes to respond to any question to which they chose to respond. Tom explained that if they exceeded their time, they will be asked to finish their point so the discussion could move forward.

The back-and-forth between the hospital representatives and the Ashland City College researchers was fairly cordial, but there definitely were some tensions between the two groups. At one point, the head of PR for the hospital informed the room, "We'll just have to agree to disagree on your interpretation of the facts."

"Excuse me," Dr. Russell started. "You can't just make up your own facts. We're not even talking about interpretation here. We're talking about science that is based on your own hospital's records. You may not like the facts as they are, but there is no interpretation here. The numbers are the numbers, and you can't just wish them away because it's expedient to do so."

After the question and answer session between Tom and panelists was completed, attendees were given the opportunity to comment to the council members in the order in which they registered. Before they began, Tom informed the attendees, "Speakers will have one minute to talk in order to make sure we hear from everyone. A bell will sound when the speaker's time is up. At that point please step aside and let the next speaker come to the podium to speak. Only those who have registered in advance will be allowed to speak. I will read the names in the order in which people registered. Thank you."

Most speakers followed this protocol in a calm procession. Occasionally, speakers were cheered by enthusiastic and frustrated attendees. In one case, advocates for the audience who were not speaking objected to a speaker who was cut off because of the time limit despite his emotional testimony about how the health care disparity affected his life.

"My mother was healthy before she went to the hospital for a routine check-up. An error by a doctor meant she went in for emergency surgery. An infection left her sick for weeks in that hospital bed until it killed her. I have no one else . . ."

As the registered attendees began to speak one after another, the scholars and hospital representatives left the platform and exited the auditorium in which the event was held. Although the event was scheduled for two hours, at three hours the final speakers had just ended. Although the mayor stayed for much of the event, she was no longer in the audience by the end, having left unseen sometime earlier.

INJURED COMMUNITIES

Tom Forghes left the event more concerned than when he arrived. Although the event had proceeded as he planned down to the last detail, the outcome was somehow not what he expected. While attendees had the opportunity to voice their concerns, he felt they still had not been heard. In informal discussions with his district members and through emails and other outreach in the week that followed, he understood that the community was as disgruntled as ever. Their focus was now on the council members taking some "real" action. Their public relations plan was perceived as a farce. Tom was concerned not only for his public image and re-election but for the real problems faced by those in his community. He was in a position to advocate for some new strategy and he had some tough decisions to make to determine how to proceed.

DISCUSSION QUESTIONS

1. What was the original problem faced by the council members?
2. What are the pros and cons of the public relations strategy used?
3. Did the public forum event foster trust and credibility for the city council members amongst the affected communities as intended? Why or why not?
4. Based on the process used in the public forum and the results of that event, how would you recommend Tom Farghes and the other council members proceed if they want to be re-elected?

KEY TERMS

External Crisis Communication, Social Responsibility, Governmental Relations, Trust/Credibility Building

CHAPTER 10

A Watered-Down Case of Social Responsibility

Allison Clearly and Juliann C. Scholl
Texas Tech University

ABSTRACT

Karen Little, an environmentally conscious individual, is excited when she is assigned to Pure Water One, a company that claims to adopt socially responsible practices at its newest plant. However, the more she learns about this company's practices, the more conflicted Karen is about working with them. Should Karen turn a blind eye to the company's practices to keep her job, or should she speak out about the unfair practices, and thus jeopardize her position at her advertising company?

Karen Little recently graduated from college and accepted an advertising position with Deltree Advertising. Karen was excited about landing a job with such a prestigious company so early in her career. The starting salary seemed good for a person fresh out of college. Moreover, the people she met during her series of interviews were friendly and seemed genuinely impressed with her. Karen was impressed with them as well.

Among Deltree Advertising's many high-profile accounts is its largest account, Pure Water One. Pure Water One has recently grown to one of the biggest bottled water companies in the country. The company boasts that it gets its product from fresh-water streams. In addition, through various internet and social media outlets, they have publicized their new environmentally friendly bottling plants in India; this publicity has helped its growth in recent months. This marketing strategy is paying off, since more consumers are leaning toward socially responsible companies that focus on reducing dangerous emissions into the environment and that provide organic and safe products.

Karen is excited that Pure Water One is a client of Deltree's, and that she has been given some assignments regarding its latest campaign. In her personal life, Karen does what she can to be more environmentally friendly. She lives modestly to be able to make her monthly payments on her new hybrid vehicle. She recycles regularly and even has her own compost bin. Karen believes companies should be required to handle the environment responsibly and give back to communities they inhabit.

Karen started her first weeks on the job following Cindy Hritsco, Deltree's head of advertising. In their first sit-down meeting, Cindy explained, "The current ad we are working on focuses on the humanitarian approach Pure Water One has to the communities around their newest factories in India. All the water they bottle is from fresh streams in the area. The new campaign we are working on will be to show how Pure Water One is helping provide clean water to villages in India where the factories are. These people would otherwise have no access to clean water if it weren't for Pure Water One providing it."

Karen is impressed. She responds, "That is so awesome! I am so excited that our client is a company that gives back to the community. I know consumers care about where their products come from and a back story like this should be told!"

"So glad you feel that way, Karen," says Cindy, putting a mentor-like hand on Karen's shoulder. "I think you'll do a great job on this one." Both women continue to discuss the details of the campaign and the stipulations given by the client.

Alone in her cubicle, Karen decides the best way to approach this campaign is to see what the consumer feels is most important from the bottled water company they choose. Karen remembers that her city will be hosting a community art market and bazaar, an annual event that allows artists, merchants, entrepreneurs, and businesses to set up booths to advertise or sell their products or services and is attended by a variety of community members. Karen decides to set up a booth at this event to promote Pure Water One's new campaign and get customer feedback.

Karen looks forward to hosting her booth at the event. The booth has a large horizontal banner labeled, "Pure Water for All," and she has plenty of bottled water samples to distribute to people passing by. Karen cannot wait to gauge consumers' attitudes. As the crowd starts to build around the water booth, Karen begins to interview people about what they feel is important for a company to do to gain the public's trust and patronage.

When Karen engages people, she tries to be impartial in getting their opinions, but secretly hopes that they care about the environment and responsible business practices. She asks her rehearsed question: "What do you feel is most important when buying a product, affordability, social responsibility of the company, or quality of the product?"

A college-aged woman with a bag with a world peace pin on it says, "Social responsibility, of course! I want to know that some big company isn't ruining land somewhere or polluting the air just because it costs less than doing things the right way."

Her friend says, "I don't know about that. I think I would like to have a quality product first and foremost. But I don't want to be eating fruits that were grown in a lab with chemicals or drinking water that chemical waste has tampered with."

Karen is pleased that these women are so forthcoming with their opinions. She presses further: "That's great feedback! What if I told you Pure Water One bottles fresh water with no added chemical taste enhancements as well as uses environmentally friendly factories that not only provide you with fresh water, but poor villages in their area as well?"

Both women agree that that sounds great and take some samples of bottled water and some promotional pamphlets.

Later in the day, after many people had been taking samples, getting information, and filling out surveys, Karen starts talking to a young man named Rick. He holds a sign saying, "Nothing is free! Pure Water One are thieves!" Karen loves the passion protestors have. She herself had participated in a few protests while in college. Karen sees this as an opportunity to educate Rick on Pure Water One and all the good they do.

Rick says, "I get that Pure Water One has plastic that doesn't fog up the air as much as the competing brands, but there still are emissions, right?"

"Well, yes," says Karen, "but any factory would have some emissions. Pure Water One does things to counteract that like practicing responsible waste disposal, and their newest endeavor is providing fresh water to villages that have been impacted by drought in India."

Rick responds, "So, they are giving water away to people in India? Have you thought about why they even need the water? What did they do before Pure Water One was there?"

Karen searches her brain for an explanation. "Well, I supposed they only had access to unclean water."

"Have you thought about the possibility that Pure Water One are crooks and they bought all the land in the area that had any clean water and left all those people to die?" Rick says.

"Um, uh, well … I can't imagine that is the case, Rick. Pure Water One is known for …"

"For twisting the truth and making themselves look good," Rick impatiently interrupts.

Although her conversation with Rick ended politely, Karen is confused and conflicted. She returns to her original spot behind the booth and starts to wonder if Rick could be right. Could Pure Water One actually have done this? Why would they portray themselves as being so responsible and helpful if they were really the cause of the lack of safe drinking water in the first place?

The next day, Karen analyzes the data she got from the surveys. Overwhelmingly, the results suggest that consumers believe social responsibility to be the most important aspect of a company. Given these findings, Karen cannot get Rick's words out of her head all day and she decides it is her responsibility to find out if there is any truth to his claims.

Karen remembers that when she first started work on the Pure Water One campaign, she was given information on the villages that are being provided water. However, after closer review of some of the information, she notices that several of the villages have not been using the water provided them. Karen decides to dig deeper and call Mike Cantu, Pure Water One's researcher assigned to the campaign. She cannot get a hold of him on the phone so she writes him an email asking for clarification on why the villages are not using the water. After two days, Mike writes Karen this email addressing her concerns:

Dear Ms. Little,

I have looked into your request for information pertaining to why some villages in the central area near the factories have not utilized the resources. Not all villages have paid for the access to Pure Water One's resources. While Pure Water One loves to give back, some costs need to be accounted for in order to provide the fresh water to the communities.

I hope this is the information you were seeking. If you need further assistance, please let me know.

Sincerely,

Mike Cantu
Sr. Researcher

Karen is shocked that the water is not donated as a charitable item, but sold as a business transaction! Karen is curious as to what those villages are doing for water if they are not using Pure Water One's water. She knows that other than the land Pure Water One owns, there is no other clean water in the area. Karen calls Don Martin, the photographer who took all the photos in India for the campaign, to see if she can get some insight from someone who has been there.

When Karen gets in touch with Don, she notices he is not as helpful as she expected him to be. Don is reluctant to speak to Karen because he needs the steady income from Deltree Advertising. Karen ensures Don this is just for her information and she will not tell anyone else they spoke.

Don sighs, still not feeling good about talking to her. However, he explains, "Karen, the living conditions in the area are horrible. Pure Water One brought in crews to clean the area up and make it look better than it actually was before I took the photos. Many people were ill and had to be removed from the area for the pictures. Then they were brought back after."

Karen is in disbelief, but asks, "Then why don't they pay for the access to the water if it is making them that sick?"

Don heaves another sad sign, and then goes on. "Pure Water One charges much more than anyone in the area can afford for the water. The people there farm for themselves and their families to survive. You see, they don't have jobs like you or I where they get money; they barter for what they need or they just share within the community. Water is their livelihood. Without it their crops don't grow and they can't survive."

Feeling a little braver, Don continues to tell her that before Pure Water One built its new factories there last year and purchased the land, the villages had free access to the water there for irrigation, bathing, and drinking. Pure Water One bought all the land that had any fresh water on it and left the people to suffer from disease and poor crops.

Although disappointed, Karen thanks Don for his insight and repeats her promise to keep their conversation confidential. She hangs up the phone and just sits starting at her computer screen. Then the consumer surveys on her desk catch her eye once more. She still has to finish compiling and writing up the results so she can present them to Cindy, who will likely tell her what a good job she has done on her first promotional event.

Karen is still frozen in front of her computer. She wonders, *who else knows about this? Does anybody else care that the people in those villages are being forced to pay for the very resource they had free access to just a short while ago?* She feels torn. On the one hand, she was feeling so good about her job just a half hour ago; on the other hand, it appears that her values pertaining to social responsibility are in conflict with the job everyone expects her to do, which is promote the Pure Water One product and the practices of that company. Part of her wants to expose Pure Water One and hold them accountable for what they are doing in India. But is it Karen's responsibility to do so? And is this worth jeopardizing her first job? She was hired to help promote the clients of her advertising agency. Can she still call herself an advocate of social responsibility and skill keep doing the job she was assigned?

Karen remembers that her report on the event is due to Cindy the next day. The results as she would report them would show Pure Water One in a favorable light. But Karen does not know how to proceed. Just then, Cindy has been wandering the office and stops at Karen's cubicle.

"Hi, Karen," says Cindy cheerfully. "Again, nice job on the bazaar. How are those results coming along?"

Karen looks up at Cindy. At that moment, she tries to decide what to say next . . .

DISCUSSION QUESTIONS

1. How would you describe the inner conflict Karen is experiencing? What do you think of her promise to Don not to divulge what he told her in confidence?

2. Please comment on Mike Cantu's response to Karen's request for information. In what ways was Mike's message competent? What information might be missing from the message?

3. What do you think of Karen's methods for gathering customer information at the market? What other questions would you have asked to gauge customer perceptions and preferences?

KEY TERMS

Campaign, Environmental Responsibility, Marketing, Social Responsibility

CHAPTER 11

Bad Taste? Responding to Organizational Crises and Rebuilding Reputations

Lisa K. Hanasono
Bowling Green State University

ABSTRACT

When a frozen yogurt company attempts to celebrate the success of a popular Asian American football star, many customers and civil rights organizations blame the company for being racially insensitive.

❖   ❖   ❖

"What is wrong with your company!?" screamed an angry customer. "You ought to be ashamed of yourselves. I'll never shop at Tasty Temptations again! In fact, you'll hear from my lawyer about this!"

"Ma'am, please …" Emma Dowd responded, helplessly. Before she could utter another word, the angry customer stormed out of the frozen yogurt store, slamming the door behind her.

Emma's face burned bright red. What a day! As the newly hired public relations and advertising specialist for Tasty Temptations (a local frozen yogurt shop in Detroit, Michigan), Emma thought she would be developing new marketing materials and promoting the company's delicious treats to the local community. She didn't expect to deal with dozens of disgruntled customers, nosey news reporters, and civil rights attorneys. She also didn't expect to be called a racist. *They don't pay me enough to deal with this stuff!*

Brrring! Brring! The shrill ring of the company's telephone jarred Emma back to reality.

"Thanks for calling Tasty Temptations. This is Emma."

"Hi Emma. This is Rachel Reins from the Channel 5 News Team. I'm contacting you because we're going to run a story about your new frozen yogurt flavor tonight. Many people have been … uh … *talking* about it, and I want to get the company's official statement." Although Rachel was trying to be polite, Emma could tell that the reporter did not think highly of Tasty Temptations.

"Hello Ms Reins. Um … Thanks for calling." Emma responded. *Take a deep breath. You can do this.*

"Many people find your company's new frozen yogurt flavor titled 'Me Love You Wong Time" racially offensive. What does the company have to say about this?" The reporter asked in an accusatory tone.

Emma's head began to spin. How did she get into this mess?

JASON WONG: LOCAL HERO, FOOTBALL STAR ... AND FROZEN YOGURT FLAVOR?

Born in Detroit, Michigan, Jason Wong was raised by his Chinese American father and Korean American mother. Growing up, he was well-liked by his peers, teachers, and neighbors. In fact, while attending a fundraiser for his high school's football team, he saved the life of a man who had a heart attack. Wong was well-known in the Detroit area for being a nice guy and a great role model.

Several months ago, rookie quarterback Wong became the new star of a professional football team in the United States. Since his first appearance on the field, Jason led his team to a series of impressive wins. Raving about his outstanding quarterback ratings, great leadership skills, and charming personality, the media facilitated Jason's rapid rise to fame by featuring him on the covers of glossy sports magazines and talking about his successes on prime time television.

Noting that there were very few pro-football players of Asian descent, some journalists began to refer to Wong as the "Amazin' Asian." The nickname spread like wildfire. Within days, stores began to carry t-shirts, hats, and sweatshirts with the screen-printed words, "Amazin' Asian." For better or for worse, the products sold out very quickly. Following the fad, some businesses began to sell products with the phrase, "So Wong ... and So Right!" on them. Other businesses began to sell sports drinks (called "Wong Water") and protein bars (labeled "Nuts about Wong").

THE GOOD, THE BAD, AND THE UGLY

Tasty Temptations, a frozen yogurt shop in Jason's hometown, wanted to develop and market a product that would celebrate his rise to fame. Brad Connor, the owner of Tasty Temptations, organized a meeting with his creative team, Bryan Newman and Red Stevens.

"Jason Wong is a longtime customer of Tasty Temptations," Connor explained. "Growing up, every time he won a home football game, his folks would take him here to celebrate."

Stevens chuckled. "I remember. They came into the shop so frequently that I started to give them free sundaes."

"Well, I want to create a new frozen yogurt flavor in Jason Wong's honor," Connor stated. "But it's gotta be unique. You know... something special."

"Hmmmm ... Jason's favorite frozen yogurt flavor was banana. So we should probably start with that," Stevens offered.

"Okay, fine." Connor rubbed his forehead. "Newman, what do you think?"

"Well, people are calling him the 'Amazin' Asian.' Maybe we should focus on some ... ethnic flavors?" Newman suggested.

"Excellent!" Connor's eyes darted around the room. He didn't know much about Jason's Asian American heritage. Hopefully Stevens or Newman could help him out. "Like what?"

"Oh … I don't know…. How about topping the frozen yogurt with fortune cookie pieces?" Newman asked.

"Alrighty." Connor sounded excited. He could hear the cash register drawer ringing already. "Stevens, what do you think?"

"Maybe we could infuse the banana flavor with hints of *exotic* spices and mix in some mochi and fresh Asian pear?" Stevens offered.

"Fine…. That will be fine … We'll play with the recipe and make sure it tastes good," Connor said, gruffly. "The last thing we need is a name for the new flavor …We need something clever. Something catchy. Something about Wong."

Newman's face lit up. "I got it! *Me Love You Wong Time.*"

TASTY TEMPTATIONS

During its first week on the market, sales for the new frozen yogurt flavor, *Me Love You Wong Time*, skyrocketed. Connor and his team had perfected the recipe, and local customers called the frozen treat delicious, fresh, and fun. After a few weeks, the profits from the new product were so high that Connor decided to hire Emma Dowd to promote the frozen yogurt beyond the local community. That was when the complaints started.

At first, a few customers began to ask questions about the product.

"Don't you think the name of the frozen yogurt is a bit … offensive?" one customer pondered.

"Wow … The frozen yogurt tastes really good … but it seems kind of racist," another customer said.

"What do you mean?" Connor asked, shocked.

"Well … It's not just the name," the concerned customer explained. "The ingredients seem pretty stereotypical. Fortune cookies? Exotic spices? C'mon …"

In the ensuing days, the number of complaints and negative comments began to build. Regular customers stopped visiting Tasty Temptations. Someone spray-painted the word "racist" on the front door of the store. Instead of working to promote their products, Emma was engaging in damage control and attempting to resolve a growing crisis.

MELTING UNDER PRESSURE?

"Ahem … Did you hear me?" reporter Rachel Reins cleared her throat.

Emma shook her head, "I'm sorry, Ms. Reins. What did you say?"

"Many people find your company's new frozen yogurt flavor titled 'Me Love You Wong Time' racially offensive. What does the company have to say about this?" the reporter asked again.

Emily took a deep breath. What should she do?

DISCUSSION QUESTIONS

1. Tasty Temptations had good intentions when they created their new frozen yogurt flavor. However, some people found it to be offensive. In the world of public relations, to what extent do a company's *intentions* matter?

2. Why might some people dislike the new frozen yogurt product? What was specifically problematic about the frozen yogurt flavor's name and ingredients? What do *you* think about the new flavor?

3. What could have been done to prevent this problem?

4. What are the potential benefits and risks of changing the product's name and ingredients?

5. If you were Emma, what would you do now?

KEY TERMS

Social Responsibility, Reputation Management, Crisis Responsibility, PR Ethics

CHAPTER 12

Playing Chicken

Diana L. Tucker
Walden University

ABSTRACT

When a CEO of an international sandwich chain asks his new account executive to create a campaign and press conference around a global health and food issue, the account manager finds herself questioning the necessity of such a campaign.

Ellen Freemont had been at her computer all day researching avian flu. She certainly had not expected to be doing this when she was awarded the Uncle Bob's Sub Shop account last week. This was her first international account where she was the senior account manager. Ellen knew that receiving this account meant that she was a trusted and valued member of the public relations agency she worked for, Regency PR. Ellen also knew that doing well with this account meant she would soon be in line for a vice president position with the agency. Thus, the stakes were very high.

Ellen was especially excited to work on this account because, while it was an international chain, the company worked more like a small, local organization. The CEO, Bob Crawford, was involved in all aspects of the business and really seemed to understand the need for public relations. All too often, the leaders of an organization needed a lot of convincing to put money into public relations efforts and even then would not get involved in the promotion of the company through public relations activities. In addition, Bob Crawford saw community involvement as essential to good business, had instituted a very fair benefits package for his workers, and celebrated his workforce's diversity. Thus, the employees really seemed to like working at Uncle Bob's Sub Shops.

MORE ABOUT UNCLE BOB'S

Uncle Bob's Sub Shop started in 1988 as a project Bob Crawford did in his senior year entrepreneurship class at Durham University in Durham, New Hampshire. Bob received an "A" on the project and his father and uncle, both entrepreneurs and former restaurant owners, were keen to support him in opening a shop upon graduation and helping him build the company.

Bob, his father Robert Crawford, and uncle Steven Crawford opened the very first Uncle Bob's Sub Shop in Boston in 1990. Their specialty was gourmet subs that were made fresh and with meat grilled to order. They had a selection of artisan breads, cheeses, and unique sauces along with just about any topping customers could think of to put on their subs. Thus, customers could easily order a classic Italian Sub with Italian vinaigrette, peppers, provolone, and olives, or go with something more unique such as the Thai Chicken Curry Sub with grilled chicken breast, green peppers, and onions with a coconut red curry sauce drizzled over the top.

Uncle Bob's Sub Shop did very well and franchises started opening up in the Boston suburbs, then spread to other big cities on the Eastern Seaboard. However, the greatest expansion came when Uncle Bob's Sub Shop signed a deal to put franchises in some of the larger U.S. Army bases in Germany, Italy, Japan, and Korea. And with that move, Uncle Bob's became an international chain. Every year, more franchises were added until there were 507 franchises in America from Maine to California, plus 11 franchises on international military bases.

THE FIRST MEETING

Going into her first meeting with Bob Crawford, Ellen was excited and full of ideas for promoting the chain, its good deeds, its workplace ethics, and great sandwich ideas. But, right from the beginning, it was clear that the CEO had a very different concern and agenda, one that Ellen thought was not really a good direction for the company.

"Ellen, I am so glad to have you aboard and get to work on a PR campaign for our little company!" Bob Crawford exclaimed as Ellen entered his office.

"Oh, the pleasure is all mine, Mr. Crawford. I am really excited about working on this account! And it is far from 'little'!" Ellen said while shaking Bob's hand.

"Please, please, just call me Bob, no need for the formalities around here. Please have a seat and let's get down to business." Bob pointed Ellen to a seating area with a small couch, a coffee table, and two armchairs. He took an armchair and Ellen decided to take a corner of the couch so they would be directly across from one another.

"Well, Bob, I have been doing some brainstorming and reviewing of your past PR endeavors to prepare for our meeting and I think I have some great ideas for a fresh, new take on a PR campaign for Uncle Bob's Sub Shops." As she said this, Ellen began to take some samples and documents she had created out of her briefcase, laying them on the coffee table.

"Well, before you go too far, Ellen, I wanted us to discuss an issue that has concerned me recently and I really want to do a proactive type campaign with the issue first. Then we can definitely come back to some of your ideas in a few weeks or months." Bob announced.

"Oh, of course, Bob. You know, I really like how proactive and engaged you are in your company's day-to-day business. You really don't find that with many CEOs. It is very refreshing, I must say." Ellen replied.

"Yes, I am not your average CEO by any means," Bob said with a chuckle.

"So, what did you have in mind?" Ellen asked.

"Avian flu," Bob stated seriously.

"Avian flu??? What about it?" Ellen inquired.

"Well, you know there has been a bit of an epidemic going on in flocks of domesticated birds in parts of the world, Ellen. It seems especially prevalent in Asia. I really fear that people have begun to think that eating poultry and eggs, especially chicken and turkey, is dangerous and that they might get the avian flu from eating them. With our recent expansion on military bases in Asia, I am definitely concerned because they are American military bases and those American soldiers could easily spread that idea over here in America. The majority of our sales are in subs that contain chicken and turkey and then we get a large percentage from our egg breakfast subs. So, if people stopped eating them, we would be in a world of hurt. This is why I am thinking we need to do a proactive campaign to teach people about how avian flu is not contracted through eating poultry," Bob declared and then sat back with a smile.

Ellen was a little flustered as she had not seen this coming at all. Her initial reaction was to say that she did not think it was a very good idea. Her thought was that, if this idea is not in the minds of consumers now, doing a campaign on it would put the idea that avian flu can be caught by eating poultry into their customers' minds. Then, no matter what they said about the issue, the concern that it could be possible would still be there. However, Ellen realized that she really did not know enough about avian flu to rule out such a campaign altogether.

"Oh, wow, I had never thought of that," Ellen said cautiously.

"Exactly! And I doubt our customers have done the research, so by doing a safety and health campaign about avian flu and letting people know they can't get it through eating poultry or eggs, we are being proactive and helpful to the community," Bob responded.

"That is true. Now, just to play devil's advocate, because I see that as part of my job ..."

"Of course, of course!" Bob interrupted.

"If people are not thinking that they might get avian flu from eating eggs and poultry, but we put that idea out there—even though we are saying it can't happen—might we sort of be instigating a crisis by putting the very idea out there?" Ellen stated very deliberately.

"Hmmm ... No, I think the idea is already out there. And while more of a concern in some communities than others, certainly, I think by doing a fact-based campaign ourselves, we will demonstrate a concern for our customers and also be educating them about the avian flu and how what they eat should not be a concern," Bob maintained.

"Well, I have to admit that I really do not know anything about avian flu. Do you have resources and such that can verify the claim that people can't contract the avian flu from eating eggs and poultry?" Ellen questioned.

"Well, no, I haven't done that research myself, but I am 99% sure it is true. So, perhaps that will be your first step? To research avian flu?" Bob queried back.

"Yes, I suppose that would be a good place to start. Did you have any specific ideas about how you wanted to go about such a campaign if my research shows that the claim is true?" Ellen asked.

"Oh, well, I was thinking a press conference surely to initiate the campaign. Then have some kind of poster board in every shop explaining the issues surrounding avian flu and eating poultry and eggs, perhaps with a brochure people could take home. Then a public service type commercial too. Yes, one where maybe I, as a concerned CEO and community member, talk about the issue to assuage fears. Maybe we could get a health official from a big hospital to be on it too! That lends credibility certainly." Bob was definitely getting excited about the prospects.

"Okay, well, I will certainly think about all those ideas as I research. Once again, the research will determine whether we go forward with a campaign of this nature. So, why don't I go back to my office and get started on researching the issue and let you know what I find and we can go from there. Does that sound good?" Ellen was having a little bit of trouble keeping her enthusiasm up for the idea, but she was able to keep her tone light.

"Sounds like a plan!" Bob exclaimed.

They shook hands and made plans to meet again the next week.

THE NITTY GRITTY

Once back at her office, Ellen's first step was to find credible information about avian flu, especially information on how it was contracted. She figured her best bet was to start at the Center for Disease Control and Prevention's (CDC) website. As the CDC was the main government health-advocacy institution, she felt pretty sure that it would have the best information for her.

Just as she thought, the CDC had a plethora of information. Everything from the history of avian flu (how it got started and where), to the symptoms, to possible treatments, and the known ways it is spread. As she researched, she couldn't help but feel that she was wasting her time. Even if she learned that avian flu absolutely could not be contracted by eating eggs and poultry, she still believed that doing a health campaign on this topic was not something that Uncle Bob's Sub Shop would be wise to initiate. As she skimmed through the information, she heard a tap on her cubicle entrance. When she turned around, her mentor at Regency PR, Matt Schmidt, was standing there with a look of anticipation on his face. Matt was a senior VP who had taken Ellen under his wing when she first came on as an account coordinator six years ago straight out of college. She was very thankful for Matt's encouragement, challenges, and support over the years.

"So? How did it go? What are the plans for Uncle Bob's Sub Shop?" Matt asked eagerly.

"Well, I seem to have been thrown a curve ball right out of the gate, Matt." She sighed and gestured toward the computer screen. "You'll never guess what I am doing right now on behalf of Uncle Bob's Sub Shops."

Matt leaned in and read from the screen, then looked at Ellen quizzically and said, "Avian flu?"

"Yes, avian flu," She answered.

"Okay, you have to explain," Matt declared.

Ellen explained Bob Crawford's idea about doing a campaign to educate the public on avian flu. She ended saying, "But I just don't see how this is a good move for the company. Normally, you would only approach a topic like this as a company in response to a crisis. Truly, unless they had had problems with people getting sick from their food, doing a campaign like this is really out of Uncle Bob's purview. Don't you think?"

"Yes, that is true. That doesn't mean that it can't be done, if done the absolute right way. At the same time, it is risky. You should really look at the literature on risk communication when you get a chance. Risk communication focuses on how to communicate possible risks to the public before they become crises, which is what I guess Bob is trying to do. What have you found out about the bird flu?" Matt inquired.

"Well, the CDC explains that there are many different strains of avian flu and that actually, it is pretty rare that humans get infected. When they do get infected, it is most often from direct contact with infected domesticated birds such as chickens and turkeys. Luckily, it is even less likely to spread between humans." She continued, "the key here is that very few humans in the world have ever even contracted it. So, while it may be endemic in some bird flocks, it is not among humans. That seems to strengthen my claim that this sort of campaign is really not necessary."

"But what about contracting it by eating poultry and eggs? Is that even possible?" Matt pushed.

"That is the weird thing, the CDC does not come right out and say that you absolutely can't contract it by eating infected poultry and eggs." Ellen turned around to read from the computer screen. "The CDC says, 'if poultry and eggs were to be contaminated with the virus, proper cooking would kill it.' So, my question is, what if it is not properly cooked?"

"You are right, in any campaign, you would have to state exactly what the CDC says and that bit of information brings up the question: 'Is Uncle Bob's properly cooking their poultry and eggs?' I am sure they are, but you don't want to put that idea into the minds of consumers," Matt acknowledged.

"Definitely not," Ellen replied. "I hate to go in and shoot down Bob's idea on my first project with his company, but I really think the best decision is not to engage in such a campaign."

"How you deal with this will determine your entire future relationship with the key stakeholders in this account. So, plan very carefully and feel free to run your plan by me for feedback." Matt offered.

"Thanks Matt, I know I can always count on you." Ellen professed.

With that, Matt wandered off and Ellen turned back to her computer to begin developing a plan for discussing the pros and cons of doing a campaign about avian bird flu with Bob Crawford.

WEIGHING THE PROS AND CONS

Ellen decided that it was in her best interest to have two plans. One to convince Bob Crawford not to go through with the campaign and one plan for if he insisted on doing the campaign. She was going to have to pull out all the stops for both plans. Not only would she need to be creative and diplomatic in how she approached Bob to convince him not to do a campaign, but she would have to search high and low for ideas and enthusiasm for a campaign that she did not believe in, in case he was adamant about doing it.

Ellen realized she was now developing three campaigns for one client! And, they were all completely divergent from one another. One campaign was to convince one person, Bob Crawford, not to engage in a health campaign about the safety of eating poultry in the wake of avian flu outbreaks in domesticated birds. She needed Bob Crawford to see that engaging in such a campaign was just too risky for his company.

The second campaign was engaging in a socially responsible health campaign to manage an issue that could perhaps be detrimental to Uncle Bob's future sales. While she did like the idea that doing such a campaign helped to reinforce the idea that Uncle Bob's was a brand that was socially responsible and cared about the public, Ellen thought there were better issues they could work with to help maintain that image.

Finally, there was the campaign ideas she had brought with her to that initial meeting that had nothing to do with avian flu and now seemed to be on a back burner. She hoped she could entice Bob Crawford to be as enthusiastic about one of those ideas as he seemed to be about the avian flu campaign.

Now Ellen needed to decide where to spend most of her energy, on strategizing how to convince Bob Crawford to forgo the avian flu campaign, then make sure she had an excellent idea to replace it; or, should she develop a really strong plan FOR a campaign on avian flu like he wanted?

DISCUSSION QUESTIONS

1. If you were Ellen, where would you spend your time and energy? Why?

2. What kind of campaign plans would you put together either for convincing Bob Crawford and/or for doing a campaign about the safety of eating poultry at Uncle Bob's Sub Shops?

3. Based on the information Ellen found about avian flu, is she right in her thinking that doing a campaign might be dangerous? Or is Bob Crawford more correct in his thinking that they need to be proactive and do such a campaign?

4. Consider what you have learned about risk communication and issue management. How does the avian flu issue in this case use these concepts?

5. What other kind of PR campaign could Ellen suggest to Bob Crawford that might meet his desire to engage in a campaign to demonstrate social responsibility, but not chance raising public concern about eating poultry and eggs?

KEY TERMS

Risk Communication, Issue Management, Social Responsibility

PART III Public Relations and the Media

CHAPTER 13

The Broadway Musical Mishap: A Story of Corruption and Lies

Kathleen S. Tillman
University of North Dakota

Jason S. Wrench
SUNY New Paltz

ABSTRACT

Two producers, Freya Lebowitz and Frank Hunter, undertake the up-and-coming production of *Summer in Baden-Baden*, a Broadway musical destined for fame! Unbeknownst to the producers, the show quickly becomes riddled with a corrupt con-woman, a feigned primary investor, and a questionable public relations man thrust into the midst of the corruption and lies.

Freya stopped by the newsstand on the way into the office. Immediately, the headline on the *New York Times* jumped out at her, "*Summer in Baden-Baden* Going Up In Flames." *Uh oh*, she immediately thought to herself, handing the paper vendor the $3 for the paper. She unfolded the paper as she started walking up the steps and into her building.

Freya Lebowitz was a partner with Frank Hunter in the theater production company Starlight Productions. Their office was housed in an old building nestled on the same block as the Gershwin Theater, where the musical *Wicked* was still selling out nightly. Their building was a little awkward. Their office was located on the 7th floor, but the elevator only went to the 6th. She quickly read through the opening of the article on the short elevator trip.

"The Securities and Exchange Commission is looking for Ms. Amelot Favier in connection with possible fraud case filed in federal court yesterday. The legal brief alleges that Favier has conned a number of investors associated with the upcoming Starlight Productions' musical *Summer in Baden-Baden*, based on the book by Leonid Tyspkin with the same title."

The elevator came to a stop and Freya got out before turning left and walking up the short flight of stairs to her office. The light was already on inside the office. *Jack must already be here*, she thought to herself. She opened the door calling out Jack's name.

"Dammit Russell, what the hell are we supposed to do now!?" Freya heard Jack yelling from his office. *Must be talking to Russell Higginbotham*, the company's lead lawyer. There was a muffled response, but Freya couldn't hear what Jack was saying. She walked over to his office, knocked lightly on the door, and went in.

Jack was sitting behind his desk, the *Times* article opened in front of him. He looked up at Freya, clearly listening to something Russell was saying on the other end of the phone. He scratched out a message on a piece of paper and handed it to Freya. "Call Trevor now!" the piece of paper read.

Freya backed out of the room and walked down the hall to her office. She went inside, picked up the phone, and called Trevor's cell phone.

Trevor Shone was the chief executive officer of Shone Theatrical Consulting, the public relations firm Freya and Jack had hired to work on the *Summer in Baden-Baden* project.

"Trevor," a peppy voice answered on the other end.

"Trevor, it's Freya."

"Good morning, Freya," he responded.

"Not really!"

"Uh oh," he responded, hearing the tension in Freya's voice. "What's wrong?"

"I guess you haven't read the cover of the *Times* yet."

"Sorry, I can't say that I have. I just got out of the gym and am heading into my office. What happened?"

Freya was about to answer him, when men in dark suits appeared down the hall. *"Are you kidding me!?* Read the *Times*. I think the feds just got here," she said as she hung up the phone.

THE ROAD TO BADEN-BADEN

The *Summer in Baden-Baden* was the next "to be" show on Broadway, comprising Tony-nominated directors, choreographers, and actors. *The Road to Baden-Baden* was written by an obscure Russian writer, Leonid Tyspkin. The story centers on the tumultuous relationship between Fyodor Dostoyevsky and his wife, Anna Grigoryevna Snitkina. The musical tells of a weekend the two spent in Baden-Baden, a resort in southern Germany. During their stay, Dostoyevsky gambles away his wife's fortune and then begs for forgiveness. At this point in his life, Dostoyevsky suffers from serious bouts of epilepsy and Anna is pregnant with their first child.

The show has everything a Broadway audience could possibly want. The book (and musical) are told through the narrative and perspective of Tyspkin. It starts with him on a train traveling Moscow to Leningrad where he is reading the *Memoirs of Anna Dostoyevskaya*. The opening song exhibits the intensity of the Soviet-era train ride along with the Tyspkin's own love affair with one of Russia's most famous authors, Dostoyevsky. Ultimately, the focus of the book, as with the musical, is on Anna's understanding of her husband as seen through her own eyes. Her relationship with her husband is one filled with contempt, pity, awe, and, above all else, love. *I could easily get a huge star in the roles of all three of the leads*, Freya realized when she first saw the musical while in Moscow on business with her husband. She fell in love with the music, the story, and the amazing staging. She immediately called her producing partner who got on the next flight to Moscow. The two signed the contracts within the week for the sole-rights to the American version of the show. The two immediately started searching for investors while working with the show's original creators and a whole new team of Broadway veterans to make the show accessible for a U.S. audience.

Despite the show's promise, it initially encountered some difficulties with funding. The show was, however, able to get three of the top actors on Broadway to play Leonid Tyspkin, Fyodor Dostoyevsky, and Anna Snitkina. Startlight Productions also did raise enough money to start the complete audition process, including the first round of rehearsals. Freya and Jack flew in the composers to work with the show's three-time Tony Award winning director. While the show quickly shaped up, the investments really were not coming in at the rate necessary to mount the full musical.

The producers started to attend any and all formal Broadway events and meet-and-greets with highly endowed individuals, but Freya and Jack were fairly new Broadway producers and did not have the deep pockets that some of the more notable producers on Broadway had. They were small timers in the world of Broadway, they were not independently wealthy, and did not have a strong business firm or a group of dedicated investors to rely on. After months of attempting to secure funding, Jack and Freya were close to giving up. Although they had had relative success producing a small handful of musicals and plays off-Broadway and off-off-Broadway, this was to be their first real foray into the giant, multi-million-dollar world of Broadway musicals.

The tide finally started turning one evening while the producers were attending a gala at the Met. Freya was with her husband, Brian, and Jack was with his husband, Daryl. The couples were engaged in a conversation with a number of potential investors when a mysterious woman walked into the room.

There are those rare times when someone with such poise and elegance walks into a room that suddenly everyone stops breathing to take notice. Amelot Favier was one of those women. Amelot Favier knew a friend of a friend of Freya's and eventually was introduced to Freya and Jack at one point during the night. Amelot introduced herself as an international financier looking for some possible investment opportunities in the United States for a number of clients in Europe. Amelot, herself, was Parisian and glittered in the latest fashions from the fashion capital of the world.

Jack and Freya eventually turned the conversation toward *Summer in Baden-Baden*, and how they were looking for a number of investors to help mount the production. The three talked in detail about the show and how they believed it to be destined for success. Without hesitation Amelot agreed to talk to her clients about signing on to help raise funds for the show. She spoke of multiple financial connections and was highly interested in the show's promise!

The next day Amelot, dressed in traditional business attire, showed up at Jack and Freya's offices to discuss the terms of her involvement. For her involvement, she would be paid a 2% cut of all funds that she secured. She would also be able to borrow money from Starlight Productions to help secure the investments.

"You see, this was clearly written in the stars. We will make magic together," Amelot said as the contracts were signed.

In almost no time, Amelot began to secure major financial backing for the show. She met with potential investors over lunch and talked up the show. She told of the award-winning cast and the caliber of the directors and choreographers. As she explained the plot in detail, highlighting the tumultuous relationship between the two main characters, she promised the show would surely win a Tony! Almost immediately, investors lined up to support the show. In particular, one specific investor agreed to support the show to the tune of $6 million dollars. When Freya and Jack heard of the high level of financial support, they were ecstatic! They immediately shared the good news with the cast and crew and the show moved forward with its rehearsal schedule.

INVESTOR NIGHTMARES

"Jacques?" Jack heard as he picked up the phone, immediately recognizing Amelot's Parisian pronunciation of his name.

"Amelot!" Jack said happily into the phone. "I hope you bring me great news."

"But of course," she said, drawing out the phrase in a sultry manner. "I only ever bring you great news."

"That's what I need to hear," Jack continued. "The show is shaping up on our end. We just need the investors secured. Once we have the finances secured, we'll be ready to go. We've already secured both a theater and an investment from the theater's owners, so we're almost there."

"Perfect," Amelot purred. "Then, this will be great news indeed. One of my clients is interested in investing in the show. I can probably get him for at least $5 to 8 million. There's just one little hitch to the deal."

"What hitch?" Jack asked.

"It's nothing really, I just need to take this man and his family on a short ski weekend in the Swiss Alps. It's a very small detail. I'll pay for it out of my own pocket. It shouldn't be more than $20,000, so I'll just take out a small loan to pay for the trip. I'll recoup that money when he signs on the bottom line."

"Don't be silly. We'll advance you the $20,000, so you don't have to worry about getting a loan."

"Oh Jacques, you are such a dear!" Amelot squealed with delight before hanging up the phone and promising to get back to him in 10 days right after the short vacation in Switzerland.

Later, when Jack recalled this conversation to Freya, she wondered if Jack had just been swindled, but Amelot's track record had proven good so far. She'd already helped the producers raise a good chunk of the capital needed. If this final investor pulled through, the production would be green-lit and they could have the show running in six weeks.

Sure enough, ten days later Jack received a phone call telling him that Benjamin Wilderom was ready to sign the papers and had agreed to invest $6 million in the production.

Later that afternoon, Freya and Jack opened a bottle of champagne in their office, finally seeing their dream coming true. "Oh my god," Freya started. "We need to get this in the papers, or at least in the trade publications. I mean, everyone around town thought we'd never raise the capital. Look at us now!" Freya walked into her office, champagne flute in hand, and dialed the number for her PR firm, Shone Theatrical Consulting.

"Shone Theatrical Consulting, Maggie speaking."

"Maggie, it's Freya Lebowitz. Is Trevor around?"

"That's funny, he was just approving the copy design to be sent over to you with Justin. I think they're still in the back with the graphic artist. Let me check?"

"Thank you," Freya responded while she was put on hold. She put the phone on speaker, pleasant music filling her office. She looked through her email quickly. Sure enough, there was an email from Trevor. She clicked open the message and saw the mock-ups for how the show's new logo would appear on billboards, playbills, taxi cabs, and the theater itself.

"Freya, Trevor here. Have you gotten the email I sent you yet?"

"Trevor, I was just looking at the mock-ups. I think they're brilliant. I can't wait to show them to Jack."

"Great," Trevor continued. "That's what we like to hear from our clients. Once you give us the go ahead, we'll start getting these printed, so you'll be ready to go once the financing part is finished."

"Actually, Trevor, that's precisely why I'm calling," pausing for effect. "As of this afternoon, we have secured the financing!"

"Oh my gosh!" Trevor exclaimed. "Congratulations! I knew that you and Jack would get there."

"Well, you know what that means?" Freya questioned.

"I sure do! My production schedule just got pushed up."

"That it did," Freya responded with just an extra hit of giddiness in her voice. "Oh, and can you have one of your people write up a press release about the secured funding? We can't wait to see the reactions of those blowhards who thought we'd never get this far."

"Not a problem, Freya," Trevor responded. "I'll get Maggie and Justin on that this afternoon. We should have it sent to the usual media outlets by 5:00, so it can still appear in tomorrow's papers."

"Perfect!"

"What's perfect?" Jack questioned as he walked into her office and Freya hung up the phone.

"Everything!" Freya said. "We need to call Brian and Daryl. We've got to go out and celebrate."

"Ohh, I love a good couple's night."

"I know you do."

"But really, what's perfect?" Jack questioned again.

"Two things really. First, Trevor sent over the mock-ups for the PR campaign signage. They should be in your inbox. And second, he's going to get a press release written before 5:00, so the good news makes tomorrow's papers."

"That is perfection!" Jack responded, thinking, *How could it get any better than this?*

THE CURTAIN FALLS

Two weeks later, and four weeks until the first paying audience would see *Summer in Baden-Baden*, Jack stood outside the Royal Theater watching the signage go up announcing the show. Shone Theatrical Consulting had already started the marketing blitz all around New York. You couldn't walk into a store without seeing one of the placards for the show.

After hanging the signage and the cast posed for pictures out front, the producers and the artistic team hosted a brunch for the cast and crew. Well, the "brunch" was more like a small buffet between the morning and afternoon rehearsals. Jack and Freya had originally wanted to take the cast and crew to a nice restaurant, but the director said that would require consent from Actors Equity and they'd probably end up having to pay for the cast and crew's time while brunching. Instead, the cast and crew were treated to some of the best deli treats New York could muster.

Freya and Jack ended the afternoon back in their offices. Jack had just left for the day, but Freya was finishing some paperwork and double-checking the contract negotiations with the theater ushers union when the phone rang. She hit the speaker phone saying, "Starlight Productions."

"Freya?" came the all-too-familiar Parisian voice on the other end of the line.

"Amelot dear, how are you doing?"

"I'm not doing very well," the voice came through on the other end of the phone. "I just heard Benjamin Wilderom was taken to the emergency room last night."

Freya gasped. Her mind immediately raced to the possible implications to the show's finances. She immediately felt like a horrible human being for letting those thoughts invade before asking, "What happened?"

"Well, the poor dear had a small tumble when were in Switzerland. It wasn't anything big, or so we all thought. Unfortunately, the tumble appears to have fractured his pelvis."

"Oh, I can't believe this. Is he ok?" Freya asked softly.

"He should be fine, but wanted to give you and Jack a heads up."

"Thanks, I'm so glad you called. Will you email me the hospital where he's staying? For our biggest investor, we really should send flowers to him."

"Oh no, not flowers. Mr. Wilderom is quite allergic to flowers. No need to worry, I'll let him and his family know that you send your heartfelt best wishes for a speedy recovery."

The two women talked for a few more minutes before hanging up.

THE STAGE COLLAPSES

Unfortunately, the news from Amelot only got worse over the next few days. Although the surgeon originally thought Mr. Wilderom suffered from a broken pelvis, the surgeon also found that he had done nerve damage to his lower spine during surgery. After a round of surgeries Mr. Wilderom's condition just got worse and worse. He eventually caught a staph infection. The afternoon Amelot called Jack and Freya to deliver the bad news of Mr. Wilderom's passing was one of the most traumatic in the two's professional lives.

Jack immediately called Trevor and told him the horrible news. Trevor and Jack talked about possible ways to phrase the announcement of Mr. Wilderom's passing for the press in a way that would do the least amount of damage to Starlight Productions and *Summer in Baden-Baden*.

"Trevor Shone?" a voice said tentatively over the phone one day.

"Speaking," Trevor responded hesitantly, not recognizing the voice on the other end of the phone.

"Hi Mr. Shone, it's Mike Raskin from the *Times*."

"Oh, hi … Mike. It's great to finally talk to you."

Mike Raskin was starting to become a popular *Times* reporter. Mike was not a theater critic. Instead, he wrote about the happenings within the theater community. Trevor had been reading his column since he started working for the *Times* about two months ago. The *Times* had recruited Mike away from the *Chicago Tribune* when the *Tribune* decided it would no longer keep a theater reporter on staff full time.

"Do you have a minute, Mr. Shone?"

"Sure, what's this call in reference to?" Trevor questioned.

"I'm curious if you ever had an opportunity to meet the late Benjamin Wilderom."

"Unfortunately, I uh didn't. His passing happened so fast," Trevor responded, slightly taken aback by the question. "I know that Starlight Productions and *Summer in Baden-Baden* are still reeling from his death," Mike added, throwing on his PR hat.

"So, how is this going to affect the production?" Raskin asked.

Ah ha, Shone thought to himself. *This is what he's after.* "Well, I can say that Starlight Productions are in contact with Wilderom's family. All indications are that his family will continue with the investment. You should have seen this press release a few days ago."

"Hmmm," Raskin responded. "Must have misplaced that one around here. Thanks for your time."

Trevor found himself suddenly listening to a dial tone. *What an odd conversation.*

"Justin!" Trevor shouted from his office.

"Yeah?" a voice hollered back from down the hall.

"What information do we have on Benjamin Wilderom?"

"The dead guy?" Justin asked, walking into Trevor's office.

"Yes, *the investor* who passed away," Trevor responded.

Justin grimaced, having realized how callous he had sounded. "I don't think we have any information on *the investor* who passed away."

"That's odd," Trevor said. "We have bios on all of the other investors and everyone associated with *Summer in Baden-Baden*. Heck, I even have bios for the show's backstage crew."

"I can put one together for you," Justin offered.

"Thanks."

The next morning Trevor walked into his office and was immediately confronted by a hyper-manic Justin. Before he could even take his coat off, Justin started talking, "OK, so I was like up half the night trying to put together a short biography on Benjamin Wilderom. Umm, but I found nothing. I mean, when I say I found nothing, I mean I couldn't find his name anywhere. The only references that came up on Google could be directly traced back to press-releases that came out of our office. It's almost as if this guy is a ghost. You know, like Casper the Friendly Investor. Honestly, if I didn't know the Starlight producers myself, I would totally think something shady is going on over at that place."

"Justin, slow down. And, please, keep this between us," Trevor cautioned. "I need to find out some more information before I figure out how to handle this situation."

The rest of the afternoon, Trevor had both Maggie and Justin tracking down information on Amelot Favier, Benjamin Wilderom, and the other investors. Over and over again, the three came to the conclusion that all of the investors recruited by Favier were fake. Trevor tried to call Jack and Freya, but the answering machine picked up at their office. He didn't feel right leaving a message, so he decided to wait until the next morning.

THE AFTERMATH

The next morning Trevor got Jack and Freya on the phone and wanted to talk about what he'd found. He tried delving into a discussion about Favier, Wilderom, and the other investors, but Jack just cut him off, refusing to talk about the issue. Multiple times Trevor tried to broach the subject and each time he was rebuffed.

Instead, Jack and Freya were all about a new investor for the show. The new investor was some kind of fish baron down in Florida. He'd been in New York and seen one of Jack and Freya's other productions, and when he heard about Wilderom, he decided to reach out as a potential investor.

Late that afternoon, Trevor felt increasingly anxious about the looming Starlight Productions disaster. *God, that poor new sucker has no idea what he's investing in.* He gave the new investor's information to Justin to perform a quick search on his legitimacy. Justin found a lot of information on this guy. He was able to supply Trevor a small dossier including work and personal email addresses, work and home addresses, and three different phone numbers where he could be reached.

On the way home from work, Trevor decided to stop in at a coffee shop. He got his coffee and sat down at one of the computer terminals in the back of the shop. *Gotta love free computers*, Trevor thought to himself. *A Hacker's dream.* In that moment, Trevor decided to do something. He couldn't sit idly by and let this businessman from Florida sign on to something without the full facts. Trevor quickly opened an anonymous gmail account and emailed the investor:

> Dear Rick Jones:
>
> You don't know me, but I heard you were considering investing in Starlight Productions' new musical, Summer in Baden-Baden. Before signing any contracts, I would strongly urge you to dig a little into the backgrounds of some of the other producers (especially Benjamin Wilderom). Something just doesn't seem completely kosher here.
>
> Sincerely,
>
> A Concerned Theater Lover

Trevor reread his email a number of times before finally hitting send.

The next morning the *New York Times* ran a front-page story that contained some damning material that even Trevor hadn't put together. He sat riveted at his desk as he read through the investigative report by Mike Raskin. The article discussed a lot of details about Benjamin Wilderom and came to the same conclusion that the investor simply didn't exist. Not only didn't the investor exist, Raskin questioned whether the producing team of Jack Hunger and Freya Lebowitz was complicit in the whole affair. The story also mentioned that the SEC was looking to talk with Amelot Favier for her role in this scandal. Apparently, Amelot Favier had been involved in a number of financial schemes in the past and was on an Interpol watch list. *How did none of us not see this one coming?* Trevor questioned.

His cell phone buzzed. He looked down and saw Starlight Productions light-up on his phone. He took a deep breath and answered as cheerily as he could, "Trevor."

"Trevor, it's Freya."

"Good morning, Freya," he responded.

"Not really!"

"Uh oh. What's wrong?" Trying not to let on that he knew very well what was wrong (and much more).

"I guess you haven't read the cover of the *Times* yet."

"Sorry, I can't say that I have. I just got out of the gym and am heading into my office. What happened?" he lied, spinning around on his office chair.

"*Are you kidding me!?* Read the *Times*. I think the feds just got here." With that, the other end of the line went dead.

DISCUSSION QUESTIONS

1. What role should Trevor Shone take with the production at this point?
2. If you were Starlight Production's PR strategist, what would you tell them to do at this point?
3. Was it ethical for Trevor to email the Floridian investor?

KEY TERMS

Crisis Communication, Brand Management, Investor Relations, PR Ethics

CHAPTER 14

Post on Facebook, Lose Your Business

Felipe Gómez
San José State University

ABSTRACT

Personal posts on social media can create a reputational crisis for small businesses. The real-time nature of social media and the ability of publics to self-organize pose unique challenges for small businesses.

Originally from Thailand, Johnny T. was the owner of Authentic Thai, a small and unassuming Thai restaurant serving the downtown and university community of Southwestern City for over two decades. The restaurant seemed unassuming in terms of service and décor, but it was bargain priced and referenced as a good deal by Southwestern University students and the community. Throughout the years, Authentic Thai had won several awards on local restaurant polls such as the 2001 and 2003 Thai choice by readers of the major newspaper. The community regarded it as authentic Thai food at an appropriate price. During the last decade, Authentic Thai had been struggling because it had lost some clientele to Fancy Thai, a new Thai restaurant that has been established on the main street, right in front of Southwestern University.

As a foreign national trying to build his business in Southwestern City, Johnny had faced challenges and discrimination but had been able to overcome them as he developed and maintained Authentic Thai. However, he was disappointed about what he regarded as a lack of customer loyalty, given the loss of business to Fancy Thai. He felt that people were going to Fancy Thai because they were superficial and chose restaurants for the "ambiance" rather than for the food. Nevertheless, Authentic Thai was managing to stay afloat, until the school shooting occurred in a state in the northeast.

JOHNNY POSTS ABOUT THE LATEST SCHOOL SHOOTING

In the wake of the most recent in a string of horrible school shootings that have occurred around the country, people tried to make sense of the latest tragedy. The comments about the tragedy multiplied in social networks. The whole country was shocked that such a tragedy could happen and people were grieving for the senseless loss of children. Thousands of people posted comments grieving the tragedy through social media sites such as Facebook and Twitter. A young father posted, "I had to come home and hug my boy."

Within hours, the comments about the tragedy increased exponentially. For a large part of the population, it is fairly easy to post on social media … maybe too easy. As in the case of email, people sometimes do not realize their posts may be inappropriate or not well received by others until it is too late. Oftentimes, people post opinions that differ from others' beliefs and feelings and may actually offend and hurt others. Unfortunately, people do not realize that whatever they post online is never going away, even if they try to delete it themselves. Johnny T. fell into this lack of judgment when he decided to post the following comments on his Facebook timeline:

Johnny T.

1 minute ago near
Southwestern City

I'm failing to give a dam about the school shooting. I don't care if a bunch of white kids got killed. F**K Post-Racial bullshit. When kids from minority groups get shot, nobady cares. When Israel launched missles at the school in Gaza, everybody was too busy jerking off. Why should I care about people who don't give a damn about me? Personal responsibility, right? Get back to lavish X-mas shopping and believing in some false superstitions. Corporations don't want you to stop spending money on things you don't goddamn need.

Johnny had assumed that only friends would see his Facebook posts. He also assumed that friends who did not agree with him would simply disregard his comments. He was wrong. In less than ten minutes, his post had 143 responses. All of these responses expressed disagreement and disappointment with his post. About a third of the posts also included insults toward Johnny.

REACTIONS ON SOCIAL MEDIA AND JOHNNY'S RESPONSES

Social media responses to Johnny's post were immediate. The responses were not limited to his Facebook profile. People with access to his profile started to share in their own timelines and to comment on what a horrible human being he was. People also did screen captures of his post to forward it to other social media sites as a picture. Within a couple of hours, Johnny's post had spread nationally through social media. His post made it to national online news media the same day of the school shooting tragedy.

The reactions toward Johnny's post were overwhelmingly negative. The reactions were also more than simple opinions; the posts and messages suggested threats and actions against Johnny. Johnny received several death threats by people angered by his post. For others, the reaction was to create Facebook pages calling for a boycott of Authentic Thai, Johnny's restaurant. Most people responding decided to at the very least post their disgust on their timelines requesting their friends to avoid eating at Authentic Thai. Many others jumped into online restaurant reviews to post their indignation there. Although most of the critiques against Johnny were objective, many of them illustrated the same type of prejudice that they were condemning. For example, there were comments about him not being American and telling him to "go back to your country."

Johnny was stunned; he had not expected to create these reactions. Just twenty minutes after his first post, Johnny decided to respond to these criticisms with a follow-up post on Facebook. Johnny was aware of how his post had become a critical issue. He decided this time he would craft a message that would make him be perceived as objective, knowledgeable, sensitive, and non-prejudicial. About thirty minutes after his first post, Johnny had posted the following comment:

> *I have stated throughout the years in my beliefs with millions in cut to mental health programs, school programs, after school programs ... Years after years, thousands of kids in juvenile detention centers. Hundreds of them hungry tonight and have no places to sleep. Thousands are mentally and sexually abused by someone they know. Catholic churches and the Boys' Scout are hiding pedophiles everywhere. I mentioned Gaza and Israel. Aurora, Virginia Tech, and 4 other shootings since Columbine. I don't even remember. Where is the sympathy for them? It's just headline news.*

Although Johnny tried to make this message more professional and use better language, it was not an apology. Given the time constraints in terms of his perceived need to respond to others, his message was not as well written and structured as he had hoped. This new message also ended up attacking institutions like the Catholic Church and the Boy Scouts. Nevertheless, Johnny figured that most people would agree with him about the issues with at least one of these institutions and this agreement would deflect attention from his original post. However, this post did little to change the negative response toward his comments about the school shooting.

When his post did not dissuade his critics, Johnny reacted emotionally. He felt betrayed by his Facebook "friends" reacting to his posts. He was frustrated that people he had accepted as friends were now attacking him on his own wall. Also, the growing number of prejudicial and derogatory attacks on him as a person and as a foreigner angered him. In his frustration, Johnny ended up reverting to a more aggressive post:

> *If you don't like me or my opinions, I suggest you to unfriend me and f**k off. I am pretty much sick of some people telling me what to think, how to think, or how to feel today, and if you don't like my foods, f**k off and eat someplace else.*

This more aggressive emotional response did not help Johnny improve the situation. The attacks on him, and on Authentic Thai, continued. Johnny realized too late he had again made things worse by posting this emotional response. At this point, Johnny gave up posting on Facebook by saying "I think it's time for me to get out of this city for a while for a nice hike up north." Too late, Johnny also realized he had tied himself to Authentic Thai in this post. He was increasingly concerned about how people's responses would affect Authentic Thai.

JOHNNY DOES NOT WORK HERE ANYMORE

While Johnny's comments were posted on his personal Facebook account, he was closely tied to Authentic Thai. Johnny was concerned that people not liking him would affect his restaurant. What he thought he needed to do now was to disassociate himself from the restaurant. Consistent with his last Facebook post, Johnny left town and left his staff in charge of Authentic Thai. He also instructed the staff to say that he was not the owner, but a long-time chef that had moved to another town.

Both reporters and food critics started to visit Authentic Thai looking for Johnny. As Johnny had instructed his staff, the story they were told was that he used to be the chef, not the owner, and did not work there anymore. The story that Johnny was not the owner was inconsistent with Johnny's own Facebook profile. Reporters and writers started researching tax and incorporation documents and finding that Johnny was indeed mentioned in legal business documents. To counter the story of Johnny not being the owner, people started posting copies of legal documents on Pinterest and linking them to Facebook in an effort to show Johnny's continued relationship with Authentic Thai.

Just a couple of days after the school shooting tragedy, the critics of Johnny's comments had organized through social media. The objective seemed to direct their efforts at boycotting Authentic Thai. Some comments in online media now included disbelief that "this place has not closed yet!" The agenda for the online community attacking Johnny now seemed to be to force Authentic Thai out of business.

RESTRICTIONS OF ONLINE RESTAURANT REVIEWS

Because restaurant goers rely on online reviews, people reacting with disgust to Johnny's comments started posting online reviews about Authentic Thai in which they emphasized their disgust toward Johnny's comments.

Online sites dedicated to providing business reviews have rules. One of the rules of online sites about restaurant reviews is that the reviews need to be related to the service or food of the restaurant. The online reviews for Authentic Thai where people were expressing their disgust at Johnny's Facebook comments were deleted almost as immediately as they were posted. These comments were flagged as inappropriate and deleted because they did not relate to the business operations. Unfortunately, this restriction for online reviews about restaurants seemed to hurt more than help Authentic Thai. People were still committed to comment, and were also angered about the online review restrictions. Apparently, if they were not going to be able to talk about Johnny, they were determined to make up stories about how bad the food and the service were at Authentic Thai. One reviewer wrote

> *If I could give it zero stars, I would. This is the worse Thai food ever. The place is also dirty. I don't think they wash their plates and glasses too well. The few good reviews must be from the owners' friends and family. I think it's sad that his family has to resort to deceiving unknowing diners into a horrible experience.*

Several other reviews mentioned watching rats run across the restaurant. Others included finding a roach in the curry, the staff shouting angrily at people while waving metal spatulas, and the staff being as rude as the food was awful. Although the reviews now focused on the food and service, these reviews also managed to mention the owners as horrible people and to sneak in a couple of comments about Johnny's post on the school shooting. The ratings for Authentic Thai were now lower than most restaurants in Southwestern City:

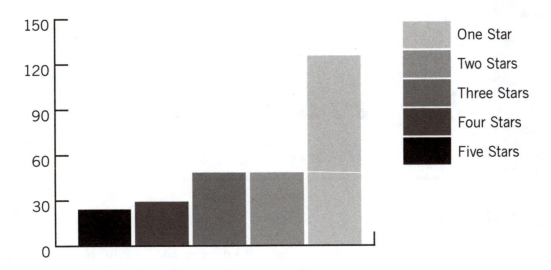

Thanks to the speed of social media, all these events happened in a less than a week. At this point, Johnny decided it was time to hire a PR firm to help him get his image back. After signing the contract, he set up a meeting to talk with his new PR firm, but he is not quite sure what they can do to help.

DISCUSSION QUESTIONS

1. As the PR consultants hired by Johnny, would you focus on restoring Johnny's image or would you focus on Authentic Thai's image? Why?
2. As the PR consultants, what types of media (social media, print, etc.) would you use to repair Johnny's image? Why?
3. As the PR consultants, how and to what degree would you monitor Johnny's personal social media communication?
4. Craft a short social media message (less than 140 characters) that Johnny could post to help him repair his image.

KEY TERMS

Crisis Communication, Reputation Management, Social Networking Sites

CHAPTER 15

Monkey Business

Roy Schwartzman and Patricia Fairfield-Artman
University of North Carolina at Greensboro

ABSTRACT

When a monkey escapes from a research center, the director and his crisis plan are ill-prepared for the consequences. The sponsoring university and the town face threats to their safety and to their image as a rapid news cycle outpaces attempts to control the damage.

Maria Mendez drives through the suburbs of Sunnyvale, eager to resume her work as a research assistant at Eastside Research Center. She had spent the weekend applying for faculty positions at some of the most prestigious universities in the country. Maria has reason to look forward to her work day. The experience she gains at Eastside will put her a notch above other job applicants. Eastside Research Center, a biomedical research institution affiliated with nearby Gibbons University, has received several prestigious grants from the National Institutes of Health and the Center for Disease Control and Prevention to investigate new drug options that could prevent, treat, or perhaps even cure the dreaded disease AIDS. As Maria pulls into the Eastside Research Center parking lot, she reflects on how lucky she is to work under the supervision of Dr. Ravinder Patel, a leading researcher in the hunt to find medications to combat the scourge of AIDS. *One day the work we do might save millions of lives. Maybe we'll even win a Nobel Prize. Imagine me, a Gibbons doctoral student, sharing the stage with Dr. Patel at the Nobel Prize ceremony!*

Maria smiles as she ponders her hopes and ambitions. She enters the facility and begins her usual routine of feeding the animals and cleaning their cages. Eastside houses many animals for use as experimental drug recipients. Guinea pigs, mice, and various species of monkeys spend their adult lives within the Research Center, recipients of various drug therapy regimens. Some of these drugs might eventually be approved for human use. Maria always looks forward to her interactions with Test Animal 7493, a ten-year-old male macaque monkey. She had nicknamed him Estefan because his face reminded her of her maternal grandfather with his fluffy gray hair and goatee. After three years, she had grown attached to Estefan, although she took all necessary precautions to protect herself from animals that carried drugs and viruses that could prove toxic to humans.

As soon as she enters the animal confinement area, Maria senses something is wrong. The macaques are screaming and jumping in their cages, their loud screeches signaling agitation and alarm. Maria has been a daily visitor since the beginning of her graduate program. The animals usually greet her joyfully, hoping for some of the treats she distributes as rewards for good behavior. This is different. Maria shivers, feeling a cold breeze uncharacteristic in the rigidly climate-controlled animal quarters. She scans the area and notices the back door, which opens to the rear parking lot. The door stands ajar, letting the chilly morning air flow directly into the compound. Maria shuts the door. *How careless! This is a serious security breach. I hope nothing was stolen.* Maria thinks of the expensive, climate-sensitive equipment that might have been stolen or damaged. On her way to report the incident, Maria detours to the macaque cages to say good morning to Estefan. To her horror, Estefan's cage door stands wide open. The cage is empty.

Oh, no! This can't be! Maria feels her throat tighten and her stomach knot up in terror. She stumbles into Dr. Ravinder Patel's office. "Dr. Patel—something terrible has happened! Come with me to the animal compound."

Ravinder has never seen Maria so agitated. She is always a model of composure. He follows her into the compound. Maria shows him the open door and the cage.

"We must assemble the entire staff immediately and search the grounds for Test Animal 7493," Ravinder declares. "Maria, take an inventory of the equipment and the test samples. List anything that you find missing or altered."

RESPONSE AND RESPONSIBILITY

A three-hour search yields no results. As director of the Center, Ravinder calls an emergency staff meeting.

"As all of you now know, sometime over the weekend the animal compound rear entrance door was not secured. Somehow one of the macaques, Test Animal 7493, escaped. Fortunately, Maria's team has not found anything else missing or damaged."

"Who could have done this? Who was the last person in the animal compound?" asked the assistant director.

Maria gulps as she questions herself. *I always work late on Fridays. Could I have left that door unsecured? And I always work a lot with Estefan. Did I lock his cage properly?*

"Isn't Elmer the only person in the Center over the weekend? As the custodian, he has unlimited access to the entire facility. And he easily could have unlatched the cage. Everybody knows how finicky those double latches are," suggests Dr. Ali Nagal, the biomedical researcher who has just received a multi-million dollar grant from the National Institutes of Health. Everyone considers him to be the next rising star in AIDS drug research.

Several voices chime in. "Yeah, that's right—must've been Elmer—everybody else knows better—he was never trained in research safety protocols—sure, it's Elmer." Maria remains silent.

Custodian Elmer Frump meekly stammers a response from the back of the room. "Uh, but I don't think that's fair. I mean, I been working here for 20 years, right there with Dr. Patel when this place opened. I've never left a cage opened, never. I need this job real bad. I got seven kids and—"

Ravinder interrupts. "Elmer, we will meet with the custodial services director to discuss disciplinary action."

"But …" Elmer's voice is drowned out by others. *Dear God, they're pinning this all on me!* Elmer thinks.

Ravinder returns to his office after the meeting and ponders his options. This incident could mar a spotless record as the founding director of Eastside Research Center. It could jeopardize not only his career but also tens of millions of dollars in research funding. If the monkey isn't recovered soon, regulatory agencies could flag Eastside as non-compliant with animal safety guidelines. This kind of breach might even threaten closure of the Center. Deep in thought, Ravinder glimpses a document that might help. He walks to the bookshelf and takes down a dusty volume dated two decades ago. The title: *Crisis Communication Plan for Eastside Research Center*. It had remained unopened since Ravinder was named Founding Director twenty years earlier. After all, nothing like this had ever happened.

He browses its pages, searching for something that might guide his actions. He highlights the following points as the central content:

1. The research at this facility will involve life-saving but also potentially dangerous drugs and technologies. If an accident or security breach occurs, trained scientists are the experts who should control the flow of communication. They are the most knowledgeable to be trusted with sensitive technical information.

2. Since the untrained lay public cannot comprehend the complicated science behind the research, maximum confidentiality should be maintained at all costs. In the hands of laypeople, technical information is subject to misinterpretation and can cause panic. To protect the public, scientific research must be the province of properly trained scientists.

3. As the most senior scientific authority, the director of the Center must authorize all communication regarding research conducted at the facility. All communication must be delayed until the director can proceed with stating the definitive information.

Ravinder feels more confident already. *OK, now we have something to work with. Good thing this plan was developed. You never know when you might need it. It's best to be prepared for the worst.* Then his secretary rushes in.

"Dr. Patel, there's a call for you on line one. It's Police Chief Janet Nguyen, and she says it's urgent."

"All right, thanks." Ravinder takes the call and encounters Chief Nguyen's voluble voice. "Hello, Janet. How are—"

"You have a lot of explaining to do. Our office has been receiving calls about some sort of monkey running around Sunnyvale. At first we thought it was a prank. But the descriptions were consistent and some came from highly respected citizens. Since we don't live in the tropics and haven't built a new wildlife preserve, I thought you might shed some light on this matter. Your center is the only place anyone can find monkeys around here. At least I've heard that's the case, since you keep them locked up in the bowels of Frankenstein's laboratory down there. Well?"

"Uh, you see, there may have been some sort of security issue here and we seem to not know the current whereabouts of one of our research animals."

"Is it a monkey?"

"Well, yes."

"When did this happen? Why wasn't my office informed immediately? Oh, that doesn't matter now. Lord knows what kind of deadly diseases you've put into that creature. I'll contact State Animal Control, since they have experience capturing exotic animals. You do realize that if this goes on for any length of time it'll cause a public panic?"

"Don't worry. We have plans for any crisis." Ravinder smiles and pats the cover of the crisis communication manual that had sat dormant in his office until today.

THE BEST MADE PLANS

The next day, Ravinder arrives at work to find a chaotic mob of news reporters, cameras, and media trucks at the entrance to Eastside Research Center. Ravinder is surprised, but confident. *How on earth did word about our mishap spread so quickly? There wasn't anything on the evening newscasts or in the morning newspaper. Good thing we have our crisis communication plan.*

Arriving at the entrance, cameras point in Ravinder's direction and microphones are thrust a few inches from his mouth. Questions launch in rapid succession. Ravinder feels prepared. *After all, I'm the expert. I know more about scientific research than all the people here.*

Someone nearby loudly begins to ask a question, causing the others to quiet down. The microphones and cameras turn in the questioner's direction. Ravinder recognizes Bubba Feng, the mayor of Sunnyvale.

"Dr. Patel, as mayor of this great city, I am concerned about the health risks this runaway monkey poses. It's a wild animal and could be dangerous if it attacks one of our citizens. But I'm also concerned about safeguarding Eastside Research Center. This facility has brought more than 150 jobs and millions of dollars in revenue to our area. We need that kind of economic benefit. So, tell everyone here how you will guarantee this animal poses no threat and how you will make certain that something like this never happens again."

"Mayor Feng, we are also very concerned. In science, we cannot offer certainties. Scientists understand that we cannot predict anything with absolute confidence, so we work with probabilities. Let me assure you that we are working with the local police and with animal control agencies. We will do everything in our power to minimize the chance that this will happen again."

The crowd looks puzzled. Ravinder hears a rapid barrage of questions. They are asked so quickly that he cannot respond.

"So, you're saying you have no idea where the monkey is?"

"Why can't you assure us that it isn't dangerous?"

"How do we know this won't happen again if even you don't know?"

"You sound like you're waffling. Just answer the questions. Are we in danger or not?"

After a few moments of silence, the questions continue in a more orderly fashion.

"We know you are researching drugs for AIDS. Does this animal have AIDS? Does it have any contagious diseases?"

"To the best of our knowledge, this animal has not tested HIV-positive."

"Are you positive this monkey has absolutely no contagious diseases?"

"Our research on Ebola hemorrhagic fever indicated that transgenic transmission of communicable diseases in these cases is extremely rare. The likelihood of contracting a disease from this monkey is perhaps one in a billion."

"Yeah, but what if you're that one?" Several voices murmur their concurrence.

"Doctor, what about the monkey? How many other wild animals do you keep imprisoned in there?"

"Let me assure you that all of our research animals are treated in accordance with all relevant federal and university protocols."

Within a few hours bloggers following the story are making posts with titles such as "AIDS Monkey on the Loose" and "Defend Yourself from the Macaque Attack." Local television newscasts accompany announcements of the missing money with footage from Ravinder's impromptu interview. Teasers for the evening news ask questions such as: "Are Sunnyvale's children at risk from Eastside's deadly monkey?"

The next day, Ravinder meets with the top administrators of Gibbons University. President Kwame Bondogo decides the university must intervene.

"Ravinder, you've been a good citizen of this university for a long time. That's why we made you the founding director when we established Eastside. And you've done a terrific job up to this point. But we have all seen how you handled the media and important stakeholders. Heck, Mayor Feng is offended because he thinks you dismissed his questions. We can't afford bad relations with the city. Effective immediately, I am placing all communication entirely in the hands of Gibbons University's Director of Public Affairs, Ellie Mays. From here onward, Ellie will handle all contacts with the media. She will prepare all our news releases and try to prevent us all from looking like idiots. The longer this continues, the more people might start to lose confidence in Gibbons and in Eastside. We might even lose donors. So, Ellie is in charge now."

This new arrangement puts Ravinder in a dilemma. *President Bondogo is my ultimate supervisor, so I should comply. This sounds like a command, so I had better obey. But our crisis plan says that I should handle communication.* Ill at ease, Ravinder hesitatingly adds, "We might even lose our federal grant funding, which could end Eastside as we know it."

President Bondogo pounds his fist on the conference table. "Exactly. That's why we need to protect our image."

ACCELERATING NEWS CYCLES

The monkey remains at large several more days. During that time, viral videos appear on YouTube and other social networking sites. As awareness of the event expands, national news media begin spreading the story. A few late-night comedians include references to "King Kong on the loose."

Because the incident involves drug research using animals, animal rights activists get publicly involved. Daily demonstrations occur at Eastside Research Center. Until this time, the Center was hardly noticed by local residents except as an economic generator. Now the national chairperson of PETA (People for the Ethical Treatment of Animals) blogs daily about how the researchers "torture" animals. PETA members picketing the site carry signs bearing gruesome photos of mangled animals. The American Society for the Prevention of Cruelty to Animals presents a petition to the Sunnyvale City Council requesting a ban on all animal research within the city limits.

Ravinder answers all public inquiries with "No comment." Internally, life at Eastside Research Center is disrupted. Elmer Frump is fired from his job as custodian. Maria Mendez harbors nagging self-doubts about whether she might have played a role in Estefan's escape. Ali Nagal quietly begins sending out job applications, concerned that his reputation as a bio-medical researcher might suffer if Eastside is discredited.

Meetings, texts, phone calls, and emails are exchanged frantically among those dealing with the crisis. Everyone recognizes that the story has acquired a life of its own. As coverage of the monkey mishap becomes more extreme, damage control becomes more and more difficult.

"We now can celebrate our one-week anniversary," President Kwame Bondogo remarks cynically as he convenes yet another of what seem like endless meetings to strategize the monkey escape incident. "Ellie, do you have anything new to tell us?"

Ellie Mays takes a gigantic gulp of her SuperSize coffee. She looks as if she hasn't slept in weeks. "As you know, I launched the 'Go with Gibbons' campaign in response to this crisis. We have a series of student, faculty, staff, and alumni videos that reassure everyone of this university's reputation as a crucial community resource. We've posted these videos on all of the university's social media. We also have bought several billboards on which we've posted the major research accomplishments of our Eastside research team."

"But how has that helped?" interjects Mayor Bubba Feng. "Yesterday my son shows me one of those so-called viral image things they're circulating all over the internet. You know, it's a mash-up of different images to look like a single picture. This one shows King Kong climbing onto Eastside Research Center. You know what King Kong is holding in his hand? They put a photo of our own police chief in there! Everything is being blown out of proportion."

"I just ignore such foolishness, but the police department looks very bad in this whole thing," adds Chief Janet Nguyen. "The gift shops around town are selling bumper stickers that say 'If the police can't find a monkey, how can they find a criminal?' This sort of thing isn't really our responsibility to begin with, but now we're stuck with it. State Animal Control has to work in tandem with us because we know the area. They supposedly have the means to subdue this monkey. And it doesn't help at all when Sunnyvale monkey videos are popping up all over the internet. We can't sort out which ones are genuine and which are hoaxes."

Ellie adds, "Our Public Affairs office staff just texted me. Evidently 'Eastside Monkey Jailbreak' is one of the top trending phrases on Twitter."

Kwame shakes his head. "Maybe we can add that accolade to one of our billboards."

MONKEY SEE, MONKEY FETCH

Ten days after the macaque went missing, Ravinder arrives home, distressed and depressed. The entire research team is preoccupied by constant concerns about the missing macaque and its consequences. The negative publicity from the incident has everyone at Gibbons University worried about the prospect of further animal research funding. He plops onto the sofa and turns on the television, searching for distraction.

"Eyewitness News 13 interrupts this program to bring you a special report. The Runaway Research Monkey has been found! Jamal Garfinkel is live on the scene. Jamal?"

"Yes, I'm here at the home of 14-year-old Tiffany Diamond. We're only a few miles from Gibbons University and the infamous Eastside Research Center. Tiffany did what the Sunnyvale Police Department and State Animal Control couldn't do. Unlike all those brainy scientists at Eastside, this eighth-grader was able to outsmart the notorious Runaway Research Monkey. That is, her five-pound Chihuahua did. Let's hear the story in Tiffany's own words." Tiffany now appears on the screen, holding a snarling brown Chihuahua adorned with a pink, rhinestone-studded collar.

"So, like, I just came home from cheerleading practice, you know? And I'm like, 'Hey, Tinkerbell—that's my dog, you know—let's go for a walk, OK?' We're in the backyard for like ten minutes and, like, Tinkerbell starts barking like crazy, you know. And I'm like, 'Tinkerbell, calm down!' And she, like, keeps barking and barking and looking up at this tree, OK? And so I look up and, like—oh my God!—there's, like this huge, creepy looking monkey way up in the tree. So I, like, call 911 'cause I'm scared that monkey might, like, jump down and attack me and eat Tinkerbell. Anyway, these guys showed up real fast. I got some photos of them grabbing that nasty monkey and posted them on Facebook."

The camera shifts to Jamal. "And you can go to the Eyewitness News 13 website to see Tiffany's photos, plus photos of our little canine hero: Tinkerbell. This is Jamal Garfinkel for Eyewitness News 13."

Ravinder shakes his head and turns off the television. *After all the hard work and misery my entire research team has been through, this is what we get? A kid's dog saves the day and gets celebrated as a hero. Meanwhile the expert scientists don't even get any credit for trying to protect the public? And how about a little acknowledgment for the work we do in testing drugs that might cure AIDS?*

Ravinder grabs his tablet and gets on Facebook, hoping to find solace from interacting with some fellow scientists. "What is this? Already?" he cries aloud when his Facebook wall pops up. A scientist at a rival research center posted a link to the video interview of Tiffany

Diamond. Ravinder then navigates to his messages and finds he has a friend request from Tinkerbell. *Who on earth is that?* Ravinder clicks the avatar of the sender to find that the "sender" is Tinkerbell Diamond, the dog that discovered the monkey. Some anonymous advocate apparently set up the dog's very own Facebook page.

"Enough!" shouts Ravinder as he shuts off his tablet. As he trudges to the kitchen to calm himself with a bowl of ice cream, Ravinder's cell phone rings. The caller ID shows the call is from President Bondogo. Ravinder decides to let the call forward to his voice mail. After finishing his second satisfying scoop of double chocolate fudge, he checks the message.

"Ravinder, this is Kwame. We need to meet as soon as possible."

Before Ravinder can return his empty ice cream bowl to the kitchen, he gets a text message from Maria Mendez telling him to come to the Research Center's animal quarantine area immediately. Test Animal 7493 is being returned. Ravinder has to be there because the communication crisis plan designates him as responsible for the Center. *But Ellie Mays has been placed in charge of communication. Still, the monkey did escape from the facility I supervise. Where do we go from here?*

DISCUSSION QUESTIONS

1. What kinds of errors are present in the ways that the various types of risks (animal safety, public health, etc.) were communicated (a) by the scientists, (b) by the university, (c) by the media? What caused these errors and how might you recommend they be avoided or corrected?

2. How should the Research Center's crisis plan have been rewritten or modified to cope better with this crisis? Which assumptions within the crisis plan might need to be reconsideration and why?

3. What should be the next action each of the characters in this case takes? How would these actions help the situation?

4. If you were hired by Gibbons University as a public relations professional to cope with this crisis, what would you do differently and why?

KEY TERMS

External Crisis Communication, Risk Communication, Crisis Communication Plans, Stakeholder Relations

TriQuinn's Tangled Web: What Do You Do if the Law and Ethics Disagree, and a Secret Is the Only Thing Separating Corporate Image Repair from Ruin?

Elizabeth Barfoot Christian
University of New Haven

Hazel James Cole
University of West Georgia

Jerry L. Allen
University of New Haven

ABSTRACT

A collision has happened between two oil tankers in the Gulf of Mexico, following a bargain purchase by one company to expand its business. Fault has not been assigned, but the media frenzy is about to ensue. Worse, things may not be what they seem, as one of TriQuinn's three owners has a secret that could make or break the company's future existence.

TriQuinn Oil & Gas is a growing company with aspirations of becoming an international corporation, although it is still a family-owned business at this point.

Reagan Quinn, brother, is CEO of the company. Alex and Jay Quinn, brothers, are partners in the company.

To become a bigger player in the business, Jay Quinn, an attorney and partner in Tri-Quinn, has decided to purchase an oil freighter so that the company can expand. After completing research on a number of possible purchases, he finds Oceans Tanker Co. has a used freighter available far cheaper than any others he can find. He advises his brothers and the board of TriQuinn of his opinion that this is a good deal for the company. They agree to meet and vote on the decision.

After his initial suggestion, Jay Quinn decides to dig a little bit deeper and finds that Oceans Tanker Co. has been cited twice in the past for faulty equipment that has been involved in environmental accidents in the Gulf of Mexico.

Upon finding out the information, Jay realizes this is most likely the reason for the price of the tanker. He looks at other prices again and realizes that the difference in going with a more reputable company will cost several million more dollars—far more than the liquid capital the company has available to expend at this time.

He decides to do no more investigating into the matter and to believe it's simply Tri-Quinn's good fortune to get such a deal on a tanker.

He, with input from the CEO of Oceans Tanker, draws up a contract. Since Jay is an attorney, he ensures that TriQuinn has no liability for the first 12 months of use and limited liability for the equipment for 24 months. Whether or not Oceans Tanker understands, Jay doesn't question or discuss this addendum he has added to the contract on page four.

The day of the vote and signing by the board comes, and Jay is running late. He arrives just as voting is being concluded.

"Jay would vote in favor of the purchase. After all, this was his idea," Reagan Quinn tells the others. "All in favor, raise your right hand."

Jay has been feeling a little guilty and has decided to tell his brothers and the board all he knows about Oceans Tanker before they sign the contract. However, by the time he arrives, it is too late. The board is already adjourning the meeting. All have signed except Jay, and by company by-laws, only two of the three brothers must consent to a written contract for it to be valid. Of course, since it was Jay's idea in the first place, there is no doubt from anyone that he will sign the contract. No one has any idea of the information he has omitted.

Jay decides to keep his mouth shut and simply let it go … without his signature. What could possibly go wrong?

Three months go by.

Williams Oil, a small independent drilling company headquartered in Louisiana, has been drilling in the Gulf for just two years. They don't have a lot of experience but have a clean track record professionally. On this day, foreman Carl Miller is in charge of moving an off-shore oil rig to a new location. The day is clear and sunny. An hour into the move, Miller sees a tanker off in the distance, but this is not an unusual sight and he doesn't think twice about it.

Hours later, a horrific accident occurs. The tanker collides with the oil rig. Millions of gallons of oil are spilling into the Gulf from the TriQuinn-owned tanker. Men from both vessels are lost and feared dead.

An emergency is declared by the President of the United States and Governor of Louisiana.

Reagan Quinn calls an emergency meeting of the board to enact a quick plan of action.

"The new is not good from the Gulf," Reagan Quinn tells his brothers. "We need to figure out what our plan is and notify the board and the companies we supply. The press is going to explode with or without a statement from us. Better for us to control it."

Reagan thinks the accident is the fault of Williams Oil, the relatively new company involved. Jay doesn't think so and must decide whether or not to come clean with what he knows about Oceans Tanker Co., since he knows that, even if the equipment isn't at fault, because of the timing and the way he worded the contract, no legal culpability will fall on TriQuinn.

However, PR is another matter.

"First, we need to make sure our concern isn't just for the oil we have lost, but we must make sure the blame falls where it rightfully should, on the Williams' foreman," Reagan says.

Alex Quinn adds, "It's a perfectly clear day. How could they hire someone so obviously inept? Of course, that's probably not the words I would use to tell the media that it's not TriQuinn's fault." He chuckles.

Jay's guilt is eating at him. He knows his brother would not be laughing if they knew what he had failed to tell them. And he knows, if it's ever found out, that his "brilliant" protection clause won't begin to fix the company's image with their buyers or with the American people.

DISCUSSION QUESTIONS

1. What is the crisis facing TriQuinn as a company?
2. If you were the public relations representative for TriQuinn, what would you advise your company to do in this situation?
3. How would you plan for the media frenzy that is about to occur? What strategies would you employ to address this crisis situation? Be sure to include a social media strategy as part of your planning strategy.
4. Who would be the identified spokesperson? What key messages would you craft to initially address the news media? Be specific.
5. How do you decide what information is for public consumption and what is proprietary?

KEY TERMS

Crisis, Issues Management, Conflict, PR Ethics

CHAPTER 17

Universally Safe Communication

Julian Jeter-Davis, Shannon M. Brogan, Erin E. Gilles, and Dotty Heady
Kentucky State University

ABSTRACT

The public relations officer of Universal Car Company is currently serving as the team manager for the "Universally Safe" campaign dedicated to featuring the innovative safety technology in the new UCC SUV's. While arranging flights for the final prep meeting before the campaign launch, the manager receives a call from the CEO of UCC that, due to manufacturing issues with the newest UCC SUV, the Reliance, the campaign must be postponed or cancelled. The team has been working on the campaign for almost a year and preparation is almost finished. Now, with one month until the campaign launch and the weight of the terrible news on his shoulders, how does the team manager communicate the bad news to everyone on his team?

Nine months ago Gary King awoke shortly before the shrill 7 am alarm, anxious to begin work with his newest employer. King had been hired as Universal Car Company's senior public relations officer. After having been in and out of work for the past five years, relying on freelance jobs and short contract stints, King was excited to be reentering the world of corporate America. Despite a history of fresh, innovative ideas, the 31-year-old man had experienced career turbulence through downsizing twice. The new PR position for UCC was a chance for him to redeem himself and continue building his portfolio in hopes of becoming an independent PR agent again with his own office.

King felt optimistic as he was assigned team manager for the Universally Safe campaign. The campaign was dedicated to the promotion of the new front and side heat-sensor technology, which was supposed to reduce accidents by drivers of the UCC Reliance SUV by 25 percent in the next three years. The front and side heat sensors were created to automatically protect against another vehicle getting too close to the Reliance. When that happened, the heat from the other vehicle would trigger the technology in the Reliance. The resulting action would be either to slow down or slightly turn the Reliance, based on the proximity and location of the neighboring vehicle. UCC's popularity among U.S. automobile owners had diminished in the past five years, and this innovative safety feature was what most employees believed UCC desperately needed. When King was assigned the task of assembling a team of professionals to create the campaign with a one-year timeline and a budget of $5 million, he jumped at the opportunity to use some of the best talent he knew.

King's decade in the industry and wide net of contacts meant that he was easily able to assemble a team. The team was going to consist of three main people, an event planner, a graphic designer (for both print and media), and a strategic marketing expert. He knew the perfect people to fill each of these positions: Donna Creel, Lance Stevens, and Elaine Ernst.

Nothing would stop Donna Creel. She was determined, hardworking, and a bit hard-headed. There were not too many people outside of her boss who could give her orders. As an event planner, she had fresh, unique ideas and an attitude that would ensure that *her* vision became a reality. Creel was sought out by Gary King to be the event-planning specialist for the Universally Safe campaign. She was a very busy lady who, because of her hard work, had made a name for herself and was requested quite frequently for her services. She resided in Palm Beach, Florida and often traveled for months at a time to manage large events.

Lance Stevens, owner of Full Print Graphics, considered himself a lucky man. His card had been sandwiched between dividers in King's desk drawer for over a year. Unexpectedly, King had stumbled across the business card while looking for an extra roll of tape. King knew that Stevens was perfect for UCC's campaign. Stevens had been a good friend of King's in college, but they had lost touch. He was now the lead graphic designer of a small PR agency in King's hometown of Austin, Texas. The agency did a full-service business, specializing in print, digital, and social media. This team would not relocate for a job, but would accommodate their clients with video chatting, email, and sending print samples through overnight mail. All of their offices, the photo studios, and the print facilities were in Austin.

Elaine Ernst was a different type of woman. She did what she was good at and not much else. She was a great writer who knew how to reach a multitude of target audiences. She had a knack for adapting the language of her writing to match her target audience, despite being an introvert who verged on being a hermit. King met her in the job he held two companies ago in Washington state. Her professionalism and insight into consumer behavior were so impressive that King had kept in touch with Ernst over the years. Whenever possible, King had hired Ernst. Despite her standoffishness with new people and preference for working alone, Ernst was an excellent asset to the team. In fact, she moved to Cincinnati where the company was headquartered to devote herself full-time to the Reliance project.

King had worked with all of the team members in the past, so he had the utmost confidence in his team and knew for certain that each and every one was hand-picked, talented, and had the necessary skills. What could go wrong?

King whistled as he shined his patent loafers before he headed out the door, filled with optimism for the week ahead.

King lived just a few blocks away from his office, so he took the opportunity to walk to work any time he got a chance. This morning, the cool autumn breeze stung at his face as he walked through the park next to his office building. He started running over his to-do list in his head. There were just two months left before the launch of the project and King's excitement was building. Yesterday, the team had their weekly meeting via Skype because half of the team did not relocate. *Skype has definitely made getting the best talent easier*, King thought to himself.

Right next door to his building was Joe's Java Hut, where he got his coffee and doughnut every morning. He walked in with his company polo on and approached the main counter.

"Hey, Joe, how's it going?" said King.

"I've been alright, Gary," Joe replied. "But, I saw the UCC news in the paper today. Are there going to be lay-offs?"

"What?" King asked quickly. "I haven't heard anything about this."

King walked over to the newsstand as Joe hollered out, "Go to the business section."

King turned to the appropriate section to see a huge headline on the front page, reading: *Universal's Reliance Proved Unreliable, NHTSA reports*. The article states that there is an issue with the latest SUV's axle alignment.

King's mouth dropped in shock. *This is terrible. This messes up the entire campaign we've constructed. Think, think, what do I do? I have more than nine months' work invested.* King's thoughts raced through his head faster than his eyes could scan the article. King stepped outside and called Jonathon Turner, CEO of UCC. After a short ring, the other end of the line picked up.

"Hello?"

"Sir, this is Gary King. I'm calling you because I just read the article in *USA Today* and I was wondering what I should do?" asked King, trying to control the note of panic creeping in.

"Gary, relax," Turner ordered. "Things like this happen all of the time. I want you to continue working in your current capacity and simply let this blow over. Once the media has calmed down, we'll launch our stellar campaign and regain the lead in the domestic SUV market."

King thanked Turner and hung up. *This call did not help at all!* thought King as he folded up the paper and tucked it under his arm.

Turner bled optimism, believing that the hard work of his employees would eventually bring the company success. However, UCC employees secretly feared that Turner's unflagging optimism in the face of shrinking sales might be angering stockholders. King walked back into the coffee shop, and responded to Joe's quizzical look.

"He said not to worry, that this is just par for the course in the auto industry," King said, with an extra dose of enthusiasm, as if trying to convince himself. "But, I'd better take this coffee to go!" He turned around and headed next door to see what the day would bring.

UNIVERSAL MAYHEM

Four weeks passed and King and his team kept plodding along, still expecting the campaign to go off without a hitch the next month. The target date for the campaign was designed to coincide with the official unveiling of the Reliance at that year's Chicago Auto Show. As the deadline got closer and closer, King felt his anxiety creeping higher and higher. King knew his team was stellar. *Heck, my team has been working hard, eating on the go and working late most nights of the week.*

With 30 days until the product release, King started setting up one final meeting with his team, a few sponsors, and the CEO. The expressed goal of this meeting was to sit down and get all the details and procedures clarified to ensure everyone was on board with the campaign. King started looking at the company's internal calendar system to determine when it would be best to arrange a meeting. He also started checking various airline schedules to see if there would be any problems flying his team to the corporate headquarters for the meeting. He was lost in thought when he suddenly became aware that his phone was ringing. He looked down at the caller ID, which read, "Jonathon Turner." As he answered, King got a sudden sinking feeling in the pit of his stomach—it was rare to get a call from Turner after 10 pm.

"Hey Jonathon, I was just looking at your schedule," King started in. "I'm trying to schedule the PR campaign launch meeting for some time in the next week—"

"Gary, I've got bad news," said Turner, cutting King off. "The media exposure turned ugly. I thought one of the reporters was our friend, but the story was more important. The article said that UCC was more focused on profits than consumer safety. They blew it out of proportion, but that's the media for you."

"So, where does this leave the campaign?"

Turner quickly averted the question, opting to drone on about the mechanical flaws affecting the project. King's thoughts raced inside his head. *This was my chance to show what I can do!? How am I ever going to open my own PR firm without this kind of national exposure? Dear god, I don't like where this is headed at all.* Suddenly, King started tuning back into what Jonathon was saying. *Why is he avoiding the question!?*

After ranting for five minutes about the problems with the vehicle, Jonathon finally answered King's question. "I'm still waiting on a final report about the problem with the SUV's axle. It's snapping under stress. We might change suppliers on the axles or use a different steel mill and see if it can be corrected in time so you can go on with the roll-out at the Chicago Auto Show. But, it may be our annealing process at the factory that is wrong. The Rockwell rate is 68 and it should be 54, so we may have to reheat the steel to 600 degrees and see if that works. If it works, it's a pretty quick fix. We just might need to postpone for another show later in the year, or recall the Reliance altogether! The heat-sensor technology works just fine and I would like for that to be demonstrated and showcased, but the axle is giving us fits. I will know something at the top of the week."

King nodded, his mind racing as Turner bombarded him with engineering data. It sounded too complicated to fix in a week, but King knew that all available engineers would be pulled from every project to address the axle defects.

Turner continued, "If the Reliance is cancelled, the priority is doing damage control with customers and stockholders. I know you've sunk almost a year into the launch, but we must focus on the most important task at hand. I'm going to be tied up focusing on this axle issue, so you've got to handle the press. Send your team my regards."

With that, Turner was gone and King was left holding the phone in shock.

King didn't even have the words to respond. He simply put his phone down and looked up at his office ceiling. All of his hard work gone down the drain and all of the effort and trust from his team gone down the drain behind it.

KING'S DECISION

King has several crucial big decisions to make. He knows that no matter which way it goes, he must tell his team that the campaign may be cancelled.

Can they fix all of the major problems with the axles on the vehicle and still hold the presentation at the Auto Show in Chicago? Does he just present the new heat-sensing technology without the full car presentation? King has flight plans and hotel rooms booked for himself and the team. Should he cancel? What will that mean for prices and availability if he has to re-book at the last minute?

What do I tell my team? When do I tell my team? Do we now need to focus on two completely different campaigns? What is our message to the public?

Perhaps most importantly, what should his media strategy be? News of the defect, if it hadn't leaked already, would soon be spread all over the internet. It could take years to rebuild public trust once it is lost. His team had been blasting news outlets nationwide with news releases outlining the new project. How can he rescind the information without damaging the public's confidence in UCC?

King's strategy will not just affect his status with UCC, but also will influence his job prospects for years to come. *Well, I wanted to play in the big leagues. I guess it's time to see if I strike out or hit a home-run.*

DISCUSSION QUESTIONS

1. What should Gary King do first? Should he make internal or external communications strategies his priority?
2. One of King's core problems is a lack of information. If you were King, how would you handle this deficit? Where would you turn for more input?
3. King has experienced past instability in his PR career. If you were in King's situation, how confident would you feel about your job security? How could this influence your decision making in this scenario?

KEY TERMS

Internal Communication, Evaluation, Media Relations

CHAPTER 18

FreshFood: A Case Study of the Organizational Image Repair Process

Corey Jay Liberman
Marymount Manhattan College

ABSTRACT

FreshFood made a grave error when it sold bad seafood to its customers. The company now must figure out how it can regain its positive image in the mind of patrons, and it decides that social media would be conducive for such apology dissemination.

Monday morning meetings were nothing new to the staff members of FreshFood, a local supermarket in the northernmost part of Delaware, which has been family owned and operated since the company's inception in 1942. Jason Crabtree, the current chief executive officer and chief operating officer of FreshFood, insists that Monday meetings provide the opportunity for all supermarket staff members, including everyone from grocery baggers to managers, to reflect on the week prior and to forecast the upcoming six days. The great majority of the dialogue that transpires during the course of such meetings centers around three large themes: sales (in what departments were sales up, in what departments were sales down, what were the items that were purchased most, what were the items that were purchased least, and what disconnected items were routinely purchased together), customer service (were there customer complaints, were there any customer-staff arguments), and innovation (what could be done to increase the sales of products in the myriad of different departments). Such meetings allow the company to pride itself on what it does well and to ameliorate the company's obvious weaknesses and struggles. At the conclusion of every meeting, Mr. Crabtree ends with his "keep up the great work and always keep your nose to the grindstone" phrase of encouragement.

This Monday, however, was quite different. Hailey Blackstone, the director of marketing and outreach for FreshFood, is, among other things, required to regularly track consumer testimonies on MarketMeasure, an online site that provides an outlet for both praise and criticism of supermarkets in the continental United States. FreshFood is often praised for the freshness of its products (its bread and produce), the friendliness of its staff, its extremely fair prices, and the quality of its meat and seafood. Based on Ms. Blackstone's recent research, here are some of the feedback remarks offered by the patrons themselves:

"The combination of FreshFood's quality and affordability keep me coming back for more."

"The friendliest staff you could ever ask for ... going to the market has become more of a joy than a dread."

"There is absolutely nothing more that you can ask for ... it is the best supermarket I have ever been to."

Very rarely does FreshFood receive much in terms of negative criticism, other than the very random customer who had a disappointing experience. However, Ms. Blackstone is well versed in marketing and communication and knows two things to be true. First, patrons who have a bad supermarket experience are more likely than those who have a positive experience to voice their complaints. This, of course, can have serious ramifications. Second, receiving one negative testimonial by a perturbed patron will have a stronger effect than several positive testimonials. As a case in point, nearly eight months ago, a supermarket patron posted the following on MarketMeasure:

"I will never ever step foot into FreshFood again. The staff members were rude, the store was extremely disorganized, the strawberries were not fresh, and it literally took me 25 minutes to get a half of a pound of Alpine Lace Swiss and a pound of honey turkey. Stay away."

Although this was the only negatively framed message posted on the site, compared to the 19 messages praising the supermarket for its excellence, sales dropped 3% the following week, coupled with a 7% depreciation in total patronage. Although it would take much more formal research to conclude that these drops were due to the negatively framed message, Ms. Blackstone was certain that it played a very salient role.

Unfortunately, Ms. Blackstone learned that there was an abundance of recent negative sentiments among the supermarket patrons regarding FreshFood's seafood from the past week. Given Ms. Blackstone's understanding of, and appreciation for, the social media world, she knew that there had to be a response on behalf of FreshFood regarding the recent complaints stigmatizing its seafood department: one that accumulates nearly 30% of the supermarket's entire revenue. The comments posted to MarketMeasure criticized the quality and taste of the past week's scallops, swordfish, and halibut. After conferring with Mr. Crabtree, Ms. Blackstone began the Monday meeting with a discussion of what could be done to regain the positive image of FreshFood in the minds of both the perturbed patrons and the patrons who became an audience for the previously mentioned complaints.

THE MONDAY MORNING MEETING

"Good morning, everyone," Hailey started. "I sure hope that you all had a great weekend. As you know, most of the time I am asking you all to think of innovative ways for us to be proactive in increasing our bottom line. This morning, however, I have some bad news. As you all know, I check MarketMeasure three times a day to see what customers are saying about their FreshFood experience. This past week, there were nine isolated remarks concerning the quality and taste of the seafood that we sold. According to the testimonials, customers were displeased and disappointed with our scallops, swordfish, and halibut."

"This is all news to me," exclaimed Amber Rosenbloom, the manager of the seafood department. "There was absolutely nothing different about this week's order, nor did I receive anything from our distributer about there being any issues. If you recall, I was notified, about three years ago, when our distributer had issues with their clams, and we temporarily stopped carrying them. However, as far as I know, there are no similar issues."

"The problem," continued Hailey, "is that it truly does not matter whether there were real issues with the seafood that we sold last week. Even if the quality was as good as we are known for, which is likely the case, we must remember that the customer is always right … as hard as that may be. In addition, it does not matter whether these were truly nine isolated complaints or whether it was one individual customer who decided to create nine different usernames on MarketMeasure, ultimately creating a potentially negative image of our store in the minds of others. The key is that we must do something both to acknowledge the issues raised and to explain what we will do to fix things."

"How will we possibly know the people who purchased seafood this past week?" asked Brad Downingtown, a recently hired grocery bagger.

"That information is quite easy to find out," answered Jack Scotch, the sales manager at FreshFood. "I can have that data for you before the end of the day."

"But that is not the answer," interjected Hailey. "Let's assume that a car manufacturer found out that its gas indicator in its most recent model was malfunctioning and providing incorrect estimates of the amount of fuel remaining in the owner's tank. From an organizational perspective, this clearly affects two populations of people: those who own the vehicle under question and those who might be future patrons. We need to apologize not only to those who bought our seafood last week, but also to all FreshFood customers after word of this incident is released. We are, I fear, about to witness one of the evils of social media, whereby such electronically mediated word-of-mouth testimony can inadvertently affect the buying habits of committed patrons."

"So you are basically saying that because we had one potentially fabricated and flawed series of negative comments about our seafood, that this could come to affect our entire company?" asked Jamie Pelegrino, a seasoned check-out clerk.

"Exactly," commented Hailey, "and that is why we need to do something … and something fast. Do we have any suggestions?"

"What if we were to hang signs at the entrance of our store both explaining the recent situation and apologizing for the issues that it created," asked Peter Adler, one of the stock boys in the produce department.

"As I see it, Peter, this could have two negative consequences," explained Hailey. "First, it could create problems where they did not exist before. In other words, this could create fear in those customers who never knew there was an issue with our seafood at all. Although not revealing information could be considered sneaky or devious, revealing information could ultimately be dangerous as well. Second, this would not reach customers who, based on the comments on MarketMeasure, have already decided to extinguish their loyalty to FreshFood, since they would not be returning to the store to see the signage. I do, however, like your recommendation, Peter. Does anyone else have a suggestion?"

"So, if I am correct, our goal would be to provide an explanation, an apology, and a rectification strategy," asked Alexis Baldwin, the manager of the dairy department.

"Exactly correct," responded Hailey.

"I have a great idea," said Sara Klein, the manager of the beauty department. "Based on data from a year ago, approximately 92% of our patrons have a rewards card, which, as we know, entitles them to discounts and deals. When signing up for the rewards card, customers must provide us with an email address. If I am not mistaken, Hailey has a database of all email addresses. We can create a team whose responsibility is to create the message that we want to send to all customers and we can send this as an email."

"But what about those who do not check their email," asked Hailey, "and what about those who will find out about this for the first time and might become disgruntled merely by message exposure."

"Well, I am getting there," explained Sara. "In addition to sending the email, let's use three of our social media outlets to communicate the same message of apology, promise, and desire. First, since we know that nearly 20% of our customers follow our daily tweets, we can use Twitter as one outlet. As we know, it is likely that those who go to a site like MarketMeasure to post and/or read customer testimonies are also the same people likely to follow us on Twitter. I think that this will get our message to quite a lot of customers. Second, we can use MarketMeasure as a social medium to communicate the same message of apology, promise, and desire. Rather than being sneaky and creating an anonymous username to argue against the nine comments degrading our seafood from last week, we will let them know that our message is coming from our director of marketing and outreach. The customers who read the negatively framed messages will also now read our message, which will likely result in renewed excitement and positivity. Third, I think that it would be extremely worthwhile to post the same message on our Facebook page, which currently has over 4,200 members. I am confident that this triangulated approach will allow us to get the message to quite a lot of customers."

"I certainly like the recommendation," stated Hailey. "Regarding the benefits of social media platforms, such an approach would certainly be high on the reach, accessibility, immediacy, and usability scales. Are there any reactions to Sara's suggestion?"

"I just want to take a moment to offer my two cents," added Mr. Crabtree. "As you know, this market has been in my family for the past seven decades. Being a wise business person, I know that it is these seemingly small, seemingly insignificant issues that can absolutely destroy a company like ours. We need to take every single step to increase the likelihood that this event is merely a small, temporary bump in the road, rather than the beginning of the end of our existence. Believe me, I am considered, by most, to be old school. If this was 30 years ago, we would publish our apology in the local newspaper, which everyone in the town would read. Today, however, we find ourselves embedded in a society of electronic communicators, which forces us to rethink the nature of organizational communication with our publics ... in this case, our customers. I think that Sara's recommendation is a great one and I fully endorse it as a communicative strategy. Barring any serious opposition, I propose to have a few people work together on framing the message, which, upon my approval, will be disseminated via Twitter, MarketMeasure, and our very own FreshFood Facebook page. Do we have any volunteers?"

Hailey Blackstone, Amber Rosenbloom, Jack Scotch, and Sara Klein all volunteered, with no objections from the other 62 full-time and part-time employees. It was clear to anyone in the meeting that three decisions needed to be made. First, how would the public apology be framed? Second, through what social media outlets would the apology be communicated? Third, when would the message be delivered? Since Mr. Crabtree made it quite clear that this was an extremely pressing issue, with extremely grave implications for FreshFood, the emergent team knew that it had to meet as soon as possible. After discussing their schedules, it was the unanimous decision that Hailey, Amber, Jack, and Sara would meet at 5 pm: the end of their respective shifts.

THE MONDAY AFTERNOON MEETING

The clock struck five and all four employees met in the break room for what they anticipated to be a very lengthy, conflict-ridden discussion. This changed, however, as soon as Hailey emerged as the leader. "To be quite honest, everyone, this is not brain surgery," began Hailey. "We have a clear problem. The problem is that we screwed up and need both to admit our error and to regain the popularity of our grocery store in the local community. Regarding the social media outlets, I think that Sara was spot-on with her recommendation of posting the message of apology on Twitter, MarketMeasure, and Facebook. By posting it on all of these outlets, we exponentially increase the likelihood that our customers will receive it. Also, as was mentioned in the meeting this morning, it is likely that only those who visit sites like MarketMeasure will know anything about the stigmatizing post about our recent stock of seafood. Therefore, those who read the postings on these social media outlets will learn of our apology and those who don't visit such social media outlets will never know that a problem existed in the first place."

"Well, what if people find out, inadvertently, and are displeased with our public relations attempts," asked Jack.

"I was thinking the same exact thing," added Amber.

"It is a good question, indeed," answered Hailey, "and one whose answer I am not certain of. If you think about the world of advertising, advertisers are not expecting 100% of customers to be exposed to their ads. From my memory of graduate school education, advertisers are lucky if 15% of their customers are exposed to their ads. Can they do anything about the remaining 85%, other than try sending the message through different media outlets? Probably not. So we are, in essence, doing the same thing. We are sending out our message with the hope that a percentage of people whom we have wronged (or potentially wronged) will receive our apology. I truly do not think that we could ask for more, nor do more."

"I completely agree," interjected Jack.

"Me too," added Amber.

"Sounds good to me," said Sara. "And I would also urge us to send this out through our social media forums as soon as possible. In fact, I am hoping that Mr. Crabtree will give us the thumbs-up this evening so that we can send the message before the start of business tomorrow morning."

"That would be amazing," claimed Amber.

"Yes it would," Jack said enthusiastically.

"Well then," stated Hailey, "there is only one thing left to do. We must decide how we are going to frame the message of apology. I really like how you, Sara, explained, in the meeting this morning, the need to craft a message that includes apology, promise, and desire."

"I really liked that too," said Amber, "and I really think that we need to incorporate all three, so as to admit our wrongdoing, promise never to have something like this happen again, and to reinstate our desire to be the supermarket with the highest quality, best customer service, and best prices around. My suggestion is that each of us works separately on drafting the message and then we reconvene when everyone is done to share our drafts. We will then collaborate our ideas and re-frame it into one final document."

All four group members agreed and decided that this strategy of group decision making was the most democratic, insofar as each member had equal opportunity to contribute to the group's decision, and the strategy was the one least likely to result in social influence. Although Jack and Sara were both done crafting their messages after 30 minutes, it took Hailey 45 minutes and Amber nearly an hour. The group reengaged in dialogue at nearly 6:15 pm and, after another 40 minutes of deliberation, came up with the following message:

> As you know, we at FreshFood pride ourselves on the quality of our products, the friendliness and helpfulness of our staff, and the most competitive prices in and around our community. It was recently brought to our attention that several of our seafood items from last week were not fresh and we deeply apologize to anyone who experienced this. If, in fact, you did experience this, please stop by within the next two weeks, with your receipt, for a full refund. We are embarrassed that this happened and just wanted to take the opportunity to formally apologize, in an effort to 'right our wrong,' and to give you our absolute word that this will not happen again. Given the seriousness of this issue, we have decided that several members of our staff will taste the fish, shellfish, produce, meat, and poultry that we receive every Sunday and Wednesday. Please know how sorry we are and please know that we will do anything and everything to regain our positive image in your minds.

After unanimously agreeing that this was the best way of publicly apologizing, the team of four sent an email to Mr. Crabtree, received his approval within the hour, and posted the message to Twitter, MarketMeasure, and Facebook. Before the four disbanded, Hailey decided to add her final thoughts. "I think that this is the absolute best that we, as a company, could have done to fix our image," claimed Hailey. "It is just crazy to think that, on the one hand, social media can destroy an organization. On the other hand, however, they can also repair an organization's image. And for all we know, and which is the craziest thing of all, this might not have even been a valid complaint about our seafood. It could have just as easily been a high school student doing a prank or merely a customer whom was disappointed with our establishment. Regardless of the reason, we must remember that we live in the electronic age with a new way of communicating with publics. It is important that we, as a company, do some additional research on social media outlets, especially in the event that our public apology is not well received. However, we can do this once I analyze the effectiveness of this public relations campaign. At this point, all we can do is wait."

DISCUSSION QUESTIONS

1. What are both the advantages and potential disadvantages of an organization using social media to publicly apologize about an issue like the one that FreshFood endured?

2. What other social media tools, in addition to Twitter, MarketMeasure, and Facebook, could FreshFood have used to circulate its message of apology?

3. How could the final message of apology have been framed differently and why would this have increased the likelihood of apology acceptance on behalf of FreshFood patrons?

4. In addition to apology, promise, and desire, what other variables could (and should) be included in an organization's message of public apology?

KEY TERMS

Public Apology, Social Media, Public Relations, Organizational Image

PART IV
Working with Stakeholders

Spinning Green along the Rio Grande: Can Corporate Social Responsibility Really Pay Off?

Kyle F. Reinson and Brett S. Vergara
St. John Fisher College

ABSTRACT

When a change in company leadership threatens the local environment and a real estate developer's positive reputation for going green, a corporate social responsibility expert faces a dilemma about what green really means.

When Clarissa Spitz checked her voicemail, she heard these words from a reporter at the *Albuquerque Record.*

"Hi Clarissa, this is Renee Banker at the *Record*, can you give me a call because I heard Allen Smythe Development is pulling funding for that bird protection project along the river. A group called 'Sustainable Bird Council' is claiming Smythe is being grossly negligent toward the environment. I'll be here until 5:30 pm, and I want to make sure I include a response from you guys in my story. Thanks."

It was just after 3 pm that day, and Clarissa knew she needed to reply to Renee before the deadline for her story on the *Record*'s popular *Insider* blog, but she was not quite sure how to respond. She had spent nearly four years working for the Allen Smythe Development Group (ASDG) as its regional corporate social responsibility officer, but a recent meeting with her new boss had resulted in some concerns. Before she could do anything, she needed to call Barney.

Barney Ruiz had just taken the helm of the southwestern real estate division of ASDG and had visited Clarissa at the company's regional office in Bernalillo County a few weeks earlier to say hello to her and get some updates on how the development approvals were going for the company's real estate venture along the shores of the Rio Grande River. ASDG was developing an upscale gated residential community called Avia Verde.

"I need to see you about this budget," demanded Barney as he shut the door to the conference room. "I need you to help me understand why, at a time when this division is still reeling from the burst of the housing bubble and losing money, that we have more than $250,000 this year for so-called 'community relations' efforts with environmental groups who might oppose our development project anyway? In my experience, you can never make these people happy. We do need to keep our investors happy, though, and we need to run a tighter ship."

Before Clarissa could reply, Barney went on a rant about how he expected his employees to manage the money of ASDG as if it were their own and how frivolous spending would simply not be part of the plan going forward. He also hinted that poor home sales at Avia Verde were going to lead to certain employee layoffs by the end of the year.

A GREAT START

Clarissa, a 15-year corporate communications veteran, had been recruited to ASDG from a California-based natural foods company called CaringFoods. CaringFoods had a strong reputation for its environmentally conscious packaging and sustainable food products like Fair Trade coffees and baked goods that were produced by union workers at a guaranteed pay rate triple that of the state's minimum wage. That company had been generating large-scale publicity from cable news networks and national news magazines as well as in the local California news outlets who touted CaringFoods as the model for a new kind of corporate environmental champion.

Several search firms had contacted Clarissa with possible job offers to jump ship at Caring Foods and as the months went by the offers become more and more lucrative, some offering her the first opportunity in her career to make more than $150,000 per year.

Bill Bantor, who had been Clarissa's boss at ASDG before he was promoted to the corporate headquarters in New Jersey to become the senior vice president of national marketing, had convinced her to leave CaringFoods nearly four years ago for the unique opportunity to help the real estate developer improve its environmental image.

At the time, Bill offered Clarissa a $200,000-per-year salary and additional benefits like large discounts on the homes that ASDG built and even a company car. Bill instantly was impressed with Clarissa's outside-of-the-box thinking and innovative ideas. He said, "I want our division to *bleed green*, and our biggest challenge is that New Mexico project. I want you to overwhelm local environmentalists with how much ASDG cares about protecting native habitats. They can be tough critics of companies like ours."

Clarissa reached out to Citizens for Zero Growth her first week on the job and made fast friends with the group's executive director Dominic Sherman, convincing him that ASDG was not like other real estate companies who rarely do much for environmental preservation efforts. Dominic liked what he heard and he and Clarissa began to have lunch together each month at a local burrito shop. He even invited Clarissa to the wedding of his only son. She beamed as Dominic told other guests at the wedding that "we can trust Clarissa will do the right thing and keep our community from sprawling out of control."

❖ ❖ ❖

By becoming close friends with the leader of Citizens for Zero Growth, Clarissa was also able to build great relationships with other non-governmental organizations at the state level and in Bernalillo County that supported the preservation of land from development. Because of Clarissa's corporate social responsibility makeover for ASDG, Avia Verde was held up as an example of responsible and sustainable development in which the community could take pride. The company won awards from the Environmental Protection Agency because the homes it was building at Avia Verde were saving home owners money on their electric and heating bills. Some of the homes with solar panels were generating more electricity than they used, which home owners could then sell back to the energy company.

"I like all of your ideas, Clarissa," Bill said. "But I *love* how they are helping us get approvals for the Avia Verde project. We've spent so much money on that riverfront land and our investors are expecting a big return."

Clarissa had truly moved mountains. She had convinced the construction managers to use solar panels on the roofs of every home, she worked with the managers to include energy-efficient home designs and appliances, and Avia Verde was already winning national awards as its first homes were completed and people started to move in. National publicity for ASDG was also positive, as the news media touted Clarissa's success in a feature story with the headline, *Queen of Green*.

BULLDOZING THE BIRDS?

As ASDG begin clearing some land for phase two of the Avia Verde project last year, bulldozer operators found evidence of two bird nests. Developers never like to see bird nests on their property because if they nest, it becomes their habitat and can halt a development project in its tracks. One was a nest of a *threatened species*, the Mexican spotted owl, and the other was the nest of the yellow-billed cuckoo, a bird that is considered *a species of concern* due to its dwindling populations. The local environmental community is always raising money to protect these two birds. Henry Fay, the land conservation supervisor, called Clarissa in a fit of anger.

"I just cannot believe this."

"What is wrong, Henry?"

"Our guys found a spotted owl and a cuckoo nesting on the property."

"So what does that mean?"

"We will need to report this, because if we do not we can get into a lot of trouble. The bad part is that we are already behind schedule and I am playing catch up. I did not need a delay."

"But what about phase two?"

"If the 'enviros' hear about this we can pretty much say *arrivederci* to phase two of Avia Verde."

As Clarissa ended the call on her smartphone, she quickly researched the legal matter of species protection and called Bill right away.

"Hi Bill, we've got bird problems."

"What?"

"A spotted owl and a cuckoo have nested at Avia Verde."

"I'm sure we can get through this, you've done a great job keeping the locals and the news media favorable to our project, I have to run to a meeting with the advertising agency, so text me later on how you will handle it. We'll pay any price to protect our environmental reputation in Bernalillo County, you have a blank check."

Clarissa called Dominic, and all of the other contacts she had made since she came to New Mexico to let them know what Henry had found on the property. She also called Renee at the *Albuquerque Record*. Because of the relationships she had developed since her arrival, most of the responses were positive, and even Renee wrote a favorable story about ASDG with the headline, *Local Developer Pledges to Save Birds*. Because Clarissa was transparent about the bird nests, she had the community behind her and ASDG.

Clarissa also called a news conference to announce that her company would be the lead funder of the newly created Sustainable Bird Council, a broad-based group of elected officials and environmental groups in Bernalillo County. The Council's chair, Dave Sanders, stood with Clarissa to answer questions from the media. Dave concluded his remarks by praising Clarissa.

"We are really thankful for the million-dollar gift from ASDG over the next five years to bring back our spotted owl and cuckoo populations along the Rio Grande. For too long, real estate interests have turned a blind eye toward the environment. These folks are different."

Dominic and Dave quickly mobilized a group of wealthy citizens, some whom now lived at Avia Verde because of its green housing, to purchase a few acres of land around the nests and create a pocket park. Clarissa worked with Henry to change the plans and, although ASDG missed the opportunity to sell the lost real estate, the contribution of citizens kept the lost revenue from hitting the balance sheet. It was a true win-win.

POP GOES THE BUBBLE?

Barney had arrived as Clarissa's new boss amidst a corporate restructuring at ASDG. The company had moved Bill to corporate headquarters and Clarissa really wished he was in the conference room instead of Barney when Barney's rant was over.

"I have to tell you, Barney, I am really insulted that all the great work I have done at the company has been so quickly blown off. This division has been successful until recently because of my efforts proving that a great corporate social responsibility program directly feeds the bottom line. Now you show up and decide to forget history. I need some time to cool off."

Clarissa stormed out of the conference room as Barney sat stunned. As she began to drive her car away from the office, she received a call from a search firm. As angry as she was, she was ready to listen to any offer that might mean leaving ASDG. The voice on the line was Linda Bailes, one of the headhunters she had talked with before Bill hired her four years ago.

"Listen, I have a confidential client who is looking for someone exactly like you," Linda told Clarissa. "You'd be in Los Angeles and it would be double what you were making at Caring Foods. Are you interested?"

Clarissa had stopped her car to take the call along the Rio Grande River. She stepped toward the river and looked back at Avia Verde, a place where she had felt at home until Barney became her boss. She thought of what might happen to the goodwill she had built in the community if she were to leave ASDG.

Linda said, "Are you there? Clarissa are you interested?"

"Let's set something up. I can interview next week. I had a vacation planned anyway."

It would have been bad enough that she did not care for Barney as her new boss, but Clarissa also knew that the real estate development industry was in serious trouble. Avia Verde was the best-selling operation that ASDG had, and even those sales had trickled down to a few homes in the past year.

Even more than her time at CaringFoods, Clarissa felt like she had really made a difference, reshaping the way the real estate industry operated and being a well-respected professional in the Bernalillo County business community.

SAVE OUR BIRDS!

Clarissa returned from her vacation, rested and awaiting a lucrative job offer in Los Angeles. Her interview went well with her potential new employer, a big Hollywood studio. She met Dominic for lunch at their favorite burrito shop.

"I bumped into that Ruiz guy last week," Dominic said. "I guess things are changing at old Smythe, eh?"

"What do you mean?"

"He told me, and apparently four other environmental groups that are part of the Council, that you guys are not going to keep your promises. You are cutting us off at the knees."

"I was not even aware of this, I was on vacation. What did Barney say?"

"He told me to forget about all this money for the birds. He doesn't even know about all the great things you have done. What, is ASDG going out of business?"

"I don't, ah, I mean ..."

"I was hoping you were going to tell me this was not true but I see that it is. I'm not feeling all that hungry. I have an appointment."

"Dominic, please wait up!"

Dominic left the burrito shop quickly. Clarissa sat silently thinking. Her smartphone chimed. It was Barney on the other end of the line.

"Well, I am glad you have had a nice vacation. Your bird friends are picketing outside calling us liars and greedy pigs. These are the people you want to give money to? I just don't get it. You need to come to the office and deal with this."

"Fine, Barney. I am on my way."

Clarissa pulled into the parking lot only to find two dozen of the people she had considered her friends, including Dominic and Dave, shouting and holding picket signs. "Save Our Birds! Kill the Greed!"

The protesters ignored Clarissa as she crossed the picket line. She was at a loss for words. Barney greeted her as she made her way to her office where her voicemail message light was blinking with the message Renee had left for her.

"This is ridiculous, Clarissa. You need to go out there and calm these people down or I will. I am worried that the television stations are coming too. Go tell them about all the green things we do at Smythe. Explain that we cannot keep throwing our money away. Do something."

"I know you are upset, Barney. I'm sorry I blew up at you before I went on vacation. Before I go out there, I need to check my voicemail. It is probably Renee at the *Record*."

Clarissa walked into her office and told Barney she would be right back out. She closed the door and made her way to her desk. On the wall she noticed photos of the Rio Grande River, pictures of her with Dominic's family at his son's wedding. She dreaded talking to Renee. Another voicemail followed Renee's, it was from Linda informing her that there was officially a job offer on the table.

With some big decisions to make, Clarissa worried that everything she had worked hard for in her career was about to come crashing down. She wondered if there really was such a thing as authentic effort by corporations to do the right thing or if it was all just spin to make them look good. She was not sure how she could stay, but she had a lot at stake if she chose to leave.

She took a deep breath and got back to work.

DISCUSSION QUESTIONS

1. If you were Barney, how would you have handled Clarissa's angry response to your concerns about the fiscal problems at ASDG?

2. If you were Clarissa, would you take the job in Hollywood, or stay in New Mexico? What would be the implications of each decision?

3. Do you think that social responsibility efforts belong in business settings? Are there ways that corporations can be profitable and at the same time be seen as caring toward the environment?

4. How much should people expect of corporations in terms of giving back to the communities in which they operate?

5. Do you think Dave and Dominic should have given Clarissa more time to respond, based on their existing friendships? How does their reaction relate to the boundary role public relations people serve within organizations?

KEY TERMS

Corporate Social Responsibility, Environmental Responsibility, Community Relations, Boundary Role in Public Relations

CHAPTER 20

In PR All Relationships Matter: A Lesson in Governmental and Media Relations

Katherine R. Fleck
Ohio Northern University

ABSTRACT

When an employee is arrested for child endangerment, the employer, government officials, and the media all want to know what happened. Through a series of missteps and bad decisions, the Children Are #1 Daycare Center learns a tough lesson in governmental and media relations.

Ring … Ring … Ring … groggy and disoriented, Sam looked at the phone on her night stand. *The State of Ohio Dispatch* the caller ID proclaimed. She picked up the phone, wiped the sleep from her eyes, and answered, "Hello?"

"Sam Wolfe?"

"Speaking."

"Hi, this is Greggory Floyd from the *The State of Ohio Dispatch* and I was wondering if you could tell me about your employee Britannee Hasslebeck?"

"Excuse me?!" Sam questioned into the phone.

"Specifically, I am interested in finding out more about Ms. Hasslebeck's criminal and educational background. As her employer at Children Are #1 Daycare, you are responsible for ensuring that you performed adequate background checks. Right?"

"Why are you asking about Britannee?" asked Sam. "Oh no," she yelled into the phone and told the reporter she had nothing else to say to him before abruptly ending the call.

PASSING THE CHILD ACT

Ohio was losing ground on education. Year after year, test results and college placement data showed the state's students were not keeping pace with their counterparts across the country. To address this problem, Representative Amanda Wilson proposed legislation to fund a system of daycare centers for all at-risk children three years old until kindergarten.

"I believe we can spend every dime the State of Ohio takes in and we will not make progress on education until we get our most vulnerable children into early learning environments," said Rep. Wilson at her news conference announcing the bill. "This measure will fundamentally change our definition of public education by providing high-quality opportunities for learning beginning at age three."

While Governor Hinchey was not in favor of spending the state's rainy day savings fund on more governmental programs, he did share Rep. Wilson's view that early childhood education was an antidote to the state's failing education system. An unlikely coalition emerged to support the measure. However, to gain Gov. Hinchey's full support, Rep. Wilson agreed the new daycare system would not be owned and operated by the State of Ohio. Instead the State would contract with privately owned daycare centers to provide the new services.

"This is a win-win situation for our children, families, and high-quality daycare providers," said Gov. Hinchey at the signing ceremony for the bill known as the CHILD Act or Changing Hope's Individual Learning Delivery Act. "I am proud that our state's leaders came together to pass a measure to protect the future of our most vulnerable children."

STEP ONE

The new system of state-funded, privately operated daycares was named Step One. The State of Ohio developed a system of rules private daycare providers would need to follow to be certified by the state as eligible providers. The Step One rules included: mandatory criminal background checks for all employees, maintaining at least one adult for every four children on the premises at all times, bachelor's degrees in early childhood education for all instructors, and yearly first-aid training for all employees.

The Children Are #1 Daycare Center was excited to join the Step One system, but they did not have the administrative tools to do criminal background checks and needed to hire several new instructors with bachelor's degrees in early childhood education. And, they didn't have much time, as the State of Ohio limited the number of centers in each community that could get state funding. On a short timeframe, but eager to get started, the Children Are #1 owners hired an experienced human resource expert to develop human resource processes, run background checks, and check educational credentials on new employees. Shortly thereafter, they welcomed Tiffany, Stella, Britannee, and Piper as new instructors.

Children Are #1 received state approval to provide state-funded daycare under the new CHILD Act in October and began accepting children into the program in November. By mid-December the center was full of children and the owners were satisfied with their decisions and their new bustling center.

THE LATE-NIGHT PHONE CALL

After getting off the phone with the newspaper reporter, Sam went into crisis mode. By 1:03 am Sam was on the phone with Sheila Weiss, the HR expert, trying to find out all she could about Britannee's background.

"Why are you calling at this hour?" murmured Sheila.

"Britannee was arrested this evening for leaving her three-year-old son locked alone in her apartment while she went to college and then out to the bars," said Sam. "The police found her passed out in the street and when she woke in the hospital she was in a panic about her son. The doctors told the police, who broke into the apartment and found the little boy covered in food he had taken out of the refrigerator."

Sheila gasped for air, and Sam went on to recall the story the reporter relayed.

"We will need to get Britannee's background and education checked out because I'm sure the state will find out and will want copies," said Sam.

"Well … it won't be that easy," hesitated Sheila.

"What do you mean?" asked Sam.

Shelia told Sam that Britannee's background check had not been returned from the service yet and she hadn't had a chance to check her education because of all the tasks required in the startup of all the new children.

Sam was stunned. "Why is she working for us if we don't have the information?"

"You asked me to get four instructors on board as quickly as possible," replied Sheila. "These checks can take time, and we didn't have much of it," Sheila said quietly.

"Why didn't you tell me the checks weren't back?" Sam yelled. "I assumed you knew the process took time, and besides you never asked," replied Sheila flatly.

THE STATE OF THE STATE'S MEDIA RELATIONS

After Sam hung up on him, *Ohio Dispatch* reporter Greggory Floyd called the next person on his list for the story he was writing, Governor Hinchey's press secretary Jason Mazzie.

Jason didn't hesitate, he told the reporter, "We will get to the bottom of this and if it's true, we will shut this center down immediately."

Next, Greggory Floyd called Representative Amanda Wilson. Representative Wilson knew Sam at Children Are #1, and told Greggory she would personally assure him that this was a mistake and the daycare had done all the necessary checks to ensure the proper instructors had been hired. Rep. Wilson was sure this was a fluke that Children Are #1 could not have foreseen.

By daybreak, Sam and Sheila had combed the internet and placed several emergency calls to the background check vendor to get Britannee's information in their hands. By the time they reached the vendor, Governor Hinchey already had Britannee's criminal background check in his hands.

"How could this have happened?" the governor asked his assistant. "We have to do something immediately."

Rep. Wilson was having a similar conversation with her staff. She had called Sam, with whom she had gone to college, but couldn't reach her.

"If any reporters call, tell them we have no information but when we do, we will let them know," Rep. Wilson told her receptionist.

Sam and Sheila just looked at each other after reading the report for the third time. It noted that Britannee pled guilty to a misdemeanor count of child endangerment when her son was 18 months old. Further, Britannee was not working on a master's degree as she had told Sheila. She was actually completing her bachelor's degree, which made her ineligible for the job.

"We are ruined," cried Sam. "I can't tell anyone we knew about this, but I can't tell them we didn't know either. What are we going to do?" she whispered. Sheila simply looked at the floor unable to respond.

"We better call our attorney," said Sam. "We're going to need some help."

When they reached their attorney's office, Sheila and Sam were advised to send all reporter's calls to her office and she would respond.

"What will you say?" Sheila asked. "Will you tell them it was my fault?"

"No," said her attorney, "I will simply say Britannee no longer works for you and you have no further comment on the matter. Now you need to let me know if there is anyone else you don't have information on."

Sam looked at Sheila and told her to tell the attorney the truth.

"I have all the other background checks back, but the educational checks have not been completed," she admitted.

"You need to complete the educational checks immediately," said the attorney. "Let me know as soon as they are done."

Sam felt humiliated but appreciated the attorney's protection. She knew the right thing to do was to call Rep. Wilson, but she was too afraid to admit the truth.

Meanwhile, Governor Hinchey decided not to respond to the media based on his attorney's recommendation. After all, this matter might end up in litigation and anything they said could be used against them.

"We have to respond," objected Jason. "I told the reporter we would shut the center down if this was true," he reminded the governor. "And you made it clear that transparency in the system would be important for parents to trust the system," he said.

"Yes, but I meant transparency in the process," said Governor Hinchey. "I am not going to let this program go down the tubes before it really gets started because we didn't get the background check rules clear enough."

It turns out the State had licensed the daycare under the rules they developed, but the rules didn't specify how or when background checks and educational credential verifications were to be conducted. They just wanted the issue to die on its own by giving reporters the run-around until they tired of the issue and moved on to something else.

"And, we can't take responsibility for an irresponsible contractor," noted the Governor's attorney. "We will refer the media to the local police office and Children Are #1, it'll be their problem."

"It's our problem too," said Jason. "We will take a serious hit on this for dodging responsibility and not taking proactive action. I want to be on record that I believe we are making a serious mistake."

The Governor's attorney simply replied, "So noted."

Rep. Wilson was advised by her attorney to blame the gap in the rules on the Governor and the hiring of Britannee on Children Are #1. But Rep. Wilson knew that would not end the story. She admonished her attorney and said, "we worked together on this bill and now we have to stand together on the solution. I am going to call the governor and suggest we hold a news conference to address the issue and put out the fire."

After several days, Rep. Wilson finally convinced the governor to hold a news conference, but not until after all the national news organizations picked up the story and covered it on the nightly news, two major national newspapers ran lengthy articles with pictures of Britannee, and the radio talk shows railed about this being the worst case of government wasteful spending and worthless government contractors.

Sam eventually called Rep. Wilson to explain what happened and apologized for keeping her in the dark. Rep. Wilson told her she could not understand why Sam had not given her a heads-up in the first place. "Rule number one is tell your partners when the ship is going down," Rep. Wilson admonished Sam. "We might have been able to help if you had reached out earlier, but the governor and I are announcing we will pull your license. This needs to be over."

Sam sat in stunned silence trying to figure out all that had gone wrong and what to do next.

DISCUSSION QUESTIONS

1. When the reporter called, what should Sam have done first?
2. Did the governor use solid reasoning in his relationship with the media?
3. Should Rep. Wilson have had her own news conference when she couldn't reach Sam and the governor rejected the idea?
4. Why didn't Rep. Wilson protect Children Are #1 from losing their license?
5. Was Jason wrong to argue with the governor's attorney about the approach to working with the media?

KEY TERMS

Media Relations, Governmental Relations, Working with Legal

CHAPTER 21

Fighting the Good Fight

Leah M. Omilion-Hodges
Western Michigan University

ABSTRACT

A hospital public relations department is charged with creating a multi-year internal campaign to persuade its change-resistant members to embrace a transition from paper to electronic medical records. Decisions must be made regarding internal branding, use of opinion leaders, and the role of social media.

Christine Klimecki sat quietly during the meeting. She took detailed notes, she followed the conversation, and she nodded her head in agreement or shook it silently in dissent but she didn't say a word. How could she? She already felt buried. Christine, the public relations specialist for a large rural hospital, was presented with a mighty task. She was the lead PR practitioner on the multi-year project to transition her hospital and its affiliates from paper-based records to exclusively electronic medical records. Emmitt's View, the small hospital she was born in, was about to embark on a large change in an environment that actively opposed change.

As a child Christine made a few trips to Emmitt's View. There was the time she fell off of the swings at school while trying to swing higher than her friend Lindsay Bradford. She smiled when she thought of the minor cuts that the doctors patched up when she inadvertently put the car in reverse instead of drive and hit the basketball pole in her family's driveway. Since then, Christine had left the community to attend the state university, where she earned both her undergraduate and graduate degrees. She did internships and spent several years working in the big city, but at the end of the day, she felt a strong tie to Emmitt's View. It was a small town, practically everything was named after the founder, but to Christine it was home. When she returned from school and from her early work experiences, she felt like not a day had passed. It wasn't just the hospital that was opposed to change, it was the whole city.

After leaving the meeting, Christine found her way back to her desk to try to make sense of the enormous task awaiting her. After reviewing her notes, she realized that the task was even larger than she had originally thought. This project required more than an internal communication plan to inform employees of the transition from paper-based medical records to exclusively electronic records; she needed a full-blown campaign to establish a new internal brand for Emmitt's View. Instead of simply communicating basic information regarding the change, why it was necessary, and emphasizing the benefits, Christine realized that she had to convince an organization to change its identity and develop an internal brand. She also knew it wasn't a task that she could accomplish on her own.

THE PROBLEM

Christine had not been at Emmitt's View Hospital long, actually her second anniversary was just around the corner, but in her short tenure she had already seen how the organization reacted to change. In the first few months at Emmitt's View, the organization proposed a change to the parking situation. Ultimately, the development would result in a new and improved building for patient care, but would temporarily inconvenience employees in regard to parking. It wasn't that the employees didn't put patient care first—in fact they were thrilled about the opportunity to expand, but it was a fact that a period of change was necessary before any new innovations could be implemented.

Christine also recalled the time that administration had decided to go with a new linen vendor. The new vendor was able to provide the same quality that the employees were used to, but at a better rate. "The patterns are different," "They use different detergent," and "I don't think they're as welcoming," were the comments generated by employees. Much to their chagrin, administration ended up using the previous linen vendor just to quiet the dissent from employees.

Christine sat in her office recalling the outrage over parking and over the linens and felt paralyzed. "How do you convince the hospital that this is a change that will help them? A change that is good for employees AND patients?" Christine realized that once she answered that question, she would at least have a fighting chance of success.

DRAFTING A GAME PLAN

After several weeks of consideration, Christine felt that she had a rough idea of how she might go about this huge undertaking. She requested a meeting with her manager, Dawn Rogers. Dawn was a great leader—she was intelligent, fair, and gifted at strategic public relations planning.

Christine sat down and forced a smile. Dawn saw straight through it.

"I know how big this is, but that's why I assigned it to you," explained Dawn. "You are respected by everyone—you left Emmitt's View, earned advanced degrees, and held some pretty impressive jobs before coming back. You're one of them too. They trust you and they respect you. That's why I put you as the point person—I want you to fight the good fight," Dawn said with a smile.

Christine instantly felt better—more confident, more in control. She sat back and started to tell Dawn about her tentative game plan.

"We need to make sure that while we emphasize the patient benefits of electronic medical records, that we also do the same for employees and especially the physicians. They are so logical and analytical, that if we can persuade them that only good can come from electronic medical records—then they will be hard-pressed to argue against them," stated Christine.

"But what's more important? We need to convince the physicians that it's the best decision, but also that it's a good thing! It's not just something that they need to do, but something that they want to do," finished Dawn.

"Yes, we need to find a way to enlist them as partners. If some of the most respected physicians get behind the project, then it becomes a lot easier to have others support the project as well," stated Christine.

"How do we do this?" asked Dawn.

"We ask them. We make them a key part of the team. I think we have some emails to send. Let's have a kick-off meeting!" Christine said excitedly. For the first time since she learned of the project, she felt excited.

COMPILING A TEAM

Christine spent the next week doing research—a mock election of sorts. She asked physicians, nurses, staff members and senior leadership questions such as which physician is most trusted? Which is most popular? Who has the ear of the others? Who is the trendsetter? She compiled her responses and then sent out a meeting request. In the meeting request, she also asked the physicians to respond to a short set of questions: How do you like to receive information from the hospital? What is the best time for you to meet? What is your favorite activity outside of work? And who do you like to receive messages from?

As Christine stood outside of the boardroom, she took a deep breath and smiled to herself. She didn't know how the meeting was going to go, but she felt reassured that, if she were going to be successful in helping the hospital transition from paper-based to electronic medical records, at the very least she had the right people at the decision-making table.

"It's good to know that you like to meet at 6 am, because I assure you that's not when I would have set the meeting," Christine said with a smile and laugh.

"Yes, if we have 6 am meetings we're still able to conduct our rounds before we have our own office hours," replied Dr. Don Smith, the chief of staff. "We were surprised that you are willing to meet us at this time because we've all consistently been told that 'it's too early,' but it gives us a chance to provide feedback for what the hospital's doing."

"Not a problem, Dr. Smith. And to the rest of you, we really appreciate you coming in early to sit down at this kickoff meeting," started Christine. "You might be wondering a kick-off for what? Well, Emitt's View, like many of the other hospitals, is transitioning from paper-based to electronic medical records. It's a big undertaking—we're going to work on it for the better part of two years before the transition is complete—but in order for us to be successful, in order for this to be well received and to be done right, I think that we need to have physicians as part of the team," said Christine.

Christine looked around and realized that she had their attention. Some of the doctors looked nervous. Others looked excited, perhaps realizing that they would be able to perform on par with the larger medical centers. At the very least, she recognized that they were still sitting at the table and willing to hear more.

"I want to go over some of the responses to the initial questions I asked. It appears that one of the most popular extracurricular activities is golf. Does that sound about right?" Christine had to smile at all of the physicians nodding their heads in unison. "Well, great, I think that we should use that as a theme in order to help some of the other physicians buy into this new change. Do you think that would be received well?"

"Just because we like golf doesn't mean that we like change," retorted Dr. Bill Zagat.

"I tend to agree. Also, golf is fun—completely changing our way of working is not," echoed Dr. Thomas Fitzpatrick.

"I hear what you're saying, but what we have to remember is we're not changing your entire way of working. Not even close. We're actually innovating. Electronic medical records are going to save you time and energy. They'll also help you to provide a higher level of care to your patients. No longer are you going to have to wait for forms or send a request to access a patient's x-rays," said Christine.

"Yes, this will take some time. But like I said, we're going to do it over a period of 18 months, so over a year and a half we have to find the best way to convince some of your colleagues that electronic medical records are a positive thing. And in the spirit of full disclosure, whether they like this or not, it's the way that the medical community is going. So I was hoping that by a assembling an all-star team with all of you," Christine paused to gesture to all of the employees present, "that we would be able to make this not only a palatable change, but we could also try to have some fun in the process. This is not only what's best for our patients, but for your own personal work life and for Emmitt's View as a whole."

Christine was warmed by the response. She realized that many of the physicians were nodding and some were even smiling. Of course some expressed concerns and some even openly opposed the transition, but by and large those present felt that this was going to be a positive change for the hospital.

Before they concluded the kickoff meeting, Christine passed around a sign-up sheet. The sign-up sheet asked if they would be willing to be a permanent part of the team to create and implement the public relations and communication plan.

IDEA GENERATION

Of the 18 physicians who were invited to the initial meeting, 12 of them committed to becoming permanent members of the steering committee. Christine realized in subsequent meetings that she had the right team. She had Dr. Smith, the chief of staff, and Dr. Michael Tomas who was well regarded for his international training. There was also Dr. Weaver who was respected for her charitable work in the community. Finally there was Dr. Ryan Jones, who was the youngest of the bunch, but also was the one who helped other physicians figure out how to use their smartphones, their tablets, and their laptops. If there was anyone who could convince them that social media belonged in part of this internal campaign, it was Dr. Jones.

The group was working successfully together and making a lot of progress on the campaign. However, despite all of their great strides, there certainly were some sticking points that the group was having difficulty in reaching a consensus over. By example, some felt that an internal campaign was silly. Some even referred to it as frivolous. "Why is it necessary to spend all of this time and all of these resources in generating a campaign that will be unknown to the community? Not to remind you that those people we serve are the ones who help to generate the revenue for the hospital," commented Dr. Smith.

While initially many of the physicians echoed his concern, with time Christine was able to convince them that, if they didn't have full buy-in from the medical community of Emmett's View, the change was going to be resisted and at the very least seen in negative terms. "In the matter of a few months this is going to be visible to everyone, not just those internally. That is, if physicians don't know how to enter prescription orders or if they don't know how to access the patient's medical records, then we're going to let down those whom we serve," argued Christine.

With time the group decided that a comprehensive internal public-relations campaign was necessary and that the golf theme was likely to be preferred by physicians. It was also decided that there needed to be persuasive messages created for word-of-mouth delivery from a physician to his or her peers. They also decided that internal branding documents such as newsletters, brochures, and clipboards would help to inform physicians of the benefits of the change.

After two months of frequent meetings, the steering committee came to senior leadership and presented their suggestions. While the committee had worked very hard, had done their research, and felt that all audiences were represented, they still needed a commitment from senior leadership to implement their plan.

IMPLEMENTING TOUGH DECISIONS

"It's our pleasure to present two months of hard work to you today. I want to preface this by saying that every member of this team has provided great ideas that we know will increase our success in effectively communicating the change and in garnering buy-in from the remainder of Emmitt's View employees," started Christine.

The meeting that was originally intended to last 60 minutes was nearing 150 minutes in length. While they had reached some areas of agreement, such as allocating resources, including employees and financial backing, for a comprehensive public relation campaign, there was still a lot of discussion about who would lead the campaign, how many phases would be present in the campaign, what the role of social media would be, and how best to utilize opinion leaders.

Christine left the meeting optimistic, but realized that she had several tough decisions to make. She had to decide if the campaign would be viewed as more credible if it was led by senior leadership or a group of physicians rather than the public relations department. She then had to decide on the best way to roll-out the campaign. That is, were there going to be multiple phases such as an introduction, a middle, and an end or was it going to be one large campaign that used the same message or messages throughout? She also had to make some decisions regarding the role of social media. While she was comfortable with social media and suggested that a Facebook page and a Twitter account would be helpful in educating physicians and other staff members about the electronic medical records, there was a large amount of dissent from the older physicians. Considering their perspective, she didn't know if it would make sense to use social media as a tactic or if she would better serve her audience by using only traditional media. Her final major decision rested on the role of opinion leaders. She had 12 physicians that she knew were highly regarded by their peers, but she didn't know the best way to involve them in the campaign. Should they be the faces of the campaign? Should they go from practice to practice and from floor to floor at the hospital to speak about the benefits of the electronic medical records? Should they give impromptu speeches to their peers? She wanted to make sure that she involved them in some capacity because they were trusted and because they were seen as credible, but she didn't know to what extent and in what regard.

Christine went back to the public relations department and asked her team to sit down and help her to make some suggestions. She said, "Before we leave here today, I'd like to make some suggestions regarding 1) the role that public relations plays in driving this campaign, 2) the proposed phases of the campaign, 3) the role of social media in the campaign, and 4) the role played by internal opinion leaders."

"I realize this is going to be a lot of work, but at the end of the day we're making decisions that will help our neighbors, our families, and ourselves in regard to the standard of care that we receive. And that's something that we can feel really good about. Now let's make some decisions," suggested Christine.

DISCUSSION QUESTIONS

1. What type of research should Christine and the public relations department collect before, during, and after this longitudinal campaign?

2. While organizations typically use social media to reach their external stakeholders, Christine thinks it may be a good idea for this internal change management campaign. If you were a member of the public relations department, what suggestions or advice would you give regarding the use of social media for internal stakeholders?

3. Christine helped the organization to realize that the transition to electronic medical records would require a multi-year campaign. What are the various phases that you would recommend? How would you assess the effectiveness of each phase? What outcomes would need to be achieved for you to feel as though you could successfully conclude the campaign?

KEY TERMS

Internal Branding, Change Management, Stakeholder Relations

CHAPTER 22

A Case of Discrimination: Fostering an Inclusive Work Environment

Dotty Heady, Erin E. Gilles, and Shannon M. Brogan
Kentucky State University

ABSTRACT

When a corporate executive's mother is given a job in public relations, the new vice president of marketing is forced into dealing with someone who cannot write. This case explores what occurs when unqualified people end up in occupations that directly interact with the public.

KF, or Kid-Friendly, Toys manufacturing company is located in a small town in Indiana, with a population of approximately 7,000 people. It is ideally situated in the middle of a triangle between Indianapolis, Indiana; Louisville, Kentucky; and Cincinnati, Ohio. KF Toys is owned by brothers Timothy and Gilbert Elpers. The company specializes in high-quality wooden educational toys. Their most successful line is a collection of basic-to-intricate puzzles and ergonomically shaped wooden pieces designed for physical therapy sessions. Throughout the company's 46-year history, it has maintained its family-owned-and-operated feel. However, the brothers are getting close to retirement age. Neither brother has children who are interested in taking over the company, so the brothers are looking to sell KF Toys to a larger toy outfit. Although the employees are sad to see the Elpers retire, they would rather see the company be sold and remain in business than for the company to close its doors. Before this happens, the Elpers brothers are focused on streamlining operations and improving the social media "buzz." The employees know that they need to make a good impression on any prospective executives who come to visit the facilities.

Marka Francis has been the HR manager for KF Toys for more than a decade. Francis is about to lose a major player from her team, Joanna Tanale, who is ready to have her baby. She will be out for 10 weeks under the Family Medical Leave Act, and Francis is not sure whether Tanale will want to come back to work once the baby is born.

The goal of the public relations department at KF Toys is to get all the promotion and media coverage they can without paying for it. They do what they can to take toys out for demonstrations, presentations, public meetings, county fairs, and Kiwanis and Chamber of Commerce meetings, to get press coverage and pictures in the papers.

Last year, the company overhauled its website and is working on enhancing its social media presence. Tanale has been working on keeping a daily presence on social media, so her replacement will need to be well versed in all the major social media applications.

ALL IN THE FAMILY

The vice president of marketing, Annabelle Hoskins, called Francis on the intercom and said she was walking down the hall toward her office and wanted to know if Francis would meet her in the hall because she was on her way out to lunch with her mother. Francis responded in the affirmative and headed for the door. She saw Hoskins walking toward her with a short woman with spiky gray hair and lively brown eyes. Hoskins introduced her mother, Aurorata Sydwoski, approximately age 61 or 62, who had been living with her sister in Florida ever since her husband (Hoskins' father) passed away. She had just completed a bachelor's degree in marketing while in Florida, and now was moving back here to live in the old family home and needed a job.

Sydwoski was quiet and soft-spoken in the brief introductory meeting with Francis in the hall at KF Toys, accompanied by her daughter. Hoskins announced that Sydwoski would be Tanale's replacement during her maternity leave.

"You'll fit in here perfectly," Hoskins said cheerfully. "This place is just like a family. Who knows, Mom. There just may be something permanent for you!"

"Oh, that's great!" Francis replied. "I'm sure you'll feel right at home in no time." Francis was caught off guard and felt ambushed! She was cut out of the loop. As HR manager, she should have had an opportunity to help evaluate job candidates. But, Hoskins was capable, so why shouldn't her mother be equally valuable? *After all, it is the vice president of marketing's mother!*

POOR GRAMMAR IS CAREER SUICIDE

A few weeks later, Sydwoski relocated to Indiana and began her duties with KF Toys. Francis decided to have Sydwoski help her with a press conference for a new toy that they had just produced and had not yet been shown to the public. Eight members of the press from several towns around the area had said they were coming. Five others might show up without calling back to say one way or the other.

There is a meeting room at KF Toys with up to 20 seats where visitors can be brought in to showcase a new product.

Sydwoski was put in charge of "meeting and greeting," while Francis was getting the backdrop and stage ready to showcase the toy. While Francis was carrying a box of brochures behind the logoed company backdrop for the news conference, Francis overheard Sydwoski talking to a group of journalists.

"They done a good job on this new toy, but it ain't going to be out on the market before September for the Christmas rush," Sydwoski said.

"Oh, no!" was all Francis could think when she heard the awful grammar. She felt the blood rush to her cheeks as she cringed. She had not spent much time with Sydwoski because she had been spending a lot of time organizing the news conference. She really had not heard her speak more than, "Yes, ma'am," "Please," "OK," and "Thank you." Francis was kicking herself for not spending more time with Sydwoski. And, not only was the grammar poor, but Sydwoski had no business undermining KF Toys in front of the press. *Isn't that PR 101?* In all of Francis' years with the company, no matter how far behind they were, they always got the toys ready in time for the holiday rush.

Now, what will I do? thought Francis. I just need to figure out some way to make this work. Let's face it, she's my boss' mother.

NAVIGATING CORPORATE CULTURE

There had been signs from the start that Sydwoski didn't fit into the corporate mold. From the beginning there were little issues that Francis should have picked up better on. Francis specifically needed someone who could manage the company website; Sydwoski could barely navigate word processing software. Since she had joined the company, Sydwoski had opened a virus email and infected her computer, irretrievably deleted a key file on marketing research, and locked the marketing team out of the printer interface. *Her blunders would almost seem funny if they weren't doing so much damage.*

And, on the first day of official work since she was hired, she drove an old, beat-up pick-up truck to work with an oversized bumper sticker that said, "Coalition of Rights for Women Over 50." Francis thought, *What do we have here? Sydwoski belongs to the Coalition of Rights for Women Over 50, also known as CRWO-50.* Francis did not know much about this group, but she figured it might be rather radical. Sydwoski had mentioned off-handedly last week that last year CRWO-50 held a protest outside four large companies. Francis wondered if it were a union, a group, or if it had much power. She thought, *I have been warned! I had better look this group up online to see what trouble I have caused for myself.*

There is a clash over the expected knowledge that Francis feels Sydwoski should have since she just graduated with a marketing degree, and the knowledge she doesn't have at all.

In the meantime, how can Francis minimize the impact of Sydwoski on clients, the press, and basically ANYONE outside the company? *What will I do? Can I let her go? What do I say to her? Can Sydwoski unlearn a lifetime of poor grammar? What do I tell my supervisor? Will this impact the potential sale of the company? I am in a pickle!*

DISCUSSION QUESTIONS

1. In what ways can the interactions between employees and clients help or harm a company's image?

2. How might factors like grooming, dress, grammar, and even topics of small talk send negative or positive messages?

3. Is the fact that Aurorata Sydwoski is the vice president of marketing's mother likely to influence how KF Toys handles this situation? How should Francis deal with the situation? Should she speak to Sydwoski's daughter, Annabelle Hoskins, directly, consult with the brothers who own KF Toys, or give Sydwoski time to get acclimated to her new position? Defend your answer.

KEY TERMS

Discrimination, Ageism, Social Media

CHAPTER 23

Spotlight on a Solar Energy Company: Investor Relations Crisis

Joan Schuman
Joan Schuman Associates and SUNY New Paltz

ABSTRACT

Two days before Solar Global Industries, a publicly traded company, planned to announce its Q4 earnings report, its stock share price mysteriously plummets. Dealing with the immediate response is the first step; second is the suspicion of insider trading.

Wednesday morning, 6 am, Maria's cell phone rings. Without breaking stride in her morning run, she sees it's from her coworker Vince, chief legal counsel to the company.

"Hey, Vince, what's up?"

"Did you check the stock prices yet, Maria?" asked Vince.

"No, I was waiting until I cleared my head. I only got four hours of sleep last night. The meeting didn't end till after 1 am."

"Well the stock price is down almost 10% in overnight trading."

"What? How could that happen? Oh no."

"I don't know what happened, but I scheduled a meeting in an hour. I think your whole PR team should be there. I'll be there with all the legal staff. And of course, I've spoken with President Juarez and our CFO, Cohen. "

"Ok. Thanks. I'll call the new college interns too, and we'll all be there within the hour."

SOLAR GLOBAL INDUSTRIES BACKGROUND

Solar Global Industries started as an entrepreneurial two-person company more than seven years ago. Billy Juarez and his partner, Sean Montrose, are American designers of solar technology. By the end of their second year in business together, they partnered with others in South America and Europe, and have plans now to expand throughout Asia. They have taken the best of engineering design, and combined it with solar know-how developed in Germany, Great Britain, the United States, Mexico, and Brazil. This global company focuses on expanding market share within each of these countries, and in specific industries with which they have developed trusted relationships. These include the military, various government agencies, as well as private energy sectors. Their products are constantly evolving as the technology improves, and they focus on targeting the needs of each new client. According to President Juarez, "We found that if we take the time and pull all our resources into solving one customer's needs, we can use that solution to solve many other similar business and government problems across the board."

To complement their global approach to technology and solar energy solutions, Solar Global has offices in cities in three different countries (Berlin, New York, Rio de Janeiro). And their staffing and marketing reflect both their global and their environmental approaches. Maria, as chief public relations officer and vice president for investor relations (IR) makes sure their website is in six different languages and their news releases are bilingual. Working with human resources, they make sure that most of their engineering as well as sales staff are bilingual too.

Maria pushes the president on the environmental issues, so their corporate offices are 90% solar powered, even in northern hemisphere cities, such as New York and Berlin. They recycle and reuse 100% of paper waste. They recycle 100% of scrap metal and 80% of the water from the factory processes.

Maria always touts the company's environmental efforts, awards, and recognition in every blog, the website, and all news releases. She helps brand their environmental responsibility as part of their corporate image.

The corporate goals and objectives also include positioning Solar Global Industries alongside its partners and competitors as a key manufacture and technical know-how resource. To do this, Maria and her team are frequently educating the general public, media, and politicians about the need for solar energy. They are continuously selling the story to investors and the media, and in the process help elevate awareness of the issues involved.

Part of her combined job handling public relations and investor relations also includes quarterly conferences, letters from the CEO, financial press releases, and maintenance of the IR section on the corporate website. Solar Global frequently posts videos of their solar panel installation processes with customer interviews. The PR team, plus President Juarez and CFO Cohen, go on frequent road trips selling the Global Solar story to investors and financial conferences.

As Maria quickly got dressed, she thought of the stellar PR image she and her team had worked so hard to maintain for Global Solar. She hoped it was not tarnished.

Maria appreciated that, at the start, Global Solar built a strong public relations team of professionals. She oversaw the hiring of each and every one. And because they believe in the future, and the value of investing in education, they frequently hired students from the nearby college as interns in various departments. Greg and Sara were the first interns Maria had in the PR/IR department. And she quickly put them on maintaining the blog and Twitter accounts.

Could that be the problem? Maria wondered.

Once in the car she thought about the social media tools the interns were using on behalf of the company. She hadn't trained them yet on fair disclosure laws and the company's code of ethics involving material information. She could recite the laws in her sleep. Simply, any information that could impact the buying, selling, or holding of a share of stock has to be released to everyone—shareholders, media, the public—at the same time. This is called material information. And if one or just a few people have material information, and trade stock based on it, it is called insider trading and it is illegal.

Maria knew it was very important to update the interns on the importance of this. She was so busy, working late into the night to get ready for this end of year report that she had planned to educate the interns right after the Q4 release.

Was something leaked on the blog? Did the interns or someone else on her team or legal release material information?

She called Vince on his cell using the Bluetooth connection on her car dashboard as she drove downtown to the office.

"Vince, did you check the blog?" she asked before he even had a chance to say hello.

"Maria, it's the second thing I did this morning. Nothing unusual. No new postings."

"Whew. OK, Vince. Thanks. By the way, what's the first thing you did?"

"Well, actually, after I saw the numbers I needed some time to catch my breath. Then I checked the news release you finalized with your team last night. It's all as we discussed. It simply states the Q4 supply and shipping problems delay, and the expectation for increased profit first quarter next year."

"I know we are not the first tech and solar energy company to have these issues. I guess we're lucky it's the first time. But I don't feel lucky right now. A drop of almost 10% overnight is just too suspicious. And too much of a coincidence for me," Maria said.

"Me too," said Vince. Then he added, "Maria, I have to use the word, could there have been a leak of material information? You know I have to pursue that."

"I know Vince," said Maria. "I agree."

"Well, I'm glad you trained the interns so they know to be careful, very careful, and not say anything about our Q4 numbers until they are released. I've always been afraid of social media."

All Maria could say was a weak, "See you in five."

Maria arrived at the office front door just as Vince did. They briefly waved to each other as each kept walking. Maria knew she had to put the nagging fear of a leak in the back of her mind.

"Everyone, in my office—now," she said as she walked down the hall to her office.

"I don't know what happened. Both the PR/IR and legal teams will look into that after we get this release out and after the conference call. So right now stay focused on the job we have to do today."

Fortunately, there was enough time for Maria and her team to work together and to quickly draft, proof, and edit a revised Q4 news release. From that they then put together a quick list of talking points for the proposed end-of-day conference call.

DEVELOPING THE PR/IR STRATEGY: A MEETING WITH THE PRESIDENT AND CFO

Sitting around the conference table at 7 am were Maria and all her colleagues involved in the PR, marketing, IR, and legal issues concerning Solar Global. They had worked well together for years. Some were surprised to see Maria's two new interns Greg and Sara, and assumed Maria had brought them up to speed on protocol. Maria greeted everyone by name and then waited for the president to start

"Okay everyone. And no, it's not a good morning. I want to know what happened between the time I went to sleep at 11 pm and woke up at 5 am," said President Juarez, almost shouting.

Maria looked around the room and realized that this was her crisis, and her time to lead. She said, "My team and I worked till after midnight last night drafting the final version of the press release, which should have been in your email at around 1 am."

"Yes, I got it," said President Juarez. "No surprises in it. Everyone here knew we were announcing the fact that we didn't meet Wall Street expectations this past quarter. To repeat, several large customer orders didn't come through, plus raw material problems and the fact that other orders had to be postponed until next fiscal year all came together and caused the Q4 problem."

President Juarez then turned to Maria and Vince, who were sitting next to each other.

"But," he said, "We consistently met expectations every year since going public. Up until today, our stock was trading at an all-time high. So, when the CFO and I met with both of you, Maria and Vince, you didn't think this would be much of a problem."

"I still don't think this would have been a problem," Vince said. "Our history, plus the economic strength of the company, plus in-house orders that go through the next few years already on the books, plus the explanation, well ... it could have meant a small dip in stock price ... if any, but not a loss of almost 10%."

"Do we sit tight or do we make an announcement now?" asked President Juarez, looking at each person as he scanned the room.

"We can't wait for Friday to release the quarterly numbers," Maria quickly said. "My inbox is already full of queries from media, analysts, and even our employees who didn't know about the numbers. I've got CNBC calling every few minutes."

"We modified the release just a few minutes ago, and most importantly, drafted some talking points for an end-of-day conference call. My staff will send out invites to the media, the analysts, our large investors, and post an open-to-the-public invite on the website and the blog and Tweet it. "

Vince interrupted, adding, "My group is checking over the news release Maria's team drafted and the talking points. We will also communicate with the SEC. I'll have corrected copy on your and CFO Cohen's desk with SEC comments in 40 minutes or so."

"Gayle, what's your opinion?" asked President Juarez.

Gayle Cohen, CFO, spoke slowly, but loudly, "I strongly disagree. I'm concerned with an even bigger drop in share price if we release today. I still think we should go end of week as planned, when fewer people are around and trading. That will give us the weekend to talk with everyone and hopefully allay their fears. I also think we will look weak if we release early. Our numbers are still strong. I don't want our public image to be that we made mistakes."

"I hear your opinion, Gayle, but I agree with the IR and legal teams," said Juarez. "Let's see what they come up with in a few hours, before end of day. Then we can decide to get it out there today and hopefully stop this hemorrhaging, or hold until Friday.

He then added, "And because we are divided on this, I don't want anyone, no one, talking with the media until we decide to release our numbers."

"But we have to respond to the telephone calls now. There are dozens of them," said Maria.

"They can wait until we are good and ready to talk to them," said Juarez.

Everyone grabbed their notebooks, ipads, pens, and cell phones and pushed back their chairs. Just as the first person reached the door, President Juarez said, "Wait."

All heads turned to him. "So far we've discussed the handling of issue number one. But I am fully aware we have a bigger problem. Somebody leaked information. There is just no other way this could this have happened. I will oversee an internal audit and I may call in outside assistance on this. You are all responsible for controlling the flow of material information and for making sure there are no leaks."

THE QUESTION OF INSIDER TRADING

For everyone involved, the day went by in almost a blur.

Maria and her team were disappointed and upset about the media relations directive. They had to ignore what press queries they could and those they couldn't were told only that information would be released before end of day. Many of the media representatives Maria had courted for years were now angry with her. She was fearful what this was doing to their long-term relationship. But now she had to do what the CFO and president directed.

Slowly, but persistently, the stock prices dropped all morning.

Maria oversaw the writing and rewriting of the news release a dozen times. It was finally ready to go out by early afternoon. The team, including the interns, worked on the announcements to go on the website, on the blog, and the Twitter page.

The SEC was alerted there might be an early release. The president, the CFO, and Vince's legal team approved all the language including the talking points for the conference call.

The CFO was prepped and ready with all the numbers at her side. She still, however, wanted to keep on the planned schedule and not release numbers until Friday.

At 2 pm someone thought to bring in sandwiches. No one had eaten yet. They were all running on adrenaline and quarts of coffee.

Maria picked up one and brought it to the small office shared by the two interns. She liked working with them. They were both hired from the nearby college. Sara excelled in PR and was taking a double major in business. She was eager, bright, and appeared to be a hard worker. She and her co-intern Greg were both great writers. And they certainly knew how to handle all social media tools.

Greg had a similar background, and in addition, he came to Maria's attention through a friend of hers, Jimmy, who was a trader on the floor of the New York Stock Exchange. Greg's father and Jimmy go way back to their college days. Greg had the recommendation from Jimmy, which was certainly a leg up. Maria respected Jimmy and knew he was very familiar with Solar Global.

Maria thought it was time to talk with both interns about material information and insider trading. She was glad nothing illegal was posted on the social media sites to which they contributed. She felt very lucky. But the fear that they had a leak from her department still worried her tremendously.

"Hi guys," Maria said as she held up her sandwich. "I thought I'd take a moment and share lunch with you before we go into the next phase later today. We'll probably be pulling another late night. I have lots to review with you. I hope you both are ok with it."

Sara smiled and said, "No problem."

Greg, laughed a little nervously and said he would just cancel another dinner with Jimmy.

"You mean Jimmy, our mutual friend who's the trader at the New York Stock Exchange?" asked Maria.

"Yea," said Greg. "Geez, I canceled yesterday too. After I saw what the Q4 numbers were, I called Jimmy. I told him all hell broke loose and I thought I might not have a job to go to today, and I couldn't possibly meet him for dinner. I knew he would understand."

"Wait. What?" said Maria in state of shock. "You said what to Jimmy???"

DISCUSSION QUESTIONS

1. Who is responsible for training the interns about publicly traded companies' PR? Is the legal team responsible? Should human resources make sure they know the corporate code of ethics? Should the PR/IR director be ultimately responsible?

2. What are the advantages and disadvantages of releasing the Q4 financials early on Wednesday? What if they wait until Friday as originally planned?

3. Media were calling all morning because the stock prices dropped. There was no official statement and no one talked with the media by early afternoon. What do you think of this situation? Explain your answers.

4. Could anything have been done to prevent the premature, steady decline of stock prices on Wednesday?

5. What does Maria do now? What does she say to whom and when?

KEY TERMS

Investor Relations, PR Law, Media Relations

Reputation and Brand Management

CHAPTER 24

#CHR. Disappearing Woman? Navigating Crisis Communication Internationally

Arhlene A. Flowers and Cory L. Young
Ithaca College

ABSTRACT

Cloudbank Hotels and Resorts (CHR), a global hotel company based in New York, faces challenges as it tries to draw customers from the Middle East.

Cloudbank Hotels and Resorts is a publicly held global hotel company, with 150 hotels in 42 countries, with its corporate headquarters based in New York City. The hotel portfolio has expanded in new global markets, including the Middle East.

The CEO and founder of Cloudbank Hotels and Resorts, John Saviano, built the company for vacationers to have a family-friendly place where parents can come with their children for a destination vacation. In addition, the founder wanted to have a relaxing yet fun atmosphere for corporate executives who choose CHR as their home away from home when traveling on business. CHR also has a portfolio of hotels in leading financial and commercial markets geared to business travelers. The company prides itself on being honest and open, and depicting hotel rooms and amenities with near-perfect reflections of reality in its advertising and promotional materials. With its global presence and diverse clientele, the hotel chain is also known for its acceptance of different cultures and lifestyle preferences. The founder, a quiet and humble man, is nearing retirement, and thus relies heavily on his corporate management and regional managers (domestic and abroad) to train employees to instill these socially responsible values, so that the experiences of guests and clients mirror what they see in digital and graphic designs, and so that everyone feels welcomed and included.

THE SITUATION: DAY ONE

Abigail Becker, vice president of public relations for Cloudbank Hotels and Resorts, had just celebrated her 10th year at this global hotel chain. Based in its corporate headquarters in New York City, Abigail has seen her responsibilities increase as the hotel portfolio has expanded in new global markets. Her role also expanded to financial public relations and investor relations since the hotel company became publicly held on the New York Stock Exchange five years ago.

She arrived at her office at 8:30 am, as usual, and checked her email to discover a message with the subject line, "Now you see her, now you don't," sent from a global women's rights group. At first, she thought it was spam. But for some reason, she decided to open the email to find out what it was about. The message unveiled a before-and-after image of the cover of the brochure on CHR's new luxury resorts in Egypt. The before image showed a family (husband, wife, and two children) in their spacious suite with a view of the Red Sea. The after image was the same, except for the wife.

Below the images, the following message was posted from the executive director of this global women's rights group:

> *Our director in London was quite surprised when one of our members in Riyadh gave her Cloudbank Hotels and Resorts' new brochure of its two resorts in Egypt, with copy in English and Arabic for the Saudi Arabian market. It looked remarkably familiar since I had just received a direct mail piece from Cloudbank in English with the same brochure of the happy family, with the complete family, including the wife! Not only was the woman removed from the cover, the brochure's other images also showed a place without any adult women. In fact, Cloudbank removed women 10 times!*
>
> *This is outrageous for a supposedly sophisticated company that cares about transparency. Cloudbank Hotels has received kudos for not only being an employer of choice for women, but also for being a hotel company that really understands the needs of women, whether they are traveling on business or on vacation. How could this company just pretend we don't exist? I ask our members to share their thoughts on this outrage on our Facebook page or Twitter.*

Abigail was unaware of this Saudi Arabian version of the brochure promoting the new Egyptian resorts. She had seen the English-language version of the brochure at the annual marketing and sales meeting last month. All brochures, sales promotional literature, and advertising were handled by the company's ad agency in Boston. Although Abigail participated in strategy sessions for advertising, she was not personally involved in the process. This was overseen by the corporate vice president of advertising.

She called her direct boss, Joseph Smith, executive vice president of marketing, in the corporate headquarters to alert him about the email from this women's group. Joseph said, "Our new regional office in Africa and the Middle East is based in Rabat. This regional structure allows our management to better understand the cultural nuances and help us navigate within these diverse markets. This is probably an isolated incident, so let's hold off before we do anything."

Abigail thought back on the company's expansion within Africa and the Middle East, with new hotels in Doha, Qatar; Cairo, Egypt; Beirut, Lebanon; and two resorts in Sharm

El Sheikh and Hurghada, Egypt. Cloudbank Hotels and Resorts was already committed to building resorts in Egypt before political turmoil erupted. The political uncertainty negatively affected occupancy rates. The company was also experiencing a serious drop from its traditional U.S. and European markets since those travelers were concerned about touring Egypt on vacation. And yet another decline was occurring from its global business travelers who used to extend their stays and explore other parts of Egypt. Based on the situation, the hotel company decided to focus on promoting these resorts within the region, specifically targeting families in Saudi Arabia and other parts of the Gulf.

DAY TWO

The next day, the edited CHR brochures in Saudi Arabia were about to become a major story in the U.S. and other international markets. Abigail and her staff in the United States and worldwide received calls from Al Jazeera, CNN, BBC, and Sky TV, among other TV programs, as well as from editors of the business sections of such leading newspapers as the *Wall Street Journal*, *Financial Times*, *Wall Street*, *London Times*, *The Guardian* and the *New York Times*.

The blogosphere was buzzing with commentary from the *Huffington Post*, as well as from women's groups and advertising and public relations associations. The twitterverse's #CHR. Disappearing woman? was drawing global tweets. The women's advocacy group gained thousands of likes on its Facebook page and was attracting more shared commentary.

Abigail called Joseph and said, "This is no longer an isolated incident. We need to deal with this and talk to the media and others."

The director of reservations also called Abigail to explain that a major women's advocacy group had withdrawn its contract for a future conference. Reservationists and regional sales offices also were fielding calls and complaints. One irate female customer queried, "If women are eliminated from your brochures, are we women going to be erased from your reservation system?"

Abigail and Joseph conducted a conference call with Hassan Ghandour, director of the regional operations/Middle East and Africa, to find out how this situation evolved and the rationale. Hassan said, "Saudi Arabia has a very different culture in terms of food, drink, politics, and social norms. Women cannot dress and expose themselves the same way as women in the West. When Starbucks entered this market, it completely removed the female feature of the mermaid in its logo and just included the crown and waves of water. Other brands just show their products or services without any people or completely blur images of people. Western brands need to respect the values of this society—and, in fact, these documents are for that market. We're not airbrushing women from other markets, so I don't see the problem."

Abigail and Joseph realized that they had to address the negative reaction of their primary audiences in the United States and Europe. They needed to protect the image of the company and to convey its socially responsible values in respecting all people, particularly women. The company's sales and marketing materials contain images of people engaging in activities to illustrate the facilities, services, and amenities offered to its guests.

The CEO and founder, John Saviano, called to find out what was happening. He said, "Our company was established in 1990 to create a culture of gender equality for our workforce and offer high-quality hotels and resorts for vacationers and business executives, with an acceptance all types of people. We don't support suppressing women in any form."

Joseph said to Abigail, "We need to protect our global brand, yet face the realities of local markets. We need to determine immediate next steps to address the public, the media, our customers, and our employees worldwide."

Abigail carefully examined the commentary of the situation and reflected on the perspective shared by management. She decided to recommend ...

DISCUSSION QUESTIONS

1. What public relations strategies and tactics do you think Abigail will recommend?
2. How should Abigail, or the hotel managers, go about managing stakeholder relations—so that more groups will not cancel their reservations?
3. Given the cultural differences between the United States and the Middle East, who would be the most appropriate individual to communicate the messages? The CEO or other management? Should the spokespeople vary in different international regions? Why?
4. Based on the material you read in the case, was it appropriate to airbrush women out of the brochure? Why or why not?
5. What alternative images can be used that are still culturally relevant and appropriate, but also aligned with the CHR's mission and vision and the overall goal of the brochure?
6. Should the hotel company directly communicate with the women's advocacy group that sparked the controversy? If so, how?

KEY TERMS

Cultural Differences, Reputation Management, International Public Relations, Branding, Stakeholder Relations, Social Media

CHAPTER 25

Who's Calling the Shots? Balancing Donor Relations and Nonprofit Branding

Lacy G. McNamee
Baylor University

ABSTRACT

When a young employee of a children's charity suggests rebranding to enhance volunteer recruitment and retention, he encounters problems with a key donor.

"Eight? Are you kidding me?!" exclaimed Child Haven's Volunteer Recruiter Miguel Santos. "That's almost half of the entire class!"

"I know, I know," sighed Cynthia Cisneros, the trainer for new volunteers. "We lost six of them during the first week of training, and the others right before I was about to assign them to kids."

"Did they say why they quit?"

"Seven of them just disappeared, but then Jenny—one who made it through training—told me she was going to do Kid Pals instead, that it was what she *thought* Child Haven was in the first place. I think her friend Louise, who was also in the training class, followed suit."

Miguel rubbed his temples in an attempt to clear his mind. *This can't keep happening*, he thought. *If we keep losing volunteers at this rate, we won't be able to serve half of the kids in our area … and I'm kicking butt at recruitment!* Child Haven, a non-profit agency that trains volunteers to care for neglected and abused children, had typically lost one or two volunteers per training class, but the dropout rate seemed to keep rising despite Miguel's successful recruiting.

"Maybe I'm just a lousy trainer," said Cynthia, defeated. "In the six months that you've been here you've brought me more prospective volunteers than we've had in the past year. Gina kept saying, 'We just need to do a better job of telling the story!' Well, you've told the story—you've done your job. Maybe I'm just not doing mine."

Miguel recalled his first day on the job. Gina Torres, Community Relations Director, stressed the importance of effectively "telling Child Haven's story" when recruiting volunteers—an effort that the organization had admittedly struggled with in the past. *No kidding*, thought Miguel, when he soon realized how few people in the community had even heard of Child Haven. But thanks to Miguel's energy and creativity, recruitment numbers quickly began to rise.

"It's not you, Cynthia. The volunteers love you, and you're a fantastic trainer," replied Miguel. "

"Then what is it?" questioned Cynthia.

Miguel paused, deep in thought, then proclaimed, "The story."

"The story? What do you mean, 'the story'?"

"The *story*, Cynthia. We've got our story—our brand—wrong. We're getting a story out now. It's just not our story. If anything, it's the Kid Pals story. We're presenting a personality to the public—and our potential volunteers—that's not really us."

"I'm still not sure I follow you, Miguel," said Cynthia.

"Think about it, Cynthia. What's the story we tell when we go out into the community? When we do presentations, fairs, and the like?"

Cynthia quickly rattles off, "Making a difference in the life of a child. Being a hero for a child—a mentor, a friend, a pal—ugh, I just said pal. I think I'm beginning to see what you mean."

"Yep. If it walks like Kid Pals, talks like Kid Pals, it must be Kid Pals, right? And we're not." Miguel jumped up from the break room table. "We're not an afterschool program, a buddy system, a mentor to just hang out with you for fun. We deal with kids who have heavy issues and need much more than a buddy. We're watchful protectors. Advocates. Sure, we might end up being their friends, too, but that's not our primary role."

"But we don't tell people that," Cynthia joined in.

"Nope, we don't," echoed Miguel, "and we're losing people because of it. To put it bluntly, we're selling them Kid Pals but then giving them Child Haven."

"You're right. And then we're losing recruits like Jenny and Louise when they realize this isn't what they signed up for. So what should we do?"

"I've got some ideas," said Miguel. "Let's get with Gina about this when we have our status meeting tomorrow."

That evening, Miguel pored over his notes about branding from his undergrad public relations courses. Though most of the projects he dealt with in school were based on corporations and for-profit firms, he was sure that the same ideas could be applied to a non-profit. Miguel could barely sleep thinking about the prospect of sharing these ideas with his colleagues the next day.

HITTING A WALL

The next morning, Miguel and Cynthia joined Gina Torres in her small office for their weekly status meeting. Gina was the most seasoned employee of Child Haven, beginning as a volunteer ten years prior and then eventually working her way up to Community Awareness Director. Her previous work as a middle school gym teacher made her passionate about children but somewhat conservative in her thinking, not to mention a little intimidating.

"So how's the new training class, Cynthia?" asked Gina.

"Well, the ones we've kept are great," replied Cynthia.

"What do you mean the one's you've kept?" quipped Gina.

Cynthia glanced at Miguel, as if to say, *Okay, you take it from here.* Without hesitation, Miguel jumped in, "We lost almost half of the new class, Gina. This is a trend. Our recruitment numbers keep going up, but numbers for those who actually end up volunteering are stagnant—if not trailing off."

"How can this be? What on earth could be causing such dropouts?" Gina exclaimed.

Miguel jumped in again, sensing a return in Cynthia's self-doubt. *If we don't get this problem fixed, it won't be long before we lose Cynthia, too*, thought Miguel. "Well, it's not Cynthia—she's just as fabulous as always. And not to pat myself on the back, but I don't think it's me either. I actually think it's a problem with the entire way we are approaching community awareness—the way we are presenting ourselves to the general public."

"Miguel, you're young, and, quite frankly, a little green," said Gina, visibly ruffled by his sweeping critique. "Look, I don't mean to dismiss your opinions, but I've been around Child Haven for a long time. We're probably just going through a down time. Think about the economy. In fact, I bet every non-profit in the area is in the same boat."

"No they're not!" Miguel replied, more forcefully than he intended. "Take Kid Pals, for example. They have so many volunteers I hear that they are on the verge of turning folks away. I know that Kid Pals is a sensitive subject, but it's time we talk about the elephant in the room."

Miguel went on to share his thoughts about Child Haven's branding problems and his proposal to more accurately position the personality, mission, and scope of their work. Gina sat silent while Miguel explained the need to set Child Haven apart as a unique agency by stressing that they do difficult but meaningful work for the neediest children in the community.

"So, what do you think? When can we talk to Elena about it?" said Miguel, referring to Child Haven's executive director Elena Dameron.

"I'm sorry, Miguel, but there's no need to talk to Elena. I appreciate your enthusiasm and commitment to the Child Haven mission, but what you're proposing simply won't work," Gina stated plainly. "We tell our story the way that we do because it works, and your way simply won't. Now, if you'll excuse me, I have an appointment across town and need to head that way now. Buck up, I'm sure things will return to normal in no time."

"I can't believe this! She wouldn't even entertain the idea!" Miguel exclaimed, standing in the doorway of Cynthia's office.

"Keep your voice down, and shut the door," whispered Cynthia. "Really, get a hold of yourself."

"But, Cynthia, you know this isn't just a fluke. We're losing volunteers, and will continue to do so unless we do something." Miguel paced around, fidgeting with paperweights, pencils, and picture frames as he brainstormed. Finally, he stopped and looked up at Cynthia.

"Uh oh, I know that look," said Cynthia. "That look means you have an idea. Enough ideas for today, Miguel. For goodness sake, just leave it be."

"Sorry, Cynthia, I can't leave it be. Gina's out of the office all morning...but Elena will be here in an hour. Gotta run!"

Miguel was gone before Cynthia could voice her warnings about going behind Gina's back. *Geez, he better know what he's doing, she thought. Well, one thing is for sure. I'm staying as far away from this as I possibly can. Sorry, Miguel, you're on your own from now on.*

GOING TO THE TOP

As Miguel walked down the hallway toward Elena Dameron's, office he thought about how much he admired her. Elena left a successful career as an attorney in a neighboring town to work for Child Haven just three months before Miguel was hired. Miguel himself had pondered climbing the corporate ladder instead of slugging away at the low-pay world of non-profits, so he always felt a certain kinship with her. And though many of his coworkers seemed to like Elena as much as he did, Miguel also heard that some on the Board of Directors had reservations about hiring her due to her lack of experience in non-profit work. These thoughts gave Miguel confidence as he rapped lightly on the cracked door of Elena's humble office.

"Hey, Miguel," smiled Elena. "Come on in. What's up?"

"Busy, Elena? I just wanted to bounce some ideas off you if you don't mind," said Miguel, thinking to himself, *too late to turn back now.*

"Oh, just preparing financial statements and monthly reports. You know, the glamorous part of my job," Elena joked. "I welcome the break. What's on your mind?"

Miguel began by retelling the conversation between him and Cynthia they day before. He glossed over the disastrous meeting with Gina earlier that morning, and moved straight into his pitch toward rebranding Child Haven as a tough but worthy cause. Elena nodded and interrupted occasionally to ask questions as Miguel spoke.

"So you really think we need to overhaul the entire way that we reach out to people in the community?" said Elena when Miguel finished his proposal.

"I do, Elena. We've got to distinguish ourselves from Kid Pals—but more importantly, we've got to tell our true story. If we don't, we're going to keep recruiting people, only to lose them."

"Well, if you're right, it seems we're wasting resources and time recruiting and training people who will never be committed volunteers," said Elena, "and that's no way to run a program."

After discussing the matter for a few more minutes, Elena promised Miguel she'd pursue the matter. Miguel almost skipped out the door thinking, *I knew you'd come through Elena! We're cut from the same cloth, and together, we're going to make Child Haven a household name!*

BOSS OR BENEFACTOR?

Later that afternoon, Elena convened the weekly directors' meeting with Gina as well as program director Sandra Thompson and grants director David Crouch. After going through the regular items of discussion, Elena said, "Before we wrap up, I'd like to talk about our trends in volunteer recruitment and retention. Gina, Sandra, I understand we're doing a better job at recruitment, thanks in part to Miguel Santos, but we're struggling with keeping the people whom we recruit. Can either of you speak to this?"

"Where is this coming from, Elena?" questioned Gina. "Sure, we've had a little drop off in retaining volunteers lately, but I don't know if it's anything to be worried about. Why do you ask?"

"Well, I had an interesting conversation with Miguel this morning about this, and it's got me thinking—"

"Miguel?!" Gina interrupted. "I can't believe this. Just this morning I told him to cool it on his big ideas. That boy needs to focus on more on recruiting and less on everything else."

"So you know his position on recasting our entire brand, changing the way we talk about Child Haven altogether?" said Elena, a bit surprised by Gina's sudden outburst.

Before Gina could answer, David Crouch cut in, "Excuse me, can someone please tell me what we're talking about?"

Gina quickly recapped her morning meeting with Cynthia and Miguel, being sure to add her own opinion about the matter while retelling it. Elena, who had grown somewhat accustomed to Gina's fear of change and tendency to feel threatened by lower-level employees, tactfully offered some additional information to more accurately convey Miguel's rationale for the change.

"So, Sandra, I'm interested to get your take on the situation since you work closely with our volunteers. Have any of them said anything about feeling misled about what Child Haven is and what we do?" asked Elena, in an attempt to invite others into the conversation.

"Well, yes, in fact," said Sandra, "I have heard some comments in that vein over the years. They've always stuck out to me. I just didn't know what to do with them."

"Okay, so why not do something about it? Try something new?" questioned Elena. "Maybe Miguel is on to something."

"Because of Malcolm Riggs, that's why!" exclaimed Gina, nearly to the point of shouting. "Do you want to lose our biggest donor and two-time president of the Board of Directors?"

"I'm afraid I don't follow," said Elena.

"Gina might be right, Elena," David said quietly. "We had this conversation a few years back about re-framing our program to illuminate the heavier aspect of what we do. Focusing on tough work, not all rainbows and daisies—basically, the stuff that Miguel is talking about doing. Malcolm put an end to that conversation pretty quickly."

Gina jumped in next, summarizing the failed proposal to the board several years prior. Among others, Malcolm was the biggest voice of resistance, claiming that Child Haven would "scare away the volunteers" with such an approach. When the previous executive director suggested they might go ahead with the strategy despite Board protests, Malcolm made a public display of threatening to pull his funding.

"Yes, but it was also no secret that Malcolm didn't like Erin," offered Sandra, referring to the previous executive director Erin Marcum. "Anything she was for, he was against."

"Yes, but we couldn't risk losing his support," recalled David. "He funds over a third of our program, including a big chunk of our salaries."

After listening intently, Elena made her decision. "Well, things have changed, and I have a good relationship with Malcolm. In fact, I'm having lunch with him tomorrow. I'll bring it up then."

"Fine," scoffed Gina. "I won't say I told you so when you come back empty handed—but you *will* come back empty handed."

CASE CLOSED

Elena had always felt at ease with Malcolm Riggs, a retired county judge and longtime supporter of Child Haven, but today she was a bit on edge. The thought of losing Malcolm's funding, which was made possible by his parents' very hefty estate, was almost unfathomable. *Where would we fill the gap?* thought Elena, as she waited for Malcolm to join her at a local Italian bistro. *What am I thinking? I can't think about losing his support. Surely I can persuade him to see the need for change—*

"Well, hello, Elena," boomed the judge. "Sorry, I'm a bit late. I got caught up with some yard work. How ya doing? Something wrong?"

Elena was so deep in thought she didn't even notice Malcolm approach her table. "No, no, Malcolm. Just thinking about some things back at the office."

"Well, tell the old judge what's going on. Surely there's something I can do to help."

Elena was tentative for a moment, but then decided to forge ahead. "Malcolm, we're struggling with keeping volunteers. Recruitment numbers are up, but they drop like flies once we get them in the door. But the good news is…I think I have a good plan for how to address it."

"Of course you do! That's why we hired you," laughed the judge. "Well? Let's hear it."

"Have you ever heard of the term branding?" asked Elena.

"Sure, branded many a cattle, Elena. Grew up on a ranch. But what's that have to do with this?"

Oh boy, thought Elena. *This is going downhill fast. Keep it simple, Elena.* She stifled a nervous laugh. "Well, I mean more our brand as a program, Child Haven's *story*, our personality that gets presented to the public—to prospective volunteers. I'm worried that we are branding our self in a way that confuses us with Kid Pals, you know, like an afterschool buddy program where volunteers simply take kids on fun outings and watch their soccer games."

Typical of his blunt style, Malcolm cut in, "So what's that have to do with volunteers dropping out?

"Well, I think that story misleads people, and we end up getting a bunch of recruits who aren't ready for what they get themselves into—real children with real issues, heavy issues that need an advocate and a champion, not just a buddy." Elena cut to the chase. "Look, Malcolm, I think we need to start repositioning ourselves to the public as an agency that does serious work with troubled children—that requires volunteers with an equally serious commitment."

Elena paused to gauge Malcolm's reaction. He furrowed his brows, took a long draw from his water glass, and then responded.

"So, we're hurting for volunteers, and your solution is to tell them, 'Hey, come spend time with us. You'll put in a lot of hours, deal with scary issues, and your kid may not even like you.' Elena, pardon me for sounding a little harsh, but where did you get a hare-brained idea like that?"

"Well, uh …" Elena was flabbergasted. *Geez, I expected push-back but not insults.*

"I have to say, Elena, I'm surprised. Erin came up with some similar nonsense back in the day. Maybe y'all get in so deep you just can't see the forest for the trees. Look, if you come out with a message like that, Child Haven is done. A positive message is always best. People don't want doom and gloom. I know my dollars don't want to go to doom and gloom."

Though she couldn't be sure, Elena sensed this was a veiled threat and decided not to push the matter further. Instead, she made light of the proposed change and quickly changed the subject, thinking to herself, *Shoot, Gina was right. What a mess I've made.*

During Elena's evening jog, the lunch conversation with Malcolm Riggs kept invading her thoughts. *What was I thinking? We can't survive without his support. And now I've gone against Gina and David, two of my most loyal employees. I can't believe I took so much stock in Miguel's ideas—maybe we both just need to learn to go with the flow before we put our program and our jobs in jeopardy.* Running was usually her way of de-stressing, but the further she jogged, the more her worry mounted. She decided to cut through a neighborhood and head home early.

As soon as she walked through her door, Elena headed straight for her laptop to send an email:

Miguel,

I want to thank you for your commitment to Child Haven and your concern about volunteer retention. However, your proposal for addressing the situation is simply not feasible at this time. Perhaps we both should have consulted the input of others in the office before going full steam ahead. I appreciate your enthusiasm, but you still have much to learn about our program. Be patient, and, please, direct all your future inquiries to Gina first before approaching me.

You're doing a wonderful job at recruitment—keep up the good work.

Regards,
Elena

DISCUSSION QUESTIONS

1. If you were Miguel, how would you respond to Elena's email?
2. If you were Elena, would you forge ahead with rebranding and risk losing a major donor's support? Does she have any other alternatives?
3. What types of branding challenges are at play in this case, and, is rebranding appropriate under the current circumstances?

KEY TERMS

Branding, Investor Relations, Donor Relations, Non-profit Organizations

CHAPTER 26

A Name for Success?

"Iris" Shuang Xia and Narissra Maria Punyanunt-Carter
Texas Tech University

ABSTRACT

When a company expands and develops into a bigger one, it will try to reach different markets and target new customers. Jonny and David have to find a way to achieve these goals and remove an invisible obstacle for their company. However, it is risky to change and rebuild a brand. Jonny and David will need to make the best decision for the company.

Jefferson City is a medium-sized Midwestern city, but it is also one of the major transportation centers in the Midwest because it sits at the intersection of two major interstates. Hundreds of thousands of big-rig trucks travel through Jefferson City each year, which historically has been a huge boon to the local economy. Because of its central location between Chicago and Denver, many truckers stop overnight in Jefferson City as they traverse the country. When truck drivers come to Jefferson City, they always have dinner in a restaurant called Safe.

In 1999, Safe was just a small restaurant located near the freeway with two workers. Jonny Buchanan and David Whitman, the owner-operators, came up with many ideas to attract customers to Safe. The food was delicious and cheap, and Jonny and David paid a lot of attention to the service and management. They constantly asked customers for suggestions and advice. In order to keep customers loyal to their restaurant, they improved their food and menu by learning from other famous restaurants.

Safe was famous for its secret recipe. Instead of grilling meat, Jonny and David invented a way to steam meat with homemade sauce, which was healthier. The meat in their burger was more tender and juicy than the other burgers in the area. Since Safe was famous for their traditional Midwestern cuisine that always came with some kind of savory meat, more and more truck drivers came to Safe, and it became a real landmark on the trucker circuit. The long line of trucks outside Safe became a special scene in the city every day.

By 2003, Safe had expanded to five restaurants in Jefferson City, with three of them targeted toward specific trucking routes and the other two targeted more toward the locals than the truckers. Business was great! Jonny and David began thinking about the future of their restaurants.

"David, I am excited that we have made it this far, but I still feel like increasing the number of restaurants is not our only goal," Jonny spoke seriously to David after a busy working day in Safe.

"What do you mean it is not our goal? We did very well." David asked him. He was confused.

"Yeah, I know. I mean, perhaps we can bring our business to a higher level. We have already begun to feel the pressure and problems brought by our expansion. We have issues with hiring chefs and managing employees, and the old way of cooking our meat is not fast enough for the increasing number of customers. If we want to open more restaurants in the future, these are the problems we have to solve, otherwise we can't expand our business successfully," Jonny said.

David thought about Jonny's words for a moment, and then nodded his head: "Yes, you're right. We do have those problems. So how can we solve all of them?"

Jonny had already thought about possible solutions, so he explained: "We need experts to help us design a new way to steam meat faster. We also have to regulate the management and service."

"You mean we have to standardize the way we produce food, the way we manage the restaurants, and the way we serve our customers, like McDonald's?" David tried to understand his partner.

"Yes! Just like McDonald's! We are not only expanding the number of restaurants, but also building our brand. A successful brand that everyone in United States will know." Jonny became excited.

"Great! Let's do it!"

After the discussion, Jonny and David decided to stop expanding their restaurants for a while. In the meantime, they asked experts to help them create a new steam system to cook the meat faster. They installed this new system in the restaurants, making the cooking process faster and enabling Safe to market itself as a "fast food" restaurant. In addition, they also invited experienced managers join their leadership team, and created a handbook of policy and rules to regulate the management and service in every Safe restaurant.

When they had solved all these problems, Jonny and David felt it was time for them to expand their restaurant again. This time, they wanted to open more restaurants in Jefferson City's downtown instead of near the freeways.

"Jonny, I think we have one more problem before we open a restaurant in downtown." David said. It seemed that he had thought about this problem for a long time.

"What's the problem?" Jonny stopped the work at hand.

"We named our restaurant Safe because our first restaurant was opened near the freeway, and our main customers were truck drivers."

"Right. We thought Safe was like a blessing to truck drivers. It was the kind of name that we hoped might attract truck drivers to come to our restaurant." Jonny tried to recall why they used this name.

"However, our situation is different right now. If we are going to open restaurants in downtown, this name may not work. The people who live downtown are not truck drivers.

Our name, Safe, in my point of view, it doesn't match our target customers." David explained his worries.

"Hmm …" Jonny agreed: "We might also have to find a name that has deeper meaning. For example, we might include our value or mission in this name. What do you think?"

"That would be even better. Now the problem is, what's the best name for us?"

"This is a new beginning of our business. This business conveys our hope. We hope it will develop into a bigger and more successful business. Just like a tree, it begins as a small seed, but it will grow bigger and bigger. This is what I feel about our business right now."

"I like that metaphor. A small seed will grow into a big tree." David thought for a while: "How about The Seed? The growing of the seed, the booming of a new business!"

"Fantastic, David! I love this name!" Jonny gave David a big hug. They agreed to use The Seed as a new brand name.

The Seed appeared in Jefferson City's downtown with its new name and new logo. Its logo was a green germinating seed. Jonny and David's business was booming like they had anticipated; the seed gradually grew into a tree. The Seed became increasingly popular, and Jonny and David expanded their restaurants to other cities.

Although The Seed achieved great success, the brand was not as famous outside Jefferson City and the trucker circuit as Jonny and David had expected. It was seldom known among white-collar workers and young people from even nearby towns. Worse yet, most of its local customers were farmers and people from older generations. However, Jonny and David wanted their brand to be known by everyone throughout the Midwest and beyond. It seemed that there was an invisible obstacle that prevented The Seed from going further. In order to learn how to increase The Seed's popularity, Jonny and David spent three million dollars to invite a famous public relations and marketing company, Idea, to help them investigate.

Idea sent out a team to deal with The Seed's brand investigation. This team conducted a detailed survey throughout the Midwest and those residing in other parts of the country outside the current target market of The Seed. They evaluated The Seed's popularity among people, and investigated the entire fast food market in the United States. After the investigation, the team found that the problem resided in the brand's name.

The name The Seed meant a lot to Jonny and David; it reflected their hope and anticipation. However, it meant other things to other people. Peter Skahill, the lead consultant on the project from Idea, put it this way: "The name gives a countryside, folksy impression to some people, which is perceived as simple and friendly. However, it is not perceived as fashionable by those in the important 18 to 40 demographic. This demographic is important because a lot of them either eat fast food or are starting to have children and are getting fast food for the entire family. In the fast food market, a resonant name is very significant. Worse yet, some people perceive the name 'The Seed' as a vegetarian or vegan restaurant, which clearly puts the name out of the 'meat loving' target demographic. A good name must be easy to remember, attractive, and reflect the brand's unique characteristics. At this point, your brand just doesn't do any of those things."

This suggestion shocked people who worked for The Seed, especially at the management level. In 2006, The Seed's brand value was worth at least $20 million. Moreover, The Seed already had a significant customer base in the Midwest. Some customers even considered The Seed to be their favorite restaurant. If the name was changed, The Seed would have to confront the risk of losing those customers. The leadership team of The Seed initiated an intense debate about whether they should change the brand's name or not.

In the meeting, David started the conversation: "I think we should try a new name. This rebranding thing might bring us more customers and even help us get access to other areas of United States."

"But what about our original customers? We spent so much effort to build customer loyalty to The Seed. If we give up this name, we will give up those loyal customers as well!" Jonny was a little angry about the whole rebranding thing.

"Hey Jonny, I know that you love The Seed and this name means a lot to you. But we have to move forward and adapt to new things. This name is great, but what if we can come up with a better name?" Tim Williams tried to comfort Jonny. He was a human resources manager and a member of the leadership team.

"Tim is right. It's worth trying. We shouldn't let go of any opportunities. This opportunity might lead us to a more successful business," Sarah Green supported rebranding the company. She was a product manager on the leadership team.

"I know we should try. I just feel the risk is too high if we suddenly change everything about The Seed." Jonny knew that this was a great opportunity.

"I agree. Even though we should change the brand's name, we should be prudent in this process. It is possible that customers will not come to our restaurants," David said.

"How about we open one restaurant first to test the response of the market? If customers' responses are good, we can move on and open more restaurants using the new name, and rebrand old restaurants," Louis Hill, the marketing manager, gave a suggestion.

"This is a good idea. We can use this new-brand restaurant to test whether or not our customers accept this new name and whether or not this new name is more attractive to people," Tim said. All the team members agreed that this was the best available choice.

After this meeting, Peter's rebranding team designed several new names for The Seed. Jonny, David, and their leadership team had another meeting. They analyzed the brands' values, positioning, and customer profiles, and finally decided to use Real Juicy as the new brand's name. This name reflected the characteristics of their meat, which was juicy and real meat. These distinguishing characteristics coincided with customers' concerns about the meat they ate.

The first Real Juicy fast food restaurant was opened in 2009. During the market testing, Real Juicy's sales grew much faster than those of The Seed during the early years. However, the first Real Juicy location was in a larger market, so there was no way to determine if location had anything to do with the growth. Most of the customers had positive responses toward Real Juicy during the test. Real Juicy rapidly became popular among people (especially the 18 to 40 demographic). The restaurant's customers ranged from teenagers to grandmothers, and from farmers to white-collar workers. People were interested in Real Juicy when they heard the name for the first time.

After the relative success with Real Juicy, Jonny, David, and Peter sat down again to discuss the possible rolling out of the new brand across the current chain before opening new ones.

"You do realize that rebranding this company is going to cost between 200,000 to 500,000 dollars?" Peter started. "And that is just the rebranding part, you'll still need to retrofit your current chain stores with the new brand, so you're looking at easily spending 5 to 10 million on this project. This isn't a cheap process, so you need to know that you're ready to jump into this completely."

"Wow," David responded, looking wearily at Jonny. "You've definitely given us some things to think about."

"Peter," Jonny started, "Thanks for giving us the heads up. We'll discuss it together and then with our senior leadership team and get back to you next week."

Peter put his files back in his briefcase and left the conference room as David and Jonny just sat quietly pondering their next steps. When Peter was out the door, the two looked at each other hoping the other would know what to do next.

DISCUSSION QUESTIONS

1. If The Seed does not rebrand, what might happen?
2. What's the difference between the first rebranding and the second rebranding experience in this company?
3. How should David and Jonny evaluate the first rebranding and the second rebranding processes? Do you think these two rebranding processes are successes?
4. What do you think are the most important elements for a company to consider during a rebranding?
5. What risks are involved in a rebranding process?
6. Do you think Jonny and David should rebrand the entire company? Why or why not?

KEY TERMS

Rebranding, Brand Marketing, Management

CHAPTER 27

A Matter of Reputation

Amber Alsop
Edinboro University of Pennsylvania

ABSTRACT

A devastating crisis occurs at a local high school, causing a small town to turn upside down. A consultant is hired to help the affected individuals overcome the crisis. Not only has the crisis affected the students, but it has also affected the community and the local chapter of SADD (Students Against Drunk Driving). The consultant realizes things at Corsica Area High School are worse than she realized.

MANIC MONDAY

It is a typical Monday morning at Corsica Area High School for Superintendent Roland Smith. Prior to the students arriving, Roland always has the same routine: get the paper, make coffee, drink the coffee, and lastly, close the door to enjoy the paper before the 500 students arrive to learn for the day. Mr. Smith is calmly sitting in his office enjoying the coffee, the silence, and the newspaper. As he slowly unfolds the paper, he sees the headline, "PRINCIPAL PUCKER PUNCHES MALES AT A BAR BRAWL."

"Are you serious? This cannot be happening today!" Roland curses under his breath. He immediately picks up the phone and calls Miss Diane Crabtree, the Corsica Area High School Assistant Principal. After a brief discussion, Roland gets to the point of his phone call.

"I am afraid so," Diane informs Roland. "It seems that our principal has made front-page news."

"Great. Wait until SADD hears about this." Suddenly, his thoughts are interrupted as a second line lights up, displaying the name "Marge," Roland's secretary. He apologizes quickly to Diane and picks up the phone.

"Yes, Marge?"

"Good morning, Mr. Smith. Ms. Stigler is here to see you from the Crisis Consulting Firm."

Oh geez, I totally forgot she was coming today, Roland thinks to himself. "Send her in."

The door to Roland's office opens, and a woman in her mid-30s walks in wearing a smart two-piece business suit. She has short black hair that is cropped just above her shoulders. She extends her hand toward Roland.

"Good morning, Mr. Smith."

"Good morning, Ms. Carrie Stigler. Please take a seat," Roland responds, shaking the woman's hand while gesturing to a chair in front of his desk. "Ms. Stigler, I am sure you have heard of the predicament our school is in, yes?"

"Yes, Mr. Smith, I have," she responds, reaching into her briefcase. "When I saw the headline this morning, I figured you might need a little more help today than was originally expected. I have brought with me some measures to protect the school from losing its SADD support that is given each year. But first, I want to start from the beginning. I cannot help you unless I understand each detail of the scholarship and the incident with Mr. Jason Vocate."

Sighing, Roland looks at Ms. Stigler, not quite sure where he should begin. "There is a 99.9% chance that this donation will be pulled. I really hope you can help us, Ms. Stigler."

Sitting back and anxiously waiting to hear and see what crisis this school is faced with, Ms. Stigler puts up a clear façade, thinking to herself, *I really don't know where to begin myself. I sure hope I can help them!*

FROM THE BEGINNING

To get the full details of the story, Roland puts in a call to Miss Crabtree and asks her to join him and Ms. Stigler for a discussion about the SADD scholarship. While Roland and Ms. Stigler wait for Miss Crabtree to arrive, the two chit-chat about a variety of factors related to the school district in general. Suddenly, there's a light rap on the door and Miss Crabtree comes into the room. Roland motions to the other chair in front of his desk while the two women introduce themselves to each other.

Document after document, file after file is pulled from the filing cabinet to share the information about the SADD scholarship. It is pointed out that, in 1992, the SADD organization contracted with the school district to provide a $25 million dollar annual donation. For 20 years, SADD has been providing the school district with this money, funding that is geared toward leadership and professional scholarships for students. The money is also allocated toward extra-circular activities that enhance a student's learning ability.

Every year, Corsica Area High School is named one of the nation's top 10 schools for its students' scores on standards-based testing. This ranking is a great honor for this small-town school to achieve.

Not only does the school pride itself on its academics, but the faculty, staff, and the administration are also known for their professionalism. *Forbes* magazine has noted how professional these individuals are. They exemplify the types of role models students should have surrounding them. Since the school was built in the 1940s, there has never been a complaint, disciplinary action, arrest, drug bust, or any incident involving alcohol listed in their history. To this day, all of the students, staff, faculty, and the administration have "clean" records.

"You have a lot to be proud of, Mr. Smith. Your school district has one of the finest records that I have ever seen. This is something to be really proud of."

"Ms. Stigler, I pride myself on the record we have had for academics, integrity, and professionalism. I really do not know what I am going to do if SADD cuts our funding. We are already struggling since the state has taken more from the public schools. Because of SADD, we are able to have extra-circular activities and not charge the students anything to be involved in them."

"PUCKER" PUNCHED (BEFORE, DURING, AND AFTER THE INCIDENT)

"Hey Greg! This is Jason. I just wanted to remind you that I can't get out of the school until 4:30 pm. I'll meet you at the bar to celebrate your last night as a single man!"

"That sounds good, Jason! See you soon!"

Mr. Vocate arrives at the Wild Barn Saloon located about 20 miles from Corsica High School.

"Here he comes! It's our favorite principal!"

"Guys, don't shout out what I do! I'm not supposed to be here!" Jason responds. *I really shouldn't be doing this, but sometimes a guy just needs to relax.*

"Chillax, Jason. Have fun and enjoy the night. As one of the groomsmen, I'll see to it that you enjoy yourself!"

After the men had been drinking and doing "Pucker" shots for four hours, it's time to call it an early night for some people. All of the men are visibly intoxicated. As Jason is rounding everyone together to leave, a man yells at Jason (the principal) from across the bar.

"Who's the little guy? Is he old enough to be in a bar? Did your mom bring you?"

As a man who is shorter than average height, Jason was always a little defensive about the issue. With this drunk stranger now starting in on him, he just couldn't let it go. "You want to start? Let's take this outside."

Before you know it, Jason and his friends, along with a number of other customers from the bar, are in an all-out brawl in the parking lot. Jason may be short, but he's definitely scrappy. He ends up seriously injuring two individuals, putting them in the hospital. Not only did the men cause some serious injuries to some individuals, they also caused thousands of dollars in damage. To make matters worse, right before the cops arrive, Jason and his friends flee the scene.

"PRINCIPAL PUCKER PUNCHES MALES AT A BAR BRAWL"

"Ms. Stigler, this is the first thing I had to see on my desk when I arrived at work. I have no idea what to do. Once this leaks, the press will be all over the place." Roland looks again at the newspaper headline in dismay. *How could Jason go and do something like this!? It's so not like him!*

"Mr. Smith, I will make sure that this is handled in a professional manner. Have you talked to Mr. Vocate?" Ms. Stigler questions.

"Not yet. He hasn't even come in to work yet. According to the article, he is still being held in the county jail awaiting arraignment."

"Okay. Let us work through this step by step with the media and how the school is going to handle it."

The three quickly draw up a game plan on how the superintendent could go about handling the crisis situation. One of the important factors Ms. Stigler mentions is the necessity of putting together a concrete crisis communication plan for the future, so that the school district isn't caught off guard in the future.

Soon enough, the phone is ringing off the hook in the superintendent's office. At first, it is calls from parents who are asking that the principal be fired, and then the next concern is that this incident will cause SADD to pull their annual donation from the school.

SADD IS MAD

"Mr. Smith, the phone is for you," Marge chirps over the intercom.

"Thanks, Marge, but now is not the time. Who is it?"

"It is the CEO of SADD, sir. She would like to talk to you."

Great! Roland thinks to himself. *This is going to be a fun conversation.* "Transfer her through." Roland puts the call on speaker phone so both Ms. Stigler and Miss Crabtree can listen in on the conversation.

"Mr. Smith, how are you doing?"

"I have been better, Mrs. Clarington. How are you?"

"I was fine until I saw the news. You do realize you violated our contract. I am afraid we will have to cut the funding."

"No, please. Listen to me. I understand the circumstances we are in. Is there a way that we can set up a meeting to discuss this?"

"Just know that this type of behavior is not tolerated. You need to get rid of this principal. Understood?"

With that there is a click and the phone goes dead. "She hung up on me," Roland says in a state of disbelief.

"Mr. Smith. Do not worry. We will figure this out," Ms. Stigler reassures him.

MY NAME IS MR. VOCATE

The next day flies by like no other. Jason Vocate is released from county jail; however, it was only to get worse.

As soon as Roland hears Jason is at home, he immediately calls him. "Mr. Vocate, this is your superintendent, Mr. Smith."

"Mr. Smith, what can I help you with?"

"The CEO from SADD is coming in to meet with me and you need to be present."

"I am not helping with this," Jason replies bitterly.

"You are going to allow this money to leave this school district? That money helps students with extra-curricular activities and a chance for scholarship money!"

"I've been advised not to say anything. Please contact my attorney."

"Mr. Vocate, please let us—" Once again, there is a click and the line goes dead. *Why is everyone hanging up on me?*

Throughout the day, the phone keeps ringing non-stop. Protestors start to line up, board members are calling, and news media floods the school lawn. Ms. Stigler is feeling the pressure to save the school. Trying to keep the school from losing $25,000,000 is not easy.

DISCUSSION QUESTIONS

1. If you were hired as the consultant, in what ways would you handle the media?
2. Was it a good idea to try to contact the principal?
3. Is the media an effective tool to inform people of a crisis?
4. As the superintendent, what is the first step you would take?
5. How should the conversation with Mrs. Clarington, the CEO of Students Against Drunk Driving, have gone?
6. How would you convince Mrs. Clarington not to pull the $25 million dollars from the school's budget?
7. What should Mr. Smith do in order to help prevent these situations?

KEY TERMS

Crisis, Consultant, SADD, Strategically, Professionalism

CHAPTER 28

Can Superman Win this One?

Julio A. Rodriguez-Rentas and Paul Ziek
Pace University

ABSTRACT

Mike has been hired to fix the reputation of Manor Hill College's Student Accounts Office. Despite his dramatic changes, Mike finds himself still searching for ways to change student perception.

On a warm afternoon in mid-September, the executive director of the Student Accounts (SA) Office, Mike Webb, decides to walk to the college cafeteria to get lunch. Since the semester began two weeks ago, Mike and his team have been dealing with a steady stream of students as they added and dropped classes, paid bills, etc.

For the first few weeks of the semester, Mike hadn't had any time to get lunch out of the office and now with the lines dying down it seems like a good time. Plus, the sandwich of the month is the chicken wrap ... his favorite. As Mike walks out of his office he notices several students at the service windows taking care of last-minute items. Mike surveys the situation and said to himself: *we got through these first few weeks pretty well, our changes seem to have really taken hold.*

Standing in line at the sandwich counter ... a long line ... he overhears students talking about the SA Office.

"Hey, man. Did you switch into Dr. C's class, yet? I don't think I can go through accounting class by myself," Brian, a Manor Hill student, asks his friend.

"Ugh, I want to, but when I logged into the college intranet I noticed that I have a hold on my account. I really don't feel like dealing with this. Remember a couple years ago when trying to get into our English class?" responds his friend David.

With the memory coming to mind, Brian responds, "Oh, yeah."

"I remember I kept trying to call the Financial Aid Office, and no one picked up the phone! I remember waiting in that long line at the Financial Aid Office and the financial aid rep told me that I had to go to the SA Office to get my hold taken off."

Brian laughs, "Yeah, and then when you went to SA and waited on *their* long line, the SA rep told you that you had to get your financial aid corrected first before they took the hold off."

"I remember I spent the whole morning at both offices!"

"The typical SA runaround," remarks Brian. "Good luck with trying to get into Dr. C's accounting class this year."

Overhearing Brian and David's conversation, the editor-in-chief of the student newspaper chimes in, "Hey. I'm sorry. I couldn't help but overhear you two talking about SA. I'm Jen Biech, the editor-in-chief of the *Manor Hill Herald*." Showing her editor-in-chief ID she adds, "We're doing an article on the frustration students have with SA, and the fact that they haven't done anything to fix how they operate. Would you mind being included in the article?"

Hesitantly David responds, "Uh, sure. I guess."

Excited about a new prospect for the article, Jen asks, "Great! What time are you done with classes today?" while handing him her business card.

"3 o'clock this afternoon."

"Next customer, please!" yells one of the cafeteria cooks. "May I take your order?"

Quickly cutting the conversation, Jen answers David, "I'll let you order your food. Let's meet back here in the cafeteria. I'll give you a call, say around 3:00 pm?"

"Sure, my number is ..."

THE THORN THAT IS SA

The Student Accounts Office combines the services of financial aid, bursar services, and registrar services into one organization designed to provide student-centered, quality enrollment services. SA is dedicated to improving and streamlining processes, training staff to be cross functional, maximizing the use of new technologies, and delivering unparalleled student service.

Whether students like it or not, they still have to interface with SA, since all of their financial and academic transactions take place there.

SA is considered the worst part of Manor Hill College. Its reputation is down the drain. A student even went so far as to refer to SA as "our little slice of hell" in the *Manor Hill Herald*. SA has been the proverbial thorn in the side of many a student, and even some staff members.

Based on student feedback from SA's most recent survey, SA seems to have a bad reputation, primarily due to past delayed service, low efficiency, inconsistent messages, and disjointed transactions. College surveys from two years ago showed that nearly half (49%) of the student body was dissatisfied with SA.

SA's customer service is one of the primary issues that affects the department. In the past, SA representatives have been seen as unhelpful in trying to assist students with their accounts, have inadvertently sent the message to students that they are inconsiderate and uncaring about student frustration, and have developed a reputation known as "the SA runaround."

IT'S A BIRD ... IT'S A PLANE ... IT'S SUPERMAN

Over the years there have been protests by students demanding changes in how the SA Office operates. The student protests were eventually picked up by the community media and newspaper outlets, and therefore SA had developed a bad reputation with the external community as well. Student protests were usually followed by a leadership change or manager dismissal from college administration. Thus, for the last decade, SA has had a high leadership turnover rate. SA has had seven leaders in the past five years; three in one calendar year alone.

For two years the SA has been led by Executive Director Mike Webb. After years of moving up the ranks in the college, he has been hailed among the staff as the problem solver of Manor Hill. Being part of the college for years and knowing SA's history, Mike still took on the challenge of being the head of SA after being approached by the college administration. He wanted to change the way the department had been run for all these years.

Two years ago, the then recently installed Manor Hill College president saw the need for change. Unlike his predecessors, President Johnson wanted to take the challenge head on by convening a college-wide address announcing a change. When announcing Mike's new position to the Manor Hill College community, President Johnson even hailed Mike in the annual college address as the innovative leader who would change the way the college "does business."

"I'd like to announce that, in response to student requests, I am making a dramatic change in the college administration. The Student Accounts Office executive director will now report directly to me effective immediately. The new executive director is a well-known figure in the college community. He has been working here at the college for decades, and is well respected by the Manor Hill community. I expect much needed changes, made quickly and efficiently. Without further ado I'd like to officially announce that Mr. Michael Roberts will be the new executive director of the Student Accounts Office. I am confident that he will face the challenge head on."

Surrounded by a thunderous applause in the room, Mike walked on stage to give the president a handshake and wave to the crowd.

Mike whispered in the President's ear, "Thank you, President Johnson. I won't disappoint you."

The President whispered back to Mike, "I know you won't."

HITTING THE GROUND RUNNING

Feeling the pressure to produce right away, Mike quickly got his hands dirty, and started making much-needed changes in the division.

Looking at Manor Hill College students as internal stakeholders, SA was re-branded as the one-stop-shop student center in hopes of changing the office's reputation. Some of the new methods Mike adopted were to transition SA from paper to electronic submissions in order to make the work flow easier for students to make academic assessments, as well as increasing degree, audit, and transfer credit services and decreasing corresponding regulations.

Mike also assigned a personal SA liaison to each of the college's departments to take responsibility for the different aspects of each department's programs. This representative helps solve problems, create solutions, and implement any improvements as needed.

As the face of SA, Mike set the bar very high in the student newspaper. He even went so far as to publicize his email address and personal cell phone number throughout various campus media, including in an interview with the *Manor Hill Herald* student newspaper:

"I am publishing and promoting my email address and phone number. I will be asking people to reach me directly if they are not receiving the support they need. I will encourage students, faculty, and staff to contact me personally if they feel they have an issue that is not being addressed to their satisfaction."

The reporter asked, "That's great. Besides student satisfaction, what is your goal for SA?"

Mike answered, "My expectation is for SA to be the number one college service organization in the country in one year."

"Wow, setting the bar high, I see."

"Yes, that's what I want. In the end, the students will be the judges," Mike said with confidence.

BACK TO THE DRAWING BOARD

After two years of being the head of SA, Mike is astonished to hear the same complaints from students. Returning to the office, he convenes his core team and gives them an update on what he heard in the cafeteria. Frustrated, Mike says to his team, "We have to fix things!"

"We've done so much already," says Bob Rancer, Mike's right-hand man. "What else is there?"

"Clearly we haven't gotten our message across to our students."

Surprised, Bob asks, "Why do you say that? I think we've done a great job, actually."

"Apparently, not enough. I just came from the cafeteria, where I overheard a student talking about dreading coming to our office because of his terrible experience in the past. Now I think he's going to have an interview with the college newspaper on his past experience with the SA."

"Why didn't you say something?" asks Lisa Wright, SA's assistant director.

"What else am I going to say, Lisa? I've already done two interviews with the student newspaper about the changes that we've implemented. There must be something else we can do. Students don't know what good things we've done to help improve our services to them. We still have a bad reputation!"

"Come on, Mike … A bad reputation *still*? Really? After all we've done?" Trying to come up with an idea, Lisa asks, "Well, you've always wanted to hire a communications firm, right? Why don't we do that?"

Mike excitedly responds, "That's true. Good idea, Lisa. Let's go for it."

"I'll print out the list of the top firms!" shouts Lisa as she walks over to her desk.

Bob chimes in, "Mike, do you want to give a call to the *Manor Hill Herald* student newspaper to do another interview?"

Mike wipes the sweat off of his brow, "I need some time to think."

Lisa asks, "Are you OK, Mike?"

"I … uh … I'll be in my office."

Going back into his office, Mike starts feeling the pressure of the immediate situation. After SA's long history, is it too big to fix? He's done so much to change office processes ... then why still the bad reputation? *What is President Johnson going to think?* After all, Mike now reports to him directly. All these questions go through his mind. *Will I lose my job?*

As if it were *déjà vu*, he hears some commotion outside his office window. Peaking out the window blinds, he sees two students with a megaphone. Barely making out the muffled chant through the window, Mike hears "SA" and knows that it is geared toward him.

RING!

Mike's phone starts ringing.

The caller ID reads:

PRESIDENT JOHNSON

DISCUSSION QUESTIONS

1. What would you do if you were in Mike's shoes? Do you think he should have interjected himself into the conversation between the students?

2. Considering that Mike has been working at the college for years and is known as the problem solver, and considering the history of the SA, would you keep Mike as the executive director, or would you hire someone externally?

3. If you were hired as part of the consulting firm, what would be your recommendations in your communication plan?

4. What would you tell the college president on the phone? Would you tell the president of the day's situation?

KEY TERMS

Organizational Communication, Reputation Management, Public Relations

PART VI

Risk and Crisis Communication

CHAPTER 29

"Not in My Backyard!"

Jason S. Wrench & Austin Schatz
SUNY New Paltz

ABSTRACT

Gwen Colchimaro works as a risk communication specialist for Medi-Waste, a company that has recently placed a facility in Riddleville. When local representatives become concerned about the safety of the emissions produced by the plant, Gwen must act quickly if she is to save the facility from being shut down.

"Dear God! Are you people really that dense!?" Dr. Rebecca Punjab, the chief scientist for Medi-Waste, practically yelled at the auditorium full of concerned citizens. "If I've told you once, I've told you a thousand times already, there is nothing even remotely hazardous about the emissions produced by this plant."

"Then why do we see smoke coming out of the facility 24-7?!" an angry community member yelled out.

"Because it's an incinerator!" Rebecca replied. "The word 'incinerator' comes from the word 'incinerate,' which for the brain-trust in this room means 'to burn.' It's magic. When you burn things, there's smoke!" she continued sarcastically.

After a short, and very vocal outburst from the community present, the moderator of the event, Dr. Jillian Sage of the Environmental Protection Agency, asked for the next question.

An elderly woman approached the microphone and pulled out a small index card before she began reading. "My name is Delores Perez, and I've lived my entire life in this community," she began. "I have never before in my life, been more afraid for the health of my community than I am right now. The fact that Medi-Waste feels that it can come into this economically disadvantaged neighborhood and set up shop without any kind of repercussions is a clear indication of their arrogance. For the life of me,—"

"Would you please get to the point?" Dr. Punjab said into her microphone.

"Listen here, girly—"

"That's Dr. Punjab."

"Fine! Listen here, Dr. Girly," the woman responded. "I originally supported this effort because the facts were originally laid out in front of the community in a respectful and transparent matter. Not only am I a respected member of this community, former principal of

Riddleville High School, and known social justice advocate, I am also the councilwoman who represents this community. I currently sit on the zoning committee. After this display tonight, I will use all of my political clout to ensure that Medi-Waste is shut down in this community. In fact, I will ensure that Medi-Waste never has a facility in this region again!"

The room suddenly erupted into applause. Hoots of encouragement filled the auditorium. When the room finally died down, Delores put her note card away and stared right at Dr. Punjab. "Now, Doctor, I'm sure you're a smart woman. You need to scuttle on home to your bosses at Medi-Waste and tell them not to waste their time or money trying to operate here."

Dr. Punjab started to say something, but with a wave her hand Delores interrupted, "I think we've heard from you enough tonight." Chuckles were heard throughout the room, as people were glad to see someone finally standing up to the scientist. "As I said, this debate is officially over." With that, Delores turned from the microphone and headed up the aisle and out the back door. As if on cue, the second the door slammed shut, the entire audience stood and started exiting the building.

Gwen Colchimaro, Medi-Wastes' head of public relations, sat in the back of the auditorium watching everything unfold. *I warned them not to use Dr. Punjab*, she thought to herself.

MEDI-WASTE COMES TO TOWN

Medi-Waste was a company started in the early 1980s to help doctor's offices and hospitals dispose of medical waste properly (e.g., blood samples, needles, and other forms of waste produced in the medical environment). The safest thing to do with medical waste is to incinerate it in an effort to ensure any pathogens within the waste are destroyed. The idea of burning medical waste is hardly a new one. In fact, throughout the history of medicine, many societies have practiced burning the deceased to prevent the spread of disease and illness.

The modern practice of medical waste incineration is one that is highly regulated by the Environmental Protection Agency (EPA) in an effort to ensure that medical waste does not pollute the environment. As a company, Medi-Waste has often been hailed as a standard bearer in the field. In fact, before the EPA tightened regulations on medical incinerators in 2011, Medi-Waste had already adopted practices that went above and beyond the new regulations. For this reason, Medi-Waste was generally seen as a safe economic and environmental bet for communities. Not only would the incinerator bring new, high-paying jobs to a community, but Medi-Waste was a name that could be trusted.

When Medi-Waste originally approached the town of Riddleville about coming to the city, the town council was generally very excited. Although the town council had some basic questions about safety, the meetings with Medi-Waste proved fruitful and the council started seeking out possible locations for the facility.

When the city zoning commission originally proposed that Delores' district would be the ideal place for the incinerator, Delores immediately had a number of reservations. In a closed meeting with the town council and Medi-Waste she raised her questions.

"First, thank you for meeting with us Ms. Colchimaro."

"It's my pleasure," Gwen replied. "It's my job to help you understand the benefits of Medi-Waste along with answering any questions about the company, its history, and its track record. As you will see, we have nothing to hide."

"That's very good to hear," Delores continued. "As you can imagine, as the councilwoman whose district has been proposed to house this incinerator, my constituents are very concerned. There's a feeling in my district that placing the incinerator there isn't fair. For many years, my district has been home to the lowest socioeconomic level citizens in Riddleville. Thoughts?"

"I'm very well aware that your district has worries related to issues of fairness. Historically, people who live near major manufacturing facilities tend to be lower income, lower in socioeconomic status, and are more likely to be members of racial minority groups. At Medi-Waste, we take the issue of fairness very seriously," Gwen replied. "In order to give us insight into this population, Medi-Waste conducted a survey a month ago when your district was originally proposed."

"And what did the outcomes of your survey find?" Delores questioned, unaware that such a survey had been conducted.

"I'm actually very glad that you asked. I took the liberty to prepare a report for the town council based on our findings." Gwen opened a box that she had brought with her, pulled out a stack of nicely bound reports, and quickly distributed them to the council members. "I don't want to go into all of the specifics here, but all of the information about the survey, including the complete set of questions, findings, and our interpretation is contained within the document. Instead, if you'll look on page 3 of the report, you can see the basic executive summary from Medi-Waste's impact analysis."

EXECUTIVE SUMMARY

Medi-Waste Survey of Riddleville Community

1. Introduction

1.1 <u>Background and objectives</u>

The purpose of this study was to examine the community concerns in Riddleville about the proposed Medi-Waste facility. Key information expected from the survey included:

- Perceived understanding of how medical incinerators work.

- Perceived downsides to medical incinerators within a community.

- Actual knowledge of medical waste incinerators.

- Fears associated with medical waste incinerators.

- Perceptions of fairness in Riddle of the proposed location of the new Medi-Waste incinerator.

- Perceptions of Medi-Waste as a company.

1.2 Methodology

A random sampling technique of Riddleville community members was conducted using a database of telephone numbers purchased from the telephone company. Because of the proposed location and higher incidence of missing data due to the number of home phone numbers that have been replaced with cell phones, door-to-door interviews were also conducted within the proposed community where the Medi-Waste facility would be placed. We specifically over-sampled individuals within the target community to ensure that a broad arrange of voices from within the community would be heard. Overall, 2,000 residents in Riddleville were sampled. An additional 1,000 residents from the targeted community were also surveyed either via phone or in-person interviews.

1.3 Results

Overall, the results indicated that there are a number of serious concerns from the Riddleville community members related to the building of a Medi-Waste facility within the community.

First, residents generally did not have an accurate understanding of how medical incinerators work. Overall, residents generally had no understanding of the EPA guidelines for medical incinerators or the various protective mechanisms used by Medi-Waste.

Second, Riddleville as a whole had a number of false assumptions related to downsides of medical incinerators. In fact, a number of health myths were noted, including perceptions of increased likelihood of cancer, lung problems, and other medical problems. Although the medical research clearly has shown that these are not scientifically sound concerns, Medi-Waste realizes that community members' concerns are legitimate, and must be addressed.

Third, the community where the Medi-Waste incinerator is proposed to be located has clear perceptions that the facility isn't fair. In fact, on a scale of 1 (not at all fair) to 10 (completely fair), community members rated the fairness at a 4.4, which is an indication of this issue. Based on the other findings, we believe that this reaction is closely related to myths about medical incinerators as a whole.

Lastly, the community generally had no opinion about Medi-Waste as a company itself.

> ### 1.4 Recommendations
>
> Based on the above findings, we strongly believe that the first course of action is a clear campaign to educate community members about the realities of medical waste incinerators. Medi-Waste needs to stress clearly to the community our history of innovation and our track record of safety as independently verified by the EPA.

After reading through the executive summary, the council members asked a number of targeted questions related to the findings. Delores listened to the back-and-forth between Gwen and the other council members before finally asking the most pressing question on her mind.

"I see that you understand the perceptions and realities of the individuals within Riddleville. In fact, I'm impressed with how prepared you are today."

"Thank you Councilwoman Perez. Medi-Waste prides itself on its community investment. We don't see ourselves as individuals in the business of exploiting communities. We see ourselves as partners that help communities better themselves."

"That's all well and good, but how are going to assuage the fear that many of my constituents have about the fairness issue?"

"Good question, in my field we often refer to a concept called NIMBY, or Not In My Back Yard. Many people see the necessity of facilities like Medi-Waste, but no one really wants one right in their backyard. From what we've learned over the decades, NIMBY reactions are often out fear and/or ignorance."

"Ignorance?" Delores questioned.

"When I use the word 'ignorance,' I use it in the sense that individuals are uninformed. When people hear about medical supplies being burnt, they often have a knee-jerk reaction and assume the worst. As a company, Medi-Waste believes the strongest way to prevent these reactions is through open and honest dialogue coupled with listening to and empathizing with community members' fears. Research shows us that fear is often scientifically unfounded, but it doesn't make it any less real to those experiencing the fear."

The discussion went on for another hour as Gwen easily fielded questions and provided detailed answers to the council. At one point, Gwen admitted that she didn't have the answer to a specific question and promised to talk to one of the Medi-Waste scientists and get back to the council within 24 hours.

When all was said and done, the City Council unanimously approved the building of the Medi-Waste incinerator in Riddleville. In fact, subsequent surveys by Medi-Waste showed an increase in actual understanding of how medical incinerators work and the rigorous methods Medi-Waste uses to protect the community.

FIVE YEARS LATER

"Gwen," Joanna Pershing, CEO of Medi-Waste, said when Gwen answered the phone in her office.

"Hi, Joanna, what can I do for you today?"

"Do you remember our facility in Riddleville?"

"Geez, I haven't thought about Riddleville in ages. That was a great example of how positive risk communication can really save a company," Gwen remembered.

"Well, we have serious problems there now."

"Uh oh, what happened!?" Gwen heard Joanna shuffling through a stack of papers on her desk.

"Well, I received a phone call from Roberto Salerno, the Riddleville Medi-Waste operations officer. Apparently, a new environmental group within the community is up in arms about the facility."

"What happened there?! When we left Riddleville, everything was running so smoothly."

"Well, Gwen," Joanna continued, "Apparently, there are growing concerns that the smoke coming from the incinerator contains carcinogens that are increasing the cancer rates near the facility. Apparently, a community member who lives across the street just died of cancer and people are now blaming Medi-Waste for killing the person."

"OK, let me get my office up-to-date about what's going on here. I still have some contacts in Riddleville, so I can reach out and see what's happening. I should have a plan of attack to handle this crisis later this afternoon."

Gwen spent the rest of the afternoon in brainstorming sessions with the other individuals in Medi-Waste's PR office. Periodically, the group would be interrupted by phone calls from Gwen's contacts in Riddleville. Over the course of the afternoon, Gwen realized that the situation in Riddleville had gone from great, to bad, to nuclear disaster in just a few months. Apparently, after accusations started flying in Riddleville, Roberto Salerno issued a flat press-release denying any and all responsibility for causing cancer in the town. The press release was flat, impersonal, and a little condescending in tone. According to her contacts in Riddleville, the press release had really galvanized the community against Medi-Waste.

At 4:30 pm, Gwen called Joanna and filled her in on all of the information she had learned over the course of the day. Gwen also proposed that Medi-Waste send in a PR team to handle the situation immediately.

"Gwen," Joanna started, "I like that you want to be proactive, but I just don't think this is a complete case for PR. Clearly, the community isn't in need of a touchy-feely discussion. I think they need to hear from an expert on this issue."

"Joanna, I really don't think an expert—"

"I know you're good at your job, Gwen," Joanna interrupted. "But this is really a case for expertise. The people in Riddleville are misinformed about science, so let's let them talk to a real scientist. I've already been on the phone with Dr. Rebecca Punjab, and she's agreed to go to Riddleville to meet with the community."

Uh oh! Gwen thought to herself. Rebecca is the last person who should go to Riddleville. Gwen had known Rebecca since she started working for Medi-Waste. Although Rebecca was probably one of the smartest women Gwen had ever met, she wasn't exactly a people-person. In fact, Rebecca's lack of people skills had gotten the company into trouble previously when she referred to an anti-incinerator scientist as "one of the most moronic individuals in science. He should have his PhD revoked and then be beaten with his diploma." Gwen was ultimately able to smooth the situation over, but it took over a year of trust-building to repair the damage Rebecca had done to Medi-Waste.

"Just for the record, Joanna, I think this is a horrible idea," Gwen said flatly. "Rebecca may be smart, but her tact is not exactly her strong suit. She could easily turn a mild crisis into a huge media disaster."

"Gwen," Joanna said, sighing, "I know you two have had your difficulties in the past, but this is what is best for Medi-Waste. You can coach Rebecca on what to say. I trust you." With that Joanna said goodbye and told Gwen to get on the first flight to Riddleville.

Upon landing in Riddleville, Gwen turned on her cell phone and listened to the messages.

"Gwen, Dr. Punjab. I guess you're in the air," the voice on the other end said flatly. "I have scheduled an open forum to put this nonsense to rest. Hopefully, you'll be here before the meeting starts at 7:00 pm."

Gwen looked down at her wrist-watch. *6:50! Are you kidding me!?*

Upon disembarking from the plane, Gwen took off in a mad dash to get a cab and make her way to Riddleville High School where the meeting would be taking place. She opted to bypass getting her luggage. *I'll come back after this is over.* She quickly left the airport and got into the first taxi she could find.

After telling the driver where she was going, Gwen called Joanna.

"Joanna," the voice on the other end said.

"It's Gwen."

"Oh good, you're on the ground. Did you get a chance to talk to Dr. Punjab yet?"

"Not exactly! She left me a phone message while I was in the air."

"Oh," Joanna started, "I guess that means you know about the public forum going on tonight?"

"Yeah, I just found out." Gwen looked down at her watch noticing that it was now 7:10. "The meeting started 10 minutes ago. I should be there by 7:30 depending on traffic."

"Great!" Joanna exclaimed. "I'm just glad you'll be there to support Dr. Punjab." Gwen heard a buzzing sound on the other end of the line, "Sorry, Gwen, my other line is ringing. Have a great evening. I know you and Rebecca will make a great team and fix this whole little mess for us." With that, Joanna was gone.

Gwen stared down at her smartphone and started scrolling through the email she'd received while she'd been on the plane. As she was scrolling through her email, an address she hadn't seen in a long time suddenly caught her attention. *Chip Bryman, I haven't thought about him since the last time I was in Riddleville.*

At the time the Medi-Waste facility had been opened in Riddleville, Chip Bryman had been a reporter who actively covered the story from beginning to end. She had really relied on Chip to help her get Medi-Waste's side of the story out within the community. She quickly opened the email and read Chip's message

> Gwen:
>
> I hope this email finds you doing well. I'm sitting in the Riddleville High School auditorium waiting for this presentation to begin. I was kind of surprised to see that you weren't on the list of speakers for the event. I figured you'd be here since this was your baby during its inception.
>
> Anyway, the meeting is about to begin. It looks like the lineup is going to be some rep from the EPA and then a Dr. Rebecca Punjab here representing Medi-Waste. Is she your protégé?
>
> Chip

She was about to email him back, but suddenly her phone chirped and another message was coming through. *Another email from Chip!?* she questioned, looking down at her phone's display.

> Gwen:
>
> Who is this woman!? She is single handedly dismantling any credibility Medi-Waste had in the community. She's arrogant, unable to bring information down to her audience's level, and she really doesn't seem to have a clue about putting a community's fears at ease. I hope you're still on the payroll. This is going to be a long, painful evening.
>
> Chip

Uh oh! Gwen thought to herself. If the press is already having problems with Dr. Punjab, how is she supposed to save anything? She looked at her watch. It was already 7:30, so the presentation had already been going on for 30 minutes. She looked up from her watch and saw the high school in the distance. I hope I'm not too late!

The cab pulled in front of the high school and Gwen quickly got out after paying the cab driver and giving him a pretty substantial tip. She headed into the school, feeling as if she'd been there just yesterday having her first public meeting with the Riddleville community. She quickly found the school auditorium. She opened the doors in the back of the room as gently as possible.

"Dear God! Are you people really that dense!?" was the first thing Gwen heard as she quietly shut the door behind her. "If I've told you once, I've told you a thousand times already, there is nothing even remotely hazardous about the emissions produced by this plant," Gwen winced as she listened to Dr. Punjab talk from the front of the room.

"Then why do we see smoke coming out of the facility 24-7?!" an angry community member yelled out.

"Because it's an incinerator!" Rebecca replied. "The word 'incinerator' comes from the word 'incinerate,' which for the brain-trust in this room means 'to burn.' It's magic. When you burn things, there's smoke!" she continued sarcastically.

Oh dear!? Gwen thought to herself, finding a seat in the back row. *What does she think she's doing!?* Gwen sat in stunned silence as she listened to Rebecca talk. She could practically feel the animosity growing as Rebecca droned on.

Gwen sat in the auditorium and watched as Dr. Punjab attempted to talk down Delores Perez, a woman with whom Gwen was quite familiar. Delores was on the town council at the time that the Medi-Waste facility was being proposed. She watched as Delores finished speaking, turned, and left the auditorium. In almost stunned silence, Gwen watched as the majority of the room followed suit. She joined the throngs and raced outside immediately searching her contact list for Joanna. *I warned her this was a bad idea!* Gwen thought to herself as the phone rang and she waited for someone to pick it up on the other end.

DISCUSSION QUESTIONS

1. Could Gwen have done anything differently to change the outcome of the situation? What steps should Gwen take to remedy this situation and save the facility in Riddleville?

2. How could the use of an expert have been more effective in dealing with this situation? Why is it important to have expert credibility in PR?

3. How would you confront Joanna about this issue? What can Medi-Waste learn from this situation?

KEY TERMS

Transparency, Expert Credibility, Risk Communication, Executive Summary, Crisis Communication

CHAPTER 30

Warehouse Under Water: Promised Delivery Is Compromised

Kristin Roeschenthaler Wolfe

ABSTRACT

The recent hurricane has hit your warehouse facility. Your inventory and shipping have been affected. Orders are being delayed by weeks, even though specific dates have been promised and your company is known for its customer service and on-time delivery. It is your job to communicate this information to the media and to your customers.

Katy Wilderom sat in her boarded-up house waiting for the hurricane to stop. Her dog was snuggled next to her on the couch as she read her Kindle by the light of a candle. About two hours into Hurricane Joan, Katy had completely lost power. The first thing she did was break out the pint of ice cream she had sitting in her freezer.

Although her power was still out, she had an emergency handheld device that could keep her cell phone powered during those rare situations when she lost power. Katy was the chief operations officer for Sema-Tech, a laptop manufacturer. Her primary responsibility was the company's warehouse facility, which was located right on the Gulf of Mexico. For a second she worried about the warehouse, but she knew Daniel Simpson, her second in command, was overseeing the warehouse while she was stuck at home during the hurricane.

Katy finally got tired of reading and decided to curl up on the couch with her dog and take a quick nap. She wasn't sure how long she'd been asleep when her cell phone started ringing. She shook herself awake, her dog giving her the evil eye as she woke him from his sleep as well.

She grabbed the cell phone and looked at the caller ID. "Daniel Simpson" shone in bright letters. "Daniel, how did things fare at the warehouse?" Katy said into the phone, not even giving Daniel a chance to say hello.

"We've got problems, the warehouse is flooded, the entire first floor was wiped out," Daniel responded.

"What? Is everyone OK?" Katy asked.

"Yes, we were able to get all the employees to safety without incident, but the inventory is ruined."

Katy let out a four-letter expletive before she responded. "OK. Let me talk to Joe and the others about our next move," she replied. "I'll get back to you."

Daniel said, "Wait, there's more. Many of the employees' homes were destroyed and a lot of them have been displaced. I'm not sure who will be able to come in to work for the next several weeks. And I'm also not sure when the warehouse will be able to be reopened. We may be looking at several weeks or a month, and that's the best-case scenario at this point."

"Daniel, thanks for the update," Katy responded, really questioning her use of the word "thanks." "I'll get back to you once I've had a chance to contact corporate. Be safe."

Not only will our company take a major hit financially in the loss of inventory, the warehouse is going to need repairing, Katy thought to herself. *At least all of our employees are safe; however, their homes have been destroyed and many are going to take time off to help rebuild the area.*

"Great, this is just great," Katy muttered to herself. "Not only is everything destroyed, the employees are going to need time off and we have no inventory for the back-to-school orders."

Sema-Tech was known for on-time delivery. In fact, a recent in-house document showed that in the past 24 months a delivery date had never been missed and customers' concerns were solved quickly and with full customer satisfaction. *What will happen now?*

Katy looked at her phone and decided that it was time to call her boss, the CEO of Sema-Tech, Joe Handler. *I don't know if he is aware of the entire situation.* Sema-Tech's main offices were located in Boston, so Gulf weather-related problems often weren't on the radars of the bosses up north. Katy plugged in her headset and dialed the number.

"Hello?" a voice on the other end of the phone responded.

"Joe, we have a situation," Katy started.

"What's going on?" he asked.

"The warehouse manager just called. Hurricane Joan hit them, him them hard," Katy replied.

"Oh no, what's the damage?" Joe continued.

"Luckily, all of the employees are safe. Many of their homes have been destroyed, but no one was injured or killed. As far as the warehouse goes, the entire first floor was flooded and we lost most of our inventory."

"Oh crap. We have a lot of customers waiting for their orders to ship. We have to let them know as quickly as possible," Joe thought aloud.

"I know. How do we tell them what happened without losing valuable customers? Do you think they'll understand?" Katy asked, knowing the answer already.

"We have to tell them before someone else does. I need you to get on it right away," Joe replied. "I'm going to call the senior management and give them the heads-up. I'll talk to you this afternoon."

Great, he just dropped all of the responsibility on me, Katy realized. *I don't even know where to begin.*

Katy immediately sent out an urgent email to her team scheduling a Skype meeting in 20 minutes, hoping everyone could Skype through their cell phones if they were without power like she was. *I need to brainstorm how to fix this. The more people thinking of solutions, the better*, she hoped.

During the meeting, the team came up with several solutions. However, many of the solutions could cost the company more money than it could afford to spend with the lost inventory and repairs to the building. Not to mention the lost time and labor with employees taking emergency time off. The team tossed out ideas:

"What about offering free financing?" Jason asked.

"Or offering no interest for the first six months?" suggested Sue.

"Can we supply them with a free laptop sleeve for their trouble? We could put our logo on it for advertising," mentioned Tom.

Katy jotted down and thought about the feasibility of each idea. But they all would cost money. Money that the company was losing. And these solutions might not be enough to make the customers happy. Time and money were short and, unfortunately, so were solutions.

Katy finally told the team, "Let's go back to the drawing board and keep thinking of ideas that can help to appease our customers. Try to remember that the company is losing money with the warehouse repairs and replacement of the laptops we lost. We want to come up with a solution that may not cost us a lot of money."

The team disconnected and Katy fell back onto the couch, which raised her dog's eyebrow. Sensing she needed some affection, her dog stretched his way across the couch toward her and nuzzled up next to her. Completely exhausted from the stress, Katy started slipping back into sleep before jolting back awake. *I don't have time for that, gotta wake up.* She decided that she needed to call the head of customer service for Sema-Tech. Just as she started dialing the number, the power in her house came on. *Great timing!* She almost didn't hear the voice on the other end of the phone saying hello.

"Janet, we have a problem and it's going to affect your team the most, at the moment."

"What's going on?" Janet asked.

"The warehouse was flooded. We lost almost our entire inventory. My team is drafting messages to customers and the media, but the calls will start coming in quickly. Your team needs to be prepared."

"What kind of delay are we looking at?" Janet asked, "I need to give my employees a time-frame so that they can manage customer expectations."

"I honestly don't know," Katy replied. "The entire area was devastated by the hurricane. We have no human casualties, but many of our employees and their families have lost their homes. They are emotionally devastated and need to rebuild. I will keep you updated as we have more information to provide to the customers. My team is preparing written notification, but I'm sure you will receive calls."

"Thanks for the heads-up. I will let my staff know and hope that our customers are understanding," Janet replied.

THE AFTERMATH

In the aftermath of Joan, Katy took all precautionary measures. First, she alerted the media and sent notification to all of Sema-Tech's customers who were waiting on products. In the week that followed, bad just seemed to get worse. Not only was the shipping warehouse drowned, Sema-Tech's manufacturing plant in China was having problems as well, so production was at a halt and no shipments were going out.

Katy started receiving calls from customer services management almost hourly about customers who did not care about the warehouse and just wanted their laptops delivered. The customers were calling because the delivery date was yesterday or last week and they still did not have their laptops. One of Sema-Tech's competitors, one that was not affected by Hurricane Joan, had contacted some of these people, stating that their company could provide a laptop with free overnight shipping, and some customers had already canceled their orders.

"I don't know what to tell them," Janet moaned into the phone. "My employees are trying their best, but many customers still want the laptop when promised and some are threatening to cancel the order completely."

"Let me try to draft something for your customer service representatives to use. It will have to sound genuine and not like a script. Do you think your reps can handle that?" Katy asked her.

Janet replied, "I will work with them to make it sound genuine; they will need to put it in their own words. But I will make sure the message is consistent."

Katy hung up the phone, muttering to herself, "why don't we have something in place for this type of backlash? Now I need to come up with something quickly before we lose more business."

Katy made a quick phone call to Joe to keep him informed.

"Joe, we are losing customers even with the notifications we've put out."

"What can we do? We need to keep our customers now more than ever," Joe replied.

"I'm going to work on a statement for the customer service reps to use and I'll put together more customer communication pieces to get out ASAP. Also, I plan on getting notification out to the media that we are taking action, before our competitors tell the media outlets that we aren't. Can you think of anything else?"

"No, that's a good start. Make sure this works," Joe said, abruptly hanging up.

Katy glanced at her desk, definitely feeling the pressure. *No time to worry*, she thought to herself. *I just need to pull it together and get this ship moving again.*

When most of her management team was back at work, Katy had her secretary call a meeting for 1 that afternoon in the conference room. They have been working long hours and doing their best to keep the media informed of the company's situation and the solution being implemented.

"OK, team, we've got to come up with something for the customer service reps to use. We need to get another communication out to our customers and to the media. Time is of the essence. Tom, as head of PR, do you have any new ideas?"

Tom suggested a quick email blast update on the warehouse repairs to go to all the customers who had signed up for email communication with the company.

"That's a great idea," Katy responded. "Get on it."

"We need to get a message on the website today that provides updates daily. This way customers can check the status without calling in," said Sue. "We can even set up electronic tracking of the laptop and where it is in production."

Katy had some reservations about that, but agreed to think about it. What concerned Katy was that the customer might not feel that the production was happening quickly enough.

After the meeting, Katy sat down at her computer and started crafting a message for the customer service representatives to use. She also remembered that she had promised Sue that she would think about the website idea. *Before I start writing, I should probably check with IT.*

Katy picked up the phone and dialed Jim, the head of IT and Sema-Tech's website manager. She quickly briefed him on Sue's idea.

"So, what do you think, is the up-to-the-minute laptop status feasible?" she asked.

Jim took a moment to think about it and responded, "Not really. We don't have a connection with the warehouse computers to keep the system that updated. What we could do is provide a tracking number to the customer and to the production team. When the production team moves the product from one stage to the next, they could update the status. The customer could then log in using the tracking number and see where their laptop is at that point in time. Would that work?"

"Let me think on it. It might look like we are attempting to put the onus of checking on the progress with the customers. I need to look into other solutions, but thanks for the idea," Katy responded.

Katy once again stared at her computer screen thinking about the message she needed to craft for customer service. *I forgot to call Joe!* She immediately picked up the phone and clicked on the button next to Joe's name as her speed dial called Sema-Tech's CEO. She quickly informed Joe of that afternoon's meetings.

"Let me think about it," Joe said. "I have some concerns, but it might work."

After her conversation with Joe, Katy decided to send out an internal email alerting key players that communication would be going out and it would need to be delivered quickly whether via the website, the newswire, or an external mailing. Realizing that she'd spent the last hour procrastinating, Katy finally looked at her computer screen and started typing.

The message Katy needed to convey was that Sema-Tech appreciated the loyalty and continued support of its customers. She thought through how to demonstrate that the company, and each individual in the company, was working as quickly as possible to supply the promised merchandise. *But how do I convey that Sema-Tech understands the urgency, but we need and appreciate the customers' understanding and patience while our employees and their families rebuild and while our company strives to maintain the best possible product by not shipping out the damaged laptops but building new product for delivery?*

Katy quickly pulled out a note pad and a pen and started jotting down some of these key ideas. *I need to show understanding and compassion while demonstrating the sense of urgency needed to relate to the customers and retain their business.* Katy started writing while talking to herself. "I need to reach out to the media with my plan before our disgruntled customers reach out. Maintaining customer service, keeping our customers happy, and being the first to the media with a solution have to be my top priorities." Katy looked at what she'd just written and felt confident that this was definitely the direction she needed to head.

Katy turned to the computer monitor and started writing, just as the phone rang. She looked at the caller ID and saw that Janet was calling her back.

"Janet, what news do you have for me?" Katy responded, picking up the phone.

"More and more customers are beginning to cancel their orders. They say we are not doing enough. They don't believe we are even trying to fix the problem."

DISCUSSION QUESTIONS

1. What is the best way to alert the customers and media about this situation?
2. How do you alert the internal staff, specifically those who deal with customers, of this situation? What do they need to know? What should they tell customers?
3. How do you deal with customers who want their product now, regardless of your warehouse issues?
4. How can you save the customer relationship? What type of communication may help?
5. What should the message say?

KEY TERMS

Natural Disasters, Press Release, Crisis Communication Plans, Stakeholder Relationships

CHAPTER 31

A Wild Ride

Erin C. Bryan
University of South Florida

ABSTRACT

A university's internal communication and social media specialist races against the clock respond to an internal crisis that threatens to ruin the school's external reputation as a superior place to work.

The stories are all the same, Margeaux thought to herself as Dottie, the Barnhill campus library director, continued sharing her account of the demise of the local Barnhill branch campus of Kerrigan State University. Margeaux felt somewhat guilty for not paying close attention to Dottie, but Dottie's story was all-too familiar to Margeaux. *I've heard the same tale, what, 30, 40 times now?*

Confusion. Distrust. No communication. Feelings of abandonment. Lies. The tone and severity of the words varied, but the basic premise did not. *Faculty and staff at the Barnhill campus felt they had been hung out to dry*, Margeaux thought. *Only now the university was beginning to pay for it in ways they had not anticipated.*

Margeaux hung her head in shame. *Kerrigan State University, and the Barnhill campus in particular, has always been a great place to work. I've been very proud of my contribution to making it that way. How did this problem get so big? It doesn't represent how we normally do business. How embarrassing for all of us at KSU, especially those of us in human resources!*

Lost in her thoughts for just a moment, Margeaux snapped back to full attention the moment Dottie stopped speaking.

"I cannot thank you enough for taking the time to meet with me today, Dottie," Margeaux said in her most genuine tone. "I know this has been an extremely trying year for all of you here on the Barnhill campus, but I'm going to do my best to make the rest of your time here better."

She winced at her own words—"the rest of your time here." *The words sound like death is imminent, but that's what this really is, isn't it? A campus that has been dying a slow painful death.* The dark image in Margeaux's mind was in stark contrast to the bright sunny day she was seeing—weather so common for the Barnhill campus.

"I appreciate that, Margeaux," replied Dottie, as the wind forced her hair in her face. Pushing the strands away, she continued, "It just feels good to have someone really listen to me. I don't know how much you can do in such a little amount of time, but someone doing something is certainly better than no one doing nothing at all. I can say that for sure."

"I really will try my best, Dottie," Margeaux said as she stood and extended her hand. "Please say hello to your colleagues in the library for me." With that, Dottie stood and walked away.

Margeaux sat back down and stared off into the distance. *Why wasn't she called in earlier? How did things get this bad? Didn't anyone see this coming?* Margeaux probably asked herself these questions five times a day.

As she rose from her seat once more, she gathered her belongings and left the patio area. Exhaling loudly, she thought *I'll definitely try my best. These are good people and they deserve my best effort. But, a lot of the damage is already done.* Margeaux emerged from her thoughts, glanced at her watch, and realized that she needed to get back on the road.

Having reached her car quickly, Margeaux exited the Barnhill parking lot while reflecting on her desire simply to escape the place. It had been a long week of employee interviews as Margeaux tried to get a handle on what Barnhill staff needed most in this crisis. *What a shame*, she noted to herself dryly. *The physical beauty of this campus cannot compete with my gloomy mood after hearing the woes of these employees all week. I guess that's how the Barnhill campus faculty and staff feel every single day.*

AN UNPRECEDENTED ACT

Margeaux's previous visit to the Barnhill campus—a year and half ago—had been a very different experience. At that point, faculty, staff, administrators, and students were celebrating their newly granted accreditation. The announcement that they had received full accreditation came after several years of preparation and many months of hard work on the part of the Barnhill employees.

At the celebration, colorful balloons decorated the ceiling while the staff and faculty listened to the president of Kerrigan State formally thank the Barnhill campus' employees for their hard work. After the president's speech, many faculty and staff took to the microphone in an impromptu fashion to share their personal gratitude for the opportunity to work on such a thriving campus.

It was really a "feel-good" moment, Margeaux thought. *But who could have predicted what was to come? Probably no one—anywhere.*

At the time of the accreditation celebration, the Barnhill campus was in the middle of a major transformation. Previously only awarding associate's degrees, Barnhill was growing into a traditional four-year institution. In fact, the Barnhill campus would be enrolling its first junior-level students that coming fall semester. The hiring of more faculty and staff to support the enrollment growth was well underway too.

In fact, Margeaux recalled, *a number of those newly hired faculty and staff were at that celebration. I remember thinking how awesome it was that they were coming on board at such a vibrant time. Plus, selfishly, I was thinking how the Barnhill campus success would continue to support Kerrigan State's reputation as the region's best employer. It might have been a selfish thought, but protecting that reputation is part of my job as an internal communication and social media specialist in the human resources department of Kerrigan State. Seeing all those faculty and staff so happy to be working for Kerrigan State University at Barnhill made me happy—and my job easier.*

The cause of the celebration, seeking—and receiving—independent accreditation was a major component in the master plan to bring prominence to Kerrigan State University and more jobs and educational opportunities to the region. Separate accreditation showed the public that the Barnhill campus was now more than a satellite location of KSU—it was a significant and respectable higher education institution in its own right. No longer would Barnhill have to depend upon its colleagues at the main Kerrigan State University campus to approve its every move, especially in the way of academic curriculum. The accrediting announcement was truly a reason for Kerrigan State University, the Barnhill campus, and the public to be very happy.

Not long after the accreditation celebration, a local state representative, who also happened to be the chair of the legislature's budget committee, determined that he was not pleased with the rate of progress at the Barnhill campus. When his opinions began emerging in the media, everyone at Kerrigan State University—and especially at Barnhill—wondered in disbelief what he was talking about. The progress at the campus had been tremendous and everyone—in higher education—knew it.

But the representative had his own vision for the campus—one very different from Kerrigan State's vision for Barnhill. He managed to convince the Barnhill campus' dean that his plan for complete independence from Kerrigan State University was a good one. To convince the dean, he promised to ensure that the dean would become president of this new, separate college. In a rebellious act, the representative and dean directly approached the state university system's board of governors and requested complete independence be granted to Barnhill. The board said yes, but only after five years when Barnhill proved it could function fully on its own, apart from the resources of Kerrigan State. Infuriated by only a partial victory, the representative pressed on.

When the next legislative session began a few months later, the representative exhibited the most developed political prowess one could imagine. First introducing a bill to separate the Barnhill campus from Kerrigan State University immediately, he, as chair of the budget committee, then single-handedly crafted a state budget that cut Kerrigan State University 55% in state funding support, while cutting other state universities about 25%. In essence, the senator held the state's funding of Kerrigan State University hostage, only allowing for a reduction in Kerrigan State University's funding cut if fellow legislators voted for his bill to split Barnhill from Kerrigan State University into a separate university now—not in five years per the board of governors' plan.

Spouting promise after promise in the media and on the senate floor, the senator vowed that independence would be good for everyone. To allay fears that faculty or staff might lose their jobs, he assured everyone no jobs would be lost. The Barnhill campus would just transition over into a new, separate state college, he claimed.

A ROLLER COASTER

When the bill was introduced, the faculty and staff at Barnhill became distraught. In fact, it seemed no one anywhere within the Kerrigan State University system wanted to separate the Barnhill campus. Everyone believed that, if there were to be a split, the five-year path set out by the board of governors was a solid plan. If Barnhill could show it could exist on its own by achieving the benchmarks, then independence was warranted. If not, the campus would continue under the excellent parenting of Kerrigan State University. But the other Kerrigan State University campuses knew the proposed cuts to the Kerrigan State University budget were too steep; if they wanted to preserve their own campuses, the cut had to be lessened—55% was just too much money to lose in state funding. In fear of losing their own jobs, some at Kerrigan State University—outside of the Barnhill campus—began to believe letting that Barnhill campus go was for the best.

Further, the bill's numerous revisions allowed for wide interpretation and cause for confusion. Despite the representative's public statements that no jobs would be lost, the latest versions of the bill suggested the "new" Barnhill State College would start over with all new faculty and staff rather than keeping existing Barnhill employees.

Margeaux remembers reading the possibility in the paper. *How could that be? Start over without those who had worked so hard? That was nonsensical, and in these days nothing seemed to be too far-fetched for the state legislature to consider.*

As the legislative proposal gained steam, all the searches for new faculty and staff at Barnhill were immediately suspended. The administration couldn't possibly offer contracts to new employees when they did not even know whether the campus, as it existed now, would be around in a few short months. Who would want to come in the midst of such uncertainty anyway? The flow of admissions applications dwindled substantially; students who had already been accepted and had committed to coming began telling the Barnhill admissions staff that they weren't so sure after all.

Ironically, now that the bill had been introduced, progress at Barnhill truly *was* slow; it was like the representative's plan threw an emergency parking brake on a car moving 65 miles per hour. The whole campus practically came to a screeching halt. *That's when President Dolder came in, Margeaux remembered. He knew he needed to come down to the Barnhill campus to reassure everyone things would work out just fine. And he did a great job that day; I was proud of him!*

After all the Barnhill campus employees were assembled together in the auditorium, President Dolder proudly announced, "Regardless of what happens, all of you—our Barnhill campus family—will continue to have a job with Kerrigan State University. You are part of Kerrigan State and you will stay that way if you so desire!"

The auditorium erupted in applause. *That was quite a statement*, Margeaux thought.

Prior to President Dolder's visit and wonderful announcement, Barnhill employees had been worrying whether they would be hired on at the "new" college and whether their salaries would be comparable. But now there was a breath of fresh air. Barnhill faculty and staff didn't know exactly what the future would look like, but at least everyone at Barnhill knew they would have a job regardless of what happened with the bill.

Margeaux was relieved too. Giving the employees the relief of job security was enough to hold the campus together. Kerrigan State University and the Barnhill campus in particular was very tight-knit—truly a family. Preserving those feelings of familial support and team-work would be imperative to maintain a reputation as a leading employer in the region. Margeaux was pleased the president followed through in upholding these important Kerrigan State values. Plus she was happy her Barnhill colleagues would have jobs one way or another.

Overall, the president's announcement got the gears of Barnhill campus turning again. The campus didn't regain the momentum it had before, but it was functional and students were being well-served.

Over the next few weeks, the bill successfully made its way through both chambers of the state legislature and employees and students at Barnhill held their breath waiting to see what Governor Ortiz would do. After the ten-day waiting period for the governor to sign, veto, or do nothing to the bill, the governor did the latter; she allowed the bill to go into effect without taking a stance on it. That was all it took for Barnhill's fate to be sealed. Barnhill would be closed down as a branch of Kerrigan State University and would become a new and separate state college with all-new employees. How exactly this would be executed was unclear, but that question was one for people at a much higher pay grade than Margeaux.

A day after the governor allowed the bill to become law, the employees of Barnhill gathered for another meeting with the president of Kerrigan State University. Excited to hear the first official words from Kerrigan State University administration about how the Barnhill shut-down would be implemented and how the Barnhill employees would be integrated into jobs in other parts of the Kerrigan State University system, the faculty and staff were bright-eyed, chatty, and understandably a little nervous as they once again filtered into the large auditorium.

As President Dolder welcomed everyone, Margeaux noticed the exuberance in the room. *Wow*, she thought. *It could be much different. These people are about to go through a huge transformation—their campus is about to be closed down, and they will all be moved into different jobs in the KSU system, but yet they're all still here and seemingly happy. That's impressive and yet another testament to our outstanding workplace. If Kerrigan State University was* someplace they were not happy to work, they would have already quit, or at least be looking for new jobs. In any case, they certainly would NOT be this enthusiastic!

Everyone took their seats as President Dolder approached the podium. As Margeaux's view across the auditorium improved, she struggled to see the faces near the front of the room. *Who was that over there near the side exit door?*

It can't be, she said to herself. But it was. The vice-president of human resources and a few of the university's legal counsel were huddled together. *Why are they here? Margeaux's boss' boss—the vice-president of human resources—and the university legal counsel only came out to branch campuses when something really bad happened—and, thankfully, that was exceptionally rare.* Her thoughts stopped right there. *Something really bad has happened*, she realized, but *what was it?*

As the internal communication specialist on the human resource team, it was standard procedure for Margeaux to attend campus-wide meetings when the president would speak. However, because such events were often more celebratory and the purpose was often obvious, Margeaux was rarely briefed on the specific statements President Dolder would make. When news was bad, she was always filled in ahead of time. *So if legal counsel is here and if the vice-president of human resources is here, it appears to be bad news. So why wasn't I briefed?* Suddenly Margeaux wasn't feeling so well.

President Dolder began speaking by thanking everyone for their perseverance and diligence in serving Kerrigan State University students through the political turmoil. "Now that a decision has been made," he said. "We can finally begin moving on. No one likes the idea of closing Barnhill or Kerrigan State not having a presence in the town of Eastlawn anymore. We wish we did not have to leave, but we've been given a directive by the legislature and we must fulfill it."

"Kerrigan State University is proud to have such wonderful employees who have stuck with us through thick and thin and were working so hard to grow Barnhill into a four-year institution. We know you were working tirelessly and we appreciate every ounce of energy you expended. But unfortunately that wasn't enough for the legislature and, well, what is done is now done."

He paused for a few moments as his expression changed from one of general pleasantness to dismay. With a much more somber tone, he began again, "But it is because of the legislative directive that ..." He stopped once again and restarted. "Because we do have such a great group of employees at Barnhill ... it is with great sadness we have to say goodbye. I cannot say enough how thankful Kerrigan State is for all of you who have supported us during these years we have had a home in the town of Eastlawn."

Whispers and murmurs were instantly rampant through the large room. The president had lost the audience's attention. *Say goodbye? What in the world was he talking about? This message was not sounding like what was expected!*

People were starting to fidget in their seats. *Oh no, this is going to get really bad. This isn't going to be pretty. Why didn't I know about this before? This is why my position exists!* Margeaux's stomach was churning.

With that, Margeaux's boss' boss, the newly hired vice-president of human resources, approached the microphone as President Dolder stepped to the side. *Margeaux groaned to herself. In their few conversations, it was apparent to Margeaux that Vice-President Hatcher lacked both tact and compassion.*

Taking over the microphone VP Hatcher boomed, "Thank you all for coming to our meeting today. As you know, the bill has now become law by way of statute since Governor Ortiz chose to neither sign nor veto the bill. And so, we will be closing the Barnhill campus."

She raced on with her voice still booming, "The closure will be done in a strategic fashion so we may continue to serve our existing students as they finish their associate's degrees. As services are no longer needed on this, the Barnhill campus, the number of staff and faculty will be reduced accordingly. We will be doing our best to notify each employee of their impending layoff as early as possible."

"LAYOFFS?!" someone in the crowd stood up and shouted. "LAYOFFS?!"

"You promised us a job!" another faculty member yelled. "You said no matter what we'd have a home with Kerrigan State University!"

Echoes of these cries went through the room. The crowd was on the verge of a riot.

Margeaux was officially sick to her stomach. *How could this be happening? I heard President Dolder promise them jobs myself! And why didn't I know about this beforehand?!*

The president tried to re-approach the microphone but the vice-president blocked his way. "This was an uncertain situation for us all," VP Hatcher continued. "President Dolder wishes it were different. But the reality is, given the legislature's decision and the 25% reduction in funding for all state university budgets, there is no way that Kerrigan State University can keep everyone here on the payroll."

"Can't you give us jobs at the other campuses? Use us to fill empty positions?" a man Margeaux recognized as a facilities worker said.

"You can apply for open positions just like anyone else," the VP replied quickly.

"We don't even get any special preference? You can't even guarantee us interviews for open positions at the level we are in now?" Tanya, one of the academic advisors, spoke up and asked.

"You may apply like anyone else from the public," the vice-president reiterated.

Margeaux was aghast. *I knew the budget cuts from state's reduced funding would make things difficult this next year, but we should never have told them they would definitely have jobs if we didn't know that for sure! And not to give them any preference in finding jobs within the system? What has happened to the compassionate way Kerrigan State does business?!*

A DOWNWARD SPIRAL

Miraculously, that awful meeting ended without a riot. The pre-meeting exuberance of the employees was nowhere to be found after the layoff announcement. Margeaux was surprised more people didn't vocally express their displeasure, but after looking at the weary faces, she realized that the Barnhill employees were just too exhausted.

They put on a good front for the several months of turmoil, while they were just waiting for the final decision to be made. They thought they'd have jobs, so pressing on despite the other uncertainty was worth it. But learning the devastating news that they would all—eventually—be laid off was too much. They had no more strength to fight back.

A day after the meeting, Margeaux was back on Kerrigan State University's main campus. She cautiously approached her boss' office. Her boss, despite not attending the shocking Barnhill meeting, had heard the details.

"I just have two questions" Margeaux said to her director. "One, why wasn't I consulted about that meeting ahead of time, and, two, what is my role going to be in this process of closing down Barnhill? VP Hatcher promised Barnhill employees weekly town hall meetings for questions, a website with updates, services to help them find other jobs—all projects I should be coordinating."

Her director looked her square in the eye. "Margeaux, with VP Hatcher on board, it appears things are being done differently. I advocated for your inclusion in the pre-meeting planning, but VP Hatcher expressly said no. It seems she believed she could handle the meeting on her own."

Margeaux snorted. *Handling something and handling it well are two different things. I hardly think "well" is the word to describe VP Hatcher's approach. This woman may be a one-woman wrecking ball.*

Her boss continued, "Unfortunately it also seems that VP Hatcher has come to the conclusion that the Barnhill campus is a lost cause. She feels that because it is no longer going to be part of our Kerrigan system, we should not expend any energy there. I've been told we are supposed to continue on as usual and forget all about Barnhill."

"But ..." Margeaux protested.

"I know Margeaux. I don't like it either. It's not Kerrigan State's way of doing things. But she's in charge now. And orders are orders."

"Who is going to deliver on all those promises she made to the Barnhill employees? I'm the only one in an employee communications role for the university. Barnhill campus doesn't have someone on staff to do that stuff. And I strongly doubt the VP will coordinate the logistics of a website or town hall-style question-and-answer meetings herself."

"I don't know Margeaux. The VP didn't address that."

"This is going to really affect our ratings online!" she exclaimed, referencing the popular online site to rate your employer. It seemed more and more of the general public was turning to that site to influence whether they wanted to work somewhere or not. Kerrigan State had led the local region as the best employer for five years in a row. That accolade helped them hire the best staff and attract high-quality faculty to their system. It was an important honor the KSU system wanted to maintain.

Margeaux continued in a heated fashion, "You and I both know that continued mishandling of this awful situation will make Barnhill employees hate Kerrigan State University! It will be all over social media and all over the ratings site. You know that maintaining our ongoing ranking as the best regional employer is a main focus of my social media job responsibilities!"

"I know, I know, Margeaux. You've got to calm down. I really am on your side. But I also know what I was told. We're to stay away. Hopefully any bumps in the road will be small."

In a huff, Margeaux left her boss' office. She knew her director wasn't at fault, but Margeaux was just plain mad. *Talking about being penny wise and pound foolish!* How VP Hatcher ever made it to the top in human resources was beyond Margeaux's understanding—she had no compassion for her employees!

Two months later, Margeaux's boss called her into his office. She entered and began to sit when she was surprised to see VP Hatcher was also there. *Uh-oh. What did I do?*

Her director started to greet her—"Good ..." but VP Hatcher instantly interjected.

"I need your help, Margeaux."

"Oh?" replied Margeaux.

"Yes. The Barnhill campus is a disaster."

No surprise there, thought Margeaux. Every week more Barnhill employees blasted Kerrigan State University's handling of the situation in social media and it was making its way into traditional news outlets too. Every week, Margeaux was more and more mad she wasn't involved in the shut-down of the Barnhill campus. Staying on top of the social media was part of her job responsibilities and she had been forced to ignore glaring indicators of crisis!

The VP continued, "I just don't get it. I tell the department heads at Barnhill what I know so they can tell their employees, but it seems they still aren't happy. I'm leading the leadership team that is overseeing this shut-down and that takes all my time. I don't have time for this other stuff—town hall meetings, a website ... whatever it is they're asking for!"

You mean what they were told they were going to get ... by you! Margeaux was glad she was able to keep her thoughts in her head. She continued to listen to the VP.

"They're also complaining because no one has been told who exactly is staying on for now and who is going to be let go. But we just don't know yet! And to make matters worse, there's a bunch of people jumping ship, but we need a lot of them to stay through the end or ... well, I don't know what we'll do! We have to have the needed services staffed! And if they quit, we'll never be able to hire qualified people for jobs that will be temporary."

The VP stopped for a second and took a deep breath. *That's the first time I've ever seen her slow down or look fatigued. This Barnhill situation is taking more of a toll on her than I anticipated. I hope she's learning a big lesson!*

The VP restarted her spiel, "Ultimately, it seems the president is not happy with what's going on over there and you know he's put me in charge. Apparently he's spoken to a few people and he heard everyone at Barnhill is distraught. The media is calling us for comments. Some politicians have mentioned their concerns to him in passing. And somehow there's now a rumor that our accreditors might scrutinize KSU more carefully when they come back to visit our main campus next year due to this debacle."

Ugh! Media inquiries. Politicians asking questions. And the accreditors too? This is really bad. I can't believe I am just being asked to help now! What a mess!

The VP kept going in her relentless style, "He—President Dolder—still calls them, the Barnhill campus, our family. He said from this point forward, he expected my first responsibility to be ensuring Barnhill receives exactly the same services and support we would give to any other campus in a time of internal crisis. And now he specifically said he wanted you to be involved."

Well at least President Dolder hasn't abandoned Barnhill, or his value of strong employee relations. This is going to be quite a task, but I'm up for the challenge!

"Ok, VP Hatcher. Let's get to work."

DISCUSSION QUESTIONS

1. If you were Margeaux, what would be your plan of action now that she's completed her interviews with members of the Barnhill campus?

2. In an internal crisis, what channels of communication within the organization do you think might be most effective? Why?

3. Given the distrust the faculty and staff now have of the university administration, what strategies can Margeaux use to try to repair their relationship and build the administration's credibility?

4. Until the bridges of trust are restored between the administration and the faculty and staff, what strategies might Margeaux consider in order to communicate with faculty and staff in a way that they will believe?

5. If Margeaux had been on board with the campus shut-down process from the beginning, what could she have done to help prevent the internal crisis situation?

KEY TERMS

Internal Crisis Communication, Reputation Management, Trust/Credibility Building, Opinion Leaders

CHAPTER 32

The Vicious Valentine

Carl Glover
Mount St. Mary's University

Alfred G. Mueller, II
Neumann University

ABSTRACT

Carol Sander, CEO of the Sentiments from the Heart greeting card company, needs to respond to a crisis situation involving a mix-up in Valentine's Day greeting cards that caused young children to receive cards with offensive messages. Although a subcontractor caused the problem, her company has received word that a lawsuit is being filed by a customer whose grandchild was affected by an offensive card. The company, which grew from a small business into the third-largest greeting card company in the United States, failed to develop a crisis communication plan. What strategies and messages should the company employ to address the crisis and restore its image?

In 1993, Carol Sander was a stay-at-home mom. Her husband Jim was co-owner of a popular restaurant in Gettysburg, Pennsylvania. Their two daughters, Briana and Faith, were typical overachieving "tween-agers," active in just about everything from school sports to community service clubs. Carol spent weekday mornings with her husband, afternoons with her wide circle of friends, and evenings chauffeuring the girls from event to event. Though she was constantly busy, she enjoyed the life that Jim's restaurant had made possible for them.

Tuesday, January 19, 1993, began as any other day for Carol. She made breakfast for her family, cleared up while the girls got dressed, and then drove them to school. As usual, she returned home to find Jim reading the newspaper in his favorite chair in the living room. His chair was positioned such that she could see him reading the paper from where she normally sat at the kitchen table. As was her custom, Carol engaged him in some light chatter as she sat at the table, clipping coupons from the Sunday circulars.

She had just finished telling Jim about a casual piece of gossip she had picked up from one of the other parents at Briana's piano recital the night before, when she was startled. It sounded as if Jim had thrown the newspaper down on the floor in disgust. She looked into the living room and could no longer see him sitting in his chair. As she got up to see what had happened, she caught a glimpse of his feet near the base of the chair.

Carol rushed into the living room to find Jim face down on the carpet at the foot of his chair, the newspaper still partially clutched in his left hand. She shook him frantically, crying his name repeatedly. But Jim did not respond.

She dialed 911. Fifteen minutes later, the EMT crew had arrived. They did everything they could to resuscitate him as they hurried him to the hospital. But it was too late. The attending physician at the emergency room told her it was a massive coronary. He was dead before he hit the floor. Jim was gone at the age of only 42.

The next few days were a whirlwind for Carol. Relatives flew in from all over the country for the funeral. Friends sent condolences. Neighbors delivered trays of food. She did her best to hold it all together for her daughters.

Jim had purchased plenty of life insurance, enough to pay off the house and their cars and still leave Carol with over $1 million to cover the girls' future college needs and to provide a healthy cushion for the family until Carol could develop a career for herself. She was fortunate in that sense. But she did not know how she would move forward in life without Jim.

Everything had begun to settle down by the beginning of March. Carol and the girls had begun to adopt new daily rituals. To keep herself busy while the girls were at school, Carol began making her own holiday and birthday cards to share with family and friends. She had noted how expensive cards were in the local card store and decided that it was much cheaper for her to do it on her own. After all, she had a BFA in art, and she had always had a gift for writing just the right thing in a card.

As Easter rolled by, friends and family alike complimented her on the cards she had made for them. Everyone thought the sentiments expressed in Carol's cards were superior to anything she could have bought from the local card store. And the fact that the cards were handmade gave them that special touch. By the end of the year, Carol's friends and family members had begun asking her to make cards for them to share with their friends and coworkers.

By the Christmas holidays the following year, Carol had built up a small following. As word of mouth spread about her cards, more and more people began to ask her to make cards for them. The best part, of course, was that they were willing to pay her for her time and effort.

By the end of 1995, Carol had built a healthy small business for herself. Word continued to spread about her cards, and she became a local phenomenon in Gettysburg. Because she was getting more orders than she could handle on her own, Carol had hired two women who were talented craftspeople like herself to help her create the physical cards. But Carol retained the responsibility for creating the greetings for each set of cards. She liked to compose the greetings straight from her heart. So the following year, when a friend advised her to hire an attorney and make her business official, she called her company Sentiments from the Heart.

As time went by, Carol's business expanded out of her house into a small storefront in downtown Gettysburg. She hired many more people to help her create and print the cards. Eventually, she opened a few stores in other nearby towns. She received numerous civic awards for her hard work and dedication and became an active member of the local Chamber of Commerce.

With the dawning of the new millennium, Carol hired someone to help her take her business online. Her company began mass-producing and selling cards throughout the country. By the end of the first decade of the twenty-first century, Sentiments from the Heart was the third most-popular greeting card company in the United States. Carol was CEO. Briana had pursued an MBA from the Wharton School of Business and was working with her mother as vice president. Faith had majored in communication studies and had gone to work for her mother as director of public relations.

On February 14, 2013, six-year-old Jasmine Roberts of Harrisburg, Pennsylvania, received a Valentine's Day card in the mail from her grandmother. It was one of the new line of recordable greeting cards to come from the Sentiments from the Heart company. When Jasmine opened the card, she saw her grandmother's handwriting and a big arrow pointing to a printed button on the inside back cover of the card. When she pressed the button, she heard her grandmother's voice lovingly say, "You are such a good little girl, Jasmine. I love you. Happy Valentine's Day from Grandma!"

Jasmine loved the card. She called her grandmother right away and thanked her for sending it. She then played the card for her mother and father, and took the card into her bedroom, where she proceeded to play it repeatedly for her stuffed animals. She had gone through nearly all of her stuffed animals, everyone except the frog she had received as a birthday present from her older sister Kelly. When she pushed the button on the card to play it for her frog, Hoppy, however, she heard something very different. It was a woman's voice, but it was not that of her grandmother. This voice shouted at her: "No, I was just kidding. I don't love you. You are an awful person and I don't ever want to see you again."

Jasmine began to cry. She threw the card down on the floor and ran screaming through the hallway to her mother and father, who were making dinner in the kitchen.

On the same day in Youngstown, Ohio, eight-year-old Ben Grasson received a Valentine's Day card from his mother. It, too, was one of the new line of recordable greeting cards to come from the Sentiments from the Heart company. When Ben opened the card in his mother's presence, he saw her handwriting and a big arrow pointing to a printed button on the inside back cover of the card. When he pressed the button, he heard his mother's voice lovingly say, "Ben, I want you to know how proud I am of you. I love you very much, and I hope you have a Happy Valentine's Day."

Ben set the card on his nightstand. Although he thought of himself as a big boy now, he still thought it was nice to hear his mother's voice tell him how proud she was of him. So he played it every day before he went to school. Ben enjoyed the ego boost. A little over a week after Valentine's Day, however, that all changed. Ben pushed the button on his card, as he had every day before school, but this time it was a different woman's voice. This voice shouted at him: "No, I was just kidding. I don't love you. You are an awful person and I don't ever want to see you again."

Ben was stunned. His mind raced through all the things he could have done to deserve that statement. Tears began to well up in his eyes as he walked out of his bedroom, and he went to his mother to apologize for whatever he had done wrong.

Carol had agreed to launch a new line of recordable message cards to compete with similar cards marketed by other companies. The card was manufactured to allow the purchaser to record a message in his or her own voice to a loved one. This year's Valentine's Day card was the first card from the Sentiments from the Heart company to use the recordable technology. The instructions for recording a sentiment were printed on the back outside cover of the card. The new Valentine's Day card had been tested for months with various focus groups to ensure that the instructions were clear and easy enough for virtually anyone to follow and to verify that the technology worked properly.

When they received the first few complaints near the end of the third week of February, Carol and Briana had dismissed the issue, thinking that an older sibling had recorded the audio over the old message. But a few complaints quickly turned into hundreds. Gathering all the information they could from each complaint, Carol and Briana deduced that, in each case, a child had played with the card normally for some time. Then, suddenly, without external tampering, an angry woman's voice replaced that of a loved one. The message was always the same: "No, I was just kidding. I don't love you. You are an awful person and I don't ever want to see you again."

The Sanders were at a complete loss to explain how something like this could happen. Finally, on March 8, an internal investigation revealed that the company that produced the recordable technology for the Sentiments from the Heart line of cards also produced recordable technology for cards that were meant to be sold in a national retail chain. Those cards were designed to play a joke on an adult listener. The purchaser of the card, typically a female, would record a loving message for the adult listener, typically a male. The card would play the recorded sentiment ten times without incident. On the eleventh playback, the recorded voice would be replaced by the voice of an angry woman who said demeaning things to the recipient. Apparently, some of the recording devices for that series of cards had accidentally made their way into a number of the Sentiments from the Heart line of Valentine's Day cards. The manufacturer believed that no more than five to seven percent of the Sentiments from the Heart line would have been affected.

The problem was that hundreds of children had been affected across the country. To make matters worse, within an hour of Carol's receiving the internal report, the attorney for the Sentiments from the Heart company received notice from an attorney representing Josephine Roberts, Jasmine's grandmother, that she intended to sue the Sentiments from the Heart company.

Carol decides that she wants to tackle the problem directly. She calls Faith into her office to plan an appropriate response.

DISCUSSION QUESTIONS

1. Should Sentiments from the Heart accept full responsibility for the scandalous cards, or should the company blame the subcontractor who created this problem?

2. What strategies should Sentiments from the Heart pursue to rebuild its public image and reputation? What key message should frame the company's response?

3. What approach should the company take in dealing with its own employees and other internal stakeholders? Should the information shared within the company be different from what is made public?

4. Sentiments from the Heart did not have a crisis management or crisis communication plan. How would such plans have helped the company respond to this crisis? What should the plans include?

KEY TERMS

Crisis Communication, Crisis Communication Plan, Reputation Management

CHAPTER 33

Canaries in a Coal Mine: Crisis Communication and the Coal Industry

LaKesha N. Anderson and Mary L. Kahl
Indiana State University

ABSTRACT

When a mining accident happens in rural Virginia, an industry newcomer gains valuable insight about the importance of public relations and crisis communication principles in managing crucial situations.

"Mr. Thomas, you have a call. It's Robert Kelly at Oakwood Mine. It's urgent." Something in Mr. Kelly's voice told Lydia that her boss, Jay Thomas, CEO of Seraphin Mining Company, would need her immediately. She sat at her desk nervously; waiting for the news she expected, but hoped would not be true.

"Lydia! Get Angela McKinnis here now. Fly her in on the company helicopter. Let her know there is an emergency and the helicopter will pick her up within the hour. There has been an explosion at Oakwood. Men are trapped in the mine."

No sooner had he said the words than the phone began ringing in the office.

"Mr. Thomas, a reporter from the *Buchanan Star* is on line one."

"Tell them we do not have a comment. When we do, we will let them know." Jay wondered how the media could possibly know about an explosion at his mine when he had found out only minutes earlier. He turned on the television as he listened to the phones ringing in his outer office. The local news media were already talking about the explosion, speculating about its cause, and guessing at the number of fatalities.

He sent an email to a potential overseas business partner. Their Skype meeting would need to be rescheduled.

"Mr. Thomas, Robert is here!" called Lydia.

At just past 1 pm, Robert Kelland strode into the office. The superintendent at Oakwood Mine, Robert arrived to brief his boss on the explosion at the underground site. Best estimates put the total number of trapped miners at 38, with little indication of where in the mine they might be trapped. No one had to explain the gravity of the situation. Mining accidents are not new to the industry and mining has always been dangerous. However, growing attention to regulatory noncompliance and an increase in the number of recent large mining disasters had shaken the public's confidence in an already misunderstood industry. It was imperative that the trapped miners be recovered safely.

"Families are gathering at the mine. Reporters, too. Media are setting up trucks. What should we do?" asked Robert.

"Wait. Angela will be here soon and we will discuss our next steps. We will need to address the press at some point; hopefully she will know best how to handle it. We should also probably get in touch with Daniel because I'm sure we will need legal counsel sooner rather than later. I'll have Lydia reach out to him and see if he can join us upon Angela's arrival."

ALL HANDS ON DECK

As Angela was flying out to meet with the CEO of Seraphin Mining Company she definitely had a number of mixed emotions. She was nervous, sad, and excited about the work she knew needed to be done as a result of the mine collapse. Angela had worked for Seraphin for just a year as the director of marketing. Her job duties also entailed public relations work, as the company did not employ a separate public relations director. She felt confident in her public relations skills, but was uncertain about her ability to effectively manage crisis communication of this magnitude. She had the pulse of the mine workers, but was not so certain about public perceptions of the mining industry. She had an overwhelming sense that her future at Seraphin would depend on how well she succeeded in minimizing immediate public concerns and offering reassurance in the coming hours or days.

Lydia ushered Angela into a darkened meeting room with company's CEO, the mine superintendent, and the coal firm's attorney. Angela and Daniel were briefed on the incident at the mine and ongoing recovery efforts. Lydia then returned to brief each of them on local media that had contacted the office throughout the day and provided a report on the early media response to the incident.

"Families members are on television upset, crying. People are saying they don't have information, that they have no word from us on rescue efforts. They're also questioning the company's safety record."

"Is the company's safety record an issue?" asked Angela.

After a brief silence, Daniel spoke, "The fact is, the Mine Safety and Health Administration has issued us over 300 safety citations at Oakwood in the past three years. Most are related to ventilation of methane gas. It will be something the media will question us about. However, there is no indication that this explosion was caused by anything the company did wrong. That needs to be understood."

"Is MSHA on site now?" asked Angela.

"Yes, they were on site within an hour of the explosion. They are continually measuring the methane levels inside the mine and have begun drilling gas release shafts. Hopefully, by the time the methane levels are low enough to enter the mine; crews will have devised a plan to get food and water into safe zones and will have determined the miners' general location. Right now, it isn't safe for anyone to go into the mine."

"Because of the methane levels?" Angela asked, clearly confused about what happens when gas builds up inside a mine.

"Yes, Angela," responded Robert. "When methane levels are high, even the smallest spark, similar to static electricity in your finger, will ignite a mine explosion. If we try to go inside now, we risk setting off another explosion or dying from exposure to toxic gases."

"Our goal now," said Jay, "is to reduce damage to our company while we work to get those men out of the mine. Explosions happen, that's just mining. We can replace miners, but we can't replace the company."

The four of them sat in silence for several minutes. Angela now realized how dire the situation was for the men trapped inside the mine. She was upset to learn that the company she worked for had put so many lives at risk and had so many safety violations. However, she also knew she had a job to do. She sighed.

"First things first. We need to address the media. Mr. Thomas, we should prepare for a press conference at the mine within the next hour."

QUESTIONS OF VALUE

As their car rounded the mountain and approached the entrance to the mine, Jay and Angela got their first look at the media circus surrounding the Oakwood site. At the entrance to the mine, hundreds of community members huddled together holding signs that read "Praying for our miners" and "God bless our miners." Just past the entrance, they saw a couple of miners covered in dirt who clearly had escaped the mine during the explosion. There were women and children milling about; some crying, a few speaking with reporters. Rescue vehicles lined the sides of the road and rescue crews moved through the crowds, some speaking with family members, others meeting together in small groups. There were several MSHA officials on site, speaking with both rescue teams and drill teams while also working to seal off the site for investigative purposes.

"They'll stay all night, won't they?" Angela queried.

"Yes, they'll be here all night. More of them will join the rescue effort. They'll stay until all the miners are accounted for." Angela shuddered at Jay's choice of words.

As their car pulled up to Oakwood's main office, Jay and Angela were met by Robert as well as company Vice President Shane Davidson, Board President Michael Donnelly, MSHA official Jeremy King, and the lead drilling technician, Carl Boyd. Immediately, news reporters made their way toward the small group, asking questions about recovery efforts, and probing for information on the numbers of fatalities involved in the explosion. The seven individuals moved quickly into the mine offices to prepare for the upcoming press conference.

"Let's hear the latest," said Jay.

Robert gave Jay an update, just as he had done each hour since the accident occurred. "We still estimate that 30 men are trapped inside the mine. They've been in there for nearly six hours now. In the past hour, the hospital confirmed one more death, so we have a total of six deaths now, from among the eight men we have freed." Robert nodded to Carl. "I think Carl can speak to how drilling efforts are going."

Carl passed each person a map of the area. The map had five clear "X" spots marked. "These spots indicate where we are drilling into the mine to release trapped methane. We anticipate, barring any obstructions, that this process should be finished in the next six to eight hours, as we think it should take about 12–14 hours to drill down. Rescue crews are ready to send in 4-to-5-person teams for recovery missions once we release the gas and we can enter the mine. Hopefully we can send crews in sometime in the early morning hours, maybe 2 or 3 am."

"How will you handle the partial collapse? Will the miners survive that long? Will the gas poison them?" asked Angela.

"It's very possible that they have been poisoned. We have to work quickly if we're going to find them alive," replied Carl matter-of-factly. "Unless you have questions for me right now, I need to get back to the site." Jay nodded to Carl and he left.

"Jay, you have a mess on your hands," said Jeremy. "We have a huge investigation to complete, a number of citations and fines on this mine alone, six dead men, and a bunch more that may not come out alive. My goal is to see that this investigation goes smoothly and that this company complies with this investigation, unlike the way it complied with orders to get this mine properly ventilated. Get prepared for this press conference. Then get ready to move forward with this investigation."

"We're clear, Jeremy," said Michael. "Jay, Governor Crawford is meeting with rescue officials outside. He'll be inside in a moment for the press conference and will introduce you. The president has already made comments about the incident on national television. We've arranged to hold a meeting with family members after the press conference. There, we'll update families on recovery efforts. Right now, the next of kin are on television saying they've gotten no information. We need to inform them individually, and we need to get this press conference underway. I'll make sure we get Governor Crawford here on time. See you soon."

Why is the Governor here? Angela wondered to herself. Once again she questioned how she could uphold her values while supporting those of her company, which appeared to put profit before safety. *No time for questioning,* she thought, *you have work to do.*

"Your prepared remarks, Mr. Thomas, with some light editing given the information provided just now," said Angela, handing Jay the short speech they had worked the past 45 minutes to create. "We should get to the media room."

"You're right. We have work to do. The quicker we get this press conference over, the better it will be for us."

"For everyone," replied Angela.

A makeshift media room had been arranged in a conference room at Oakwood's company offices. At 7 pm, Seraphin's Oakwood management team, accompanied by Angela, select board members, Governor Crawford, and MSHA officials, convened to meet with reporters for the first official press conference since the mine explosion had occurred nearly seven hours earlier. By this time, several members of the local and regional media were in attendance as well as reporters from national news stations.

Governor Crawford was mindful to pay his respects to the families of the miners affected by the tragedy at the Oakwood Mine. He also noted that he was confident that Seraphin Mining Company would work with the appropriate officials to determine what caused the explosion. He then introduced Jay, whom he described as a capable CEO with the utmost concern for his miners.

Jay stepped to the podium to address the crowd. He spoke swiftly and with purpose.

> *My thanks to each of you for being here. It is under unfortunate circumstances that we gather. As you know, the Oakwood Mine, operated by Seraphin Mining Company, suffered a series of explosions and a partial mine collapse earlier today. These explosions occurred during a shift change, so while many miners were in the mine, many were also able to escape because they had yet to venture deep into the mine. We have confirmed six deaths, two injured survivors, and we know that at least 30 miners are currently trapped in the mine. At this time, five shafts are being drilled into the mine to release gasses that have accumulated since the explosion. Rescue efforts can begin once drilling is complete. At this time we do not understand what caused the explosion. However, speculation can only lead to misinformation and, given the current regulatory environment, increased speculation about the dangers of underground mining is not what the industry needs. This is a community that depends on mining and the risks associated with coal mining have been known to the residents of this community for generations. Seraphin Mining Company takes safety seriously and will work with officials to determine what caused this explosion and how to help families through this situation. Our thoughts are with the families of the miners lost in this tragic accident, as well as with the families who await word that their husbands and wives, fathers and mothers, brothers and sisters, daughters and sons, grandparents and friends have been found. We will not be taking questions. Thank you.*

As cameras flashed and tapes rolled, Jay left the room. Once back in the office where they had met previously, Jay and Angela were briefed on the planned meeting with family members. Angela pulled back a curtain in the second-floor office window and looked out over the large crowd that had gathered outside the company offices and around the mine. Rescue trucks and safety crews were everywhere. She noticed that a group of protesters had collected, too. *These are not environmentalists though,* she thought.

"Jay Thomas kills coal miners," read several signs. "Canaries in a Coal Mine," read a couple of others. Other signs quoted Oakwood's abysmal safety violation figures. Angela realized that the crisis was much larger than merely informing the public about what had happened at Oakwood earlier that day. The public was outraged. The public thought her boss was a murderer.

"Mr. Thomas," Angela spoke softly, "I'll handle the family meeting. I think it would be better if you meet with the mine foremen and MSHA investigators. Spend more time on the ground so you're better prepared for tomorrow's technical briefing to reporters."

A LATE CRISIS SPEECH

Angela headed for her meeting with concerned family members accompanied by Michael, Shane, and two local rescue crew chiefs. The men were familiar with recovery efforts and could provide information to families about loved ones who had been identified and transported to hospitals and morgues. They made their way to meet with a group of over 100 family members at nearly 10 pm, over nine hours after the blast.

The room was in chaos. Family members were crying, children were screaming, people were yelling and talking so fast and from so many directions that Angela could not determine who was speaking. She had no control of the room. After a moment, Shane rapped his hand loudly against a desk, calling attention to the front of the room.

"Please, we understand that you have questions," started Angela, "but we cannot answer them if we cannot hear you and you cannot hear us. Let us provide you with the information we have. Let me introduce you to Captains John Sewell and Joe Brach of the Buchanan Fire and Rescue Departments. They can provide you first with information on missing loved ones."

"Why bother? We got the information on the news today. We know who died, no thanks to you. We didn't hear anything from you," snarled a woman in the back of the room.

"We know who is missing. We know who died. We want to know how you're going to get them out. I want to know how you're going to get my son, and his daughter, and her brother out of there. Alive," stated a man on the side of the room gesturing to various people in the audience as he spoke.

Shane explained to the crowd that drilling crews were working to create five gas release shafts and that it was hoped that rescue crews would be able to begin their missions in five to six hours. John and Joe nodded in agreement, with John stating that they would also be delivering food and water supplies to safe zones inside the mine in case men were able to get to those zones.

"That's fine but what happens if you don't get to them? You get a fine? And it's back to business as usual? You've had 358 violations in three years, most of them related to high methane levels and poor ventilation, at this mine alone. You don't care if these men come out alive. You didn't care if they died when they went in. You care about turning a profit."

The audience became loud as they verbalized support for the speaker's statement. Angela was at a loss about what to do or say. Finally, an older citizen stood and the room became quieter.

The older man said, "I understand what you're doing here. I appreciate it. But, in a small town like this, 30 people missing and six dead is a lot of miners. That's a lot of kids without fathers and mothers, a lot of missing husbands and wives, a lot of food not on the table. This didn't happen overnight. Safety has always been an issue at Oakwood, and it's never been addressed properly. When I was a miner, it was always dangerous here. I'm thankful I didn't die in there myself. People want answers. We understand mining, so don't talk to us like we don't. It's what we've done for hundreds of years and we know it better than you do. You sell it, but we mine it. So, to come in here tonight is a little too late to make a difference."

Angela sat down in one of the chairs at the side of the room. She was conflicted; her values simply did not seem to align with Jay's values. Moreover, even with her limited public relations background, she knew crisis management should be proactive rather than reactive. Angela recalled learning about crisis rhetoric in college, but almost none of the communication that had occurred that day seemed to match what she thought she knew. She quickly reviewed what should have been said, as she jotted a few notes to herself on a piece of scrap paper. She wrote: *(1) Demonstrate understanding of the situation. (2) Establish trust with the audience. (3) Reassure the audience that the threat is being addressed capably. (4) Enumerate the steps being taken to resolve the crisis. (5) Acknowledge and calm public fear. (6) Reiterate control of the situation. (7) Call for audience support and unity in the face of the crisis.*

Angela knew that she needed to speak: the time to take control of the crisis situation was upon her. Someone would have to talk to the press again very soon, but for now she would begin by addressing the families of the miners. She stood, walked to the front of room, took a deep breath, and began in the strongest voice she could muster:

> *We are very sorry to be meeting with you under these difficult circumstances. But please bear with us as we explain what we know about this situation, how it developed, and what we are doing to fix it as fast as possible. I'm from a mining family myself, so I understand a bit about what you are going through: no mere words can adequately address your fears for your loved ones and your desire to have this crisis come to an end. I share these feelings with you and I want to assure you that the lives of your family members are of the greatest possible concern to us, the greatest possible concern to me.*

> *As you know, there was an explosion at the Oakwood Mine about 12:45 this afternoon, during a shift change. The explosion may have been caused by a build-up of methane gas, which, in turn, may have caused a partial collapse of the mine. We know this from the accounts of those miners who made it out of the mine successfully. We currently believe that 30 miners remain inside the mine, while eight miners have been accounted for. Unfortunately six of those eight who made it out have died. The families of the deceased have already been notified.*

> *We are taking all the available steps to remedy the methane build up within the mine and have called in the best rescue teams available to help us get this situation under control. Emergency health workers are also on the scene to offer immediate aid to the survivors.*

> *MSHA representatives are here, as well. Right now, five shafts are being drilled into the mine to release gasses that have accumulated since the explosion. Rescue efforts can begin once drilling is complete. We are reasonably sure that we can reach all of the miners within the next*

several hours, even though we do not yet know the precise cause of the original explosion. These next few hours will likely be very difficult for you, but I urge you to stay calm and to support each other with caring and compassion. I see members of the clergy here and I call upon them to offer you comfort as we await word from the mine.

Please believe me when I tell you that everything, everything that can be done to secure the safe rescue of your family members is being done. We have everything we need by way of manpower and equipment to get these gals and guys out and to treat their medical conditions promptly. Please stay strong and unite with me to pray for the safe return of these brave souls. I will speak with you again when I have more information to share with you. Thank you.

After she finished speaking with the miners' families, Angela found Jay and suggested that he follow her crisis management notes to construct some further remarks for the media. He argued with her, suggesting that her ideas about crisis speaking would not help him to resolve the problem at the mine. He said that talking again with reporters was the last thing he wanted to do because he did not intend to assume any blame for the mine explosion. Too tired to argue, Angela consoled herself with the thought that she had done what she could to respond to the crisis in an ethical and humane manner. She had used standard crisis speaking techniques to reach out to the miners' families and friends. In the end, this was perhaps more important than salvaging the coal company's image. As she fell asleep in her hotel room, she prayed for the trapped men and she resolved to educate her superiors about ethical and effective crisis communication.

Angela had asked the hotel staff to telephone her room when the morning newspapers arrived. When she got the call, she rushed downstairs to grab them and made her way to the conference room. As she spread them out by type—local, regional, national—she was shocked to see the press coverage.

"Virginia's Most Heavily Cited Mine Explodes"

"Methane Warnings Ignored Before Virginia Mine Blast"

"Production More Important than Safety at Oakwood"

"Men Trapped in Partial Collapse from Methane Blast at Troubled Mine"

"Mine Spokeswoman Urges Families to Stay Strong, Calm"

Remembering the previous day's communication, Angela thought: words *do* matter.

DISCUSSION QUESTIONS

1. What is the difference between a problem and a crisis? Does Seraphin Mining Company have a problem or a crisis to manage? Explain your answer.

2. Why are values important to the public relations process? Whose values should a practitioner follow?

3. Was the press conference an effective means for releasing information to the public? Explain your answer.

4. Was the statement to the miners' families an effective step toward crisis management? Explain your answer.

5. What key elements of crisis rhetoric should have been employed earlier by Seraphin officials?

KEY TERMS

Crisis Communication Plans, Man-made Disasters, External Crisis Communication, Reputation Management, Elements of Crisis Rhetoric

Author Biographies

Alisa Agozzino (Ph.D., Bowling Green State University) is an assistant professor of public relations at Ohio Northern University. Dr. Agozzino teaches a variety of classes, including Introduction to Public Relations, Public Relations Writing, Principles of Social Media, Public Relations Research, and Public Relations Campaigns. Dr. Agozzino's main research interest lies in social media tools within the public relations field. Her current research agenda examines how social media impacts different industries. From non-profits, to admissions offices, to public relations professionals, Dr. Agozzino is exploring how those using social media tools are doing so to reach their target audiences in order to build and maintain mutually beneficial relationships. Professionally, she is involved in and serves on a variety of different regional and national associations. In addition to her role as ONU's Public Relations Student Society of America adviser, she serves as the co-chair of the Central Ohio PRSA public relations committee and the editor-in-chief for the national PRSA Educator's Academy newsletter.

Jerry L. Allen (Ph.D., Southern Illinois University-Carbondale), professor of Communication at the University of New Haven, has presented more than 200 competitively selected papers at regional, national, and international conferences, and published four books and more than three dozen articles and book chapters on communication. He has been the editor of the *Journal of Intercultural Communication Research*, *Communication Quarterly*, and *Communication Research Reports*, and serves on several editorial boards. Dr. Allen served as president of the Eastern Communication Association, and has been recognized by regional, national, and international associations for contributions to teaching and research. Dr. Allen has served as a consultant on communication to several corporations, political candidates, and non-profit organizations.

Amber Alsop is currently pursuing her master's degree in communications at Edinboro University and will graduate in August 2013. She has an extensive background in marketing, member engagement, professional development, and is obtaining her certification in conflict management. As someone who has volunteered with the Mothers Against Drunk Driving organization, Amber wanted to create a scenario that tied in with the organization itself. She has also presented at university conferences based around leadership, member engagement, and recruitment. Not only has she presented at universities, but she has also presented on panels through the International Listening Association and serves as a reviewer for the National Communication Association. On the side, Amber is a marketing and business development specialist for a credit union, pageant coach, ShockWave fitness instructor, volunteer volleyball coach, and has been a cheerleading coach for five years.

LaKesha N. Anderson, (Ph.D., George Mason University), is an assistant professor of communication at Indiana State University. She teaches courses in health communication, advanced research methods, and public relations, and also serves as the faculty advisor for the Indiana

State University chapter of the Public Relations Student Society of America. Her research spans the areas of health, crisis, and risk communication and utilizes both qualitative and quantitative approaches. Dr. Anderson's articles have focused on social support and postpartum depression, risk and medication recall, and organizational crisis management, and can be found in journals such as *Health, Risk and Society* and *Journal of Community Psychology*, and in various edited volumes. Her research has been presented at numerous international, national, regional, and discipline-specific conferences.

Shannon M. Brogan (Ph.D., Ohio University) is an associate professor of speech communication at Kentucky State University. She has published in *Human Communication*, *Communication Research Reports*, and the *Journal of Family Communication*. Dr. Brogan has also written organizational case studies in *Casing Organizational Communication: Applying Theory and Research to the Modern Organization*. Her research topics include family, work, and balance, consumer education, and standardized testing.

Erin C. Bryan (M.A., University of Delaware; M.B.A., West Virginia Wesleyan College) is a learning and development facilitator at the University of South Florida, where she is also a doctoral student in the Adult, Career, and Higher Education Department in USF's College of Education. Prior to USF, she served as a visiting instructor and then assistant professor of communication at West Virginia Wesleyan College. Her interests include instructional communication, pedagogy, faculty development, and organizational communication.

Maria Butauski is pursuing her master's degree in Communication at Kent State University. She graduated from Xavier University in May 2013 with majors in public relations and organizational communication. Maria has interned with several organizations, including Hamilton County Environmental Services, LifePoint Solutions, and Hyde Park Country Club, to name a few.

Elizabeth Barfoot Christian (Ph.D., The University of Southern Mississippi) is an assistant professor at the University of New Haven where she heads the public relations and journalism course sequence. She is the editor of the award-winning *Rock Brands: Selling Sound in a Media Saturated Culture* (Lexington, 2011) and the author of a companion yearlong nationally awarded blog on music marketing published by Rowman & Littlefield. Prior to academia, Christian worked in both the public relations and journalism industries for many years. Her professional research includes work in prison communication, popular culture, and communication history. She hosts a weekly radio program on WNHU 88.7. She has published scholarly works in *Music in American Life: An Encyclopedia of Songs, Styles, Stars and Stories that Shaped our Culture* (2013, ABC-CLIO Publishing), *Encyclopedia of Social Networks* (SAGE Publications, 2011), and *The International Journal of Regional and Local Studies*, 2008. She serves on committees for the Eastern Communication Association and American Journalism Historians Association and previously served as vice-president of Louisiana Press Women.

Allison P. Cleary is a master's degree student and teaching assistant in the Department of Communication Studies at Texas Tech University. She earned a B.A. in communication studies, history, and secondary education at Texas Tech University in 2012. Her current research involves service learning and social justice in the Rio Grande Valley, Texas.

Hazel James Cole (Ph.D., The University of Southern Mississippi) is an award-winning communications professional and cultural critical scholar, with 18 years' experience in corporate public relations, crisis communication, and the academy. At the University of West Georgia, she teaches public relations courses, serves as co-faculty adviser of the Public Relations Student Society of America, and was elected to serve on the University Honors Committee. Professor Cole has held numerous leadership positions and currently serves on the board of the Mississippi Innocence Project at the University of Mississippi's School of Law, founded by attorney and author John Grisham. Her academic research interests include: crisis and corporate image repair, media criticism, diversity, and cultural studies. She has presented research at national conferences and has published scholarly works in *Race and News: Critical Perspectives* (2012, Routledge), and *Rock Brands: Selling Sounds in a Media Saturated Culture* (2011, Lexington).

Patricia Fairfield-Artman (Ph.D., University of North Carolina at Greensboro) is a senior lecturer in the Department of Communication Studies at the University of North Carolina at Greensboro. Dr. Fairfield-Artman teaches courses that offer an introduction to public relations, crisis communication, persuasion and social influence, public relations case studies, and organizational issues. Her work has appeared in *Media Literacy: A Reader*. Dr. Fairfield-Artman currently serves on the board of directors of the Tarheel Public Relations Society of America. Prior to teaching in higher education, Dr. Fairfield-Artman spent twenty years in management positions with a focus on public relations in corporate and non-profit organizations in North Carolina and Washington, DC.

Katherine R. Fleck (L.P.D., Northeastern University) joined Ohio Northern University in 2011 and serves as a visiting assistant professor. Prior to joining ONU, Fleck spent more than 25 years in professional practice in government, politics, non-profit, and private sector management. Fleck's research interests include the application of framing and agenda-setting theories to the practice of public relations, political public relations, public relations pedagogy, and crisis public relations. Fleck teaches a variety of special topic courses, from Non-profit Public Relations to Crisis Public Relations, as well as foundational classes such as Introduction to Public Relations, Advanced Public Relations Writing and Public Relations Case Studies.

Arhlene A. Flowers (M.A., The New School) is an associate professor of integrated marketing communications in the Department of Strategic Communication at the Roy H. Park School of Communications, Ithaca College, New York. Prior to joining Ithaca College in 2006, she held senior management positions at public relations agencies headquartered in New York City and also headed public relations worldwide for a publicly held company in Toronto. She represented a wide range of public and private companies, government agencies, and non-profits on all continents except for Antarctica. Her research in communications and public relations has been published in a variety of peer-reviewed academic publications. She also has presented papers at regional, national, and international communication conferences in the United States, Europe, and Asia. Born in Hawaii, she holds a Bachelor of Arts from New York University and a Master of Professional Studies from the New School for Social Research in New York City.

Erin E. Gilles (Ph.D., University of Kentucky, 2009) is an assistant professor of journalism at Kentucky State University. Her research areas examine entertainment media, health communication, and advertising through a critical theory lens. She has previously published chapters in a volume on corporate communication and case studies in the textbook *Casing Organizational Communication*. Dr. Gilles currently teaches undergraduate courses in journalism, news editing, public relations campaigns, event planning, and digital photography.

Carl W. Glover (Ph.D., University of Louisville) is Acting Chair of the Communications Studies at Mount St. Mary's university in Emmitsburg, Maryland, where he teaches courses in public relations, argumentation, rhetorical history and theory, and public speaking. He also directs the university's writing center. His published works include a range of research interests ranging from classical rhetoric to modern writing center practice. Since 1997, he has served as an AP English Language and Composition reader/table leader for the Educational Testing Service. He recently coauthored a book, *Analysis, Argument, and Synthesis*, which is designed as a college-level composition course for high school students. When he is not toiling at his academic day job, he works as the lead singer for the Fire City Jazz Band.

Luis Felipe Gómez (Ph.D., University of Texas) is an assistant professor in the Department of Communication Studies at San José State University. Dr. Gómez studies organizational learning and development through the social construction of time. He is developing the concept of temporal leadership, which involves promoting a future orientation through temporal framing and other organizational communication interventions. In his teaching, he strives to help students develop their critical thinking skills and relate the concepts and skills they are learning to their work and personal lives. Dr. Gómez has taught organizational communication, intercultural communication, and quantitative inquiry at both the graduate and undergraduate levels. He earned his Ph.D. in organizational communication from the University of Texas at Austin, his M.B.A. in international finance and marketing from Katholieke Universiteit, Leuven, Belgium, and his B.A. in business administration from ITESM Campus San Luis, San Luis Potosí, México.

Lisa K. Hanasono (Ph.D., Purdue University) is an assistant professor in the Department of Communication at Bowling Green State University. Her research interests focus on prejudice, discrimination, coping, and Asian American identities. She is also interested in communication pedagogy. She has published in journals such as *Human Communication Research*,

Communication Teacher, Communication Quarterly, Sex Roles, Communication Research Reports, the *Journal of College and Student Development,* and *Communication Research.* In addition to conducting research, Lisa loves to teach! She has taught a variety of college courses, including relational communication, persuasion, communication theory, interviewing, presentation speaking, interpersonal communication, Asian American studies, and health communication.

Dotty Heady (Ed.D., Spalding University) is a full-time instructor for Strayer University. She received her Doctorate of Education in Leadership from Spalding University and dual masters in marketing and management from Webster University. She ran an in-house marketing agency for a multi-location company for five years, and had her own food safety and security consulting business for 14 years where she travelled in Europe and worked with 40 companies in six countries teaching leadership and food safety. Dr. Heady was the Vice President of Client Services and Development at The Learning House and then became a consultant and educational designer/writer where she wrote marketing and business courses for 67 different colleges and universities. She is currently a creative writer for Pearson Publishing Company and Senior Editor for Splendid Publications.

Pauline A. Howes (Ph.D., University of Georgia) is an assistant professor of communication at Kennesaw State University in Kennesaw, Georgia, where she teaches public relations courses in the Department of Communication. Dr. Howes earned her Ph.D. in mass communication from the University of Georgia, M.B.A. from Emory University, and bachelor's degree in journalism from the University of North Carolina at Chapel Hill. She has more than 20 years of experience working in corporate public relations.

Julian Jeter-Davis is a senior mass communications and journalism major concentrating in public relations at Kentucky State University. In addition, he is pursuing a minor in speech communication.

Sarah Jolly is a 2013 graduate of Xavier University in Cincinnati, Ohio. She graduated cum laude in the University Scholars honor's program, and earned her Bachelor of Arts degree with a dual major in organizational communication and communication studies and a dual minor in business and Spanish. Her thesis focused on organizational culture as an antecedent to job satisfaction.

Mary L. Kahl (Ph.D., Indiana University) is professor and chair of communication at Indiana State University. She is co-author of *Advanced Public Speaking: A Leader's Guide* and has written several chapters in other communication textbooks. She has published research essays in the areas of political communication, gender and communication, health communication, and rhetorical theory/criticism. A former president of the Eastern Communication Association, she has chaired the Public Address Division of the National Communication Association and has been selected as the recipient of the Distinguished Scholar/Mentor Award by the

Organization for the Study of Communication, Language, and Gender. She was also named as a Distinguished Teaching Fellow, as a member of the Committee of Scholars, and as the recipient of the Distinguished Service Award by the ECA. She serves on editorial boards of international, national, and regional communication journals, including *The Quarterly Journal of Speech*, the *Journal of Intercultural Communication*, and *Communication Quarterly*.

William J. Kinsella (Ph.D., Rutgers University) is an Associate Professor of Communication at North Carolina State University, where he directs the interdisciplinary program in science, technology and society. He earned a B.S. degree in physics from Manhattan College and master's and Ph.D. degrees in communication and information studies from Rutgers University. His research and teaching interests span the interrelated fields of environmental communication, organizational communication, and science and technology communication, with a particular focus on issues surrounding nuclear energy. He has been a Fulbright Scholar at the Institute for Nuclear Energy and Energy Systems at the University of Stuttgart and has published numerous journal articles and book chapters in the area of nuclear energy communication. He is a co-editor of and contributor to *Nuclear Legacies: Communication, Controversy, and the US Nuclear Weapons Complex* (Lexington, 2007).

Anastacia Kuyrlo (Ph.D., Rutgers University) is assistant professor of communication arts at Marymount Manhattan College in New York City. In her twelve years of teaching she has taught at numerous colleges, including Borough of Manhattan Community College, Marymount Manhattan College, New York University, Pace University, Rutgers University, and St. John's University. Her research interests include the examination of stereotypes communicated in interpersonal, intercultural, and organizational contexts and the implications of these for stereotype maintenance. She also studies pedagogy and mentorship as well as emotion and culture. She has published five teaching activities, four book chapters, and her work on stereotypes appears in *Qualitative Research in Psychology*. She is a former president of the New Jersey Communication Association and serves as a reviewer or editorial board member for several journals.

Corey Jay Liberman (Ph.D., Rutgers University) is an assistant professor in the Department of Communication Arts at Marymount Manhattan College. His research focuses on the links among social networks, attitudes, and behaviors, and he has recently begun to study the communication of upward dissent within organizations. He is coauthor of *Organizational Communication: Strategies for Success* (2nd Ed.) and he has had his scholarship, dealing with social networks, health communication, communication centers, organizational culture/climate, and social branding, published in both book chapters and conference proceedings. He also has a forthcoming article in *Communication Research Reports*, focusing on methodological concerns of social network scholars. He has a forthcoming sabbatical to conduct research dealing with the communicative practices of incarcerated women in a maximum security prison.

Lacy G. McNamee (Ph.D., University of Texas at Austin) is an assistant professor of organizational communication in the Department of Communication Studies at Baylor University.

Dr. McNamee's research focuses on communication and the negotiation of tensions among members and stakeholders in non-profit and faith-based organizations. This case was informed by the author's ongoing research, board service, and volunteer experiences with several non-profit organizations. The author would like to thank the editors for their constructive feedback in preparing this chapter for inclusion in this volume.

Alfred G. Mueller, II (Ph.D., University of Iowa) is dean of the Division of Arts and Sciences at Neumann University in Aston, Pennsylvania. A professor with twenty years of experience in the college classroom, Dr. Mueller is the 2013 recipient of the Eastern Communication Association's Donald Ecroyd and Caroline Drummond-Ecroyd Teaching Excellence Award. He has served as a Fulbright Scholar in the Republic of Armenia in 2005, executive director of the Eastern Communication Association from 2008 to 2010, and as president of the Association for Communication Administrators from 2013 to 2014. He is the author of the forthcoming book *Readings in the History of Rhetoric*, also by Kendall Hunt. The case study contained in this volume was written with Dr. Carl Glover while Dr. Mueller was serving as chair of the Department of Communication Studies at Mount St. Mary's University in Emmitsburg, Maryland.

Leah M. Omilion-Hodges (Ph.D., Wayne State University) is a faculty member in the School of Communication at Western Michigan University where she teaches courses in public relations, social influence/persuasion, and leadership. Her research interests lie in communication in applied organizational settings.

Narissra M. Punyanunt-Carter (Ph.D., Kent State University) is an associate professor of communication studies at Texas Tech University in Lubbock, Texas. She teaches the basic interpersonal communication course. Her research areas include mass media effects, father-daughter communication, mentoring, advisor-advisee relationships, family studies, religious communication, humor, and interpersonal communication. She has published over 40 articles that have appeared in several peer-reviewed journals, such as *Communication Research Reports*, *Southern Journal of Communication*, and *Journal of Intercultural Communication Research*. She has also published numerous instructional ancillaries and materials. She is currently coauthoring a book on interpersonal communication and organizational communication with Flat World Knowledge.

Tyler Raible graduated from Xavier University's Scholar program in 2013 with a degree in public relations and communication studies. He is currently working toward his M.A. in communication with a focus on interpersonal communication at the University of Cincinnati. His research revolves around impression management with an emphasis on tattoos in communication.

Kyle F. Reinson (M.A., Florida Atlantic University) is an assistant professor in the Communication and Journalism Department at St. John Fischer College.

Julio A. Rodriguez-Rentas (M.A., Pace University—Westchester) serves as university course-ware designer under the purview of the Office of the Provost for all of Pace University's cam-puses in New York. His background is in the web communications field, in which he has nearly a decade of experience. Mr. Rodriguez has extensive experience in training faculty on online teaching and instructional technologies. He has also worked on staff and/or as a con-sultant to a variety of institutions such as non-profit community organizations, a NGO bank corporation, an ad agency, a regional multi-cultural dance company, as well as a law school and a private national university. Mr. Rodriguez has presented at a number of conferences on research topics and publications that he has written. He holds a B.B.A. in Information Sys-tems from Pace University—New York City, as well as a MA in Media Communication from Pace University—Westchester.

Francesca Rogo graduated in 2013 from SUNY New Paltz with a degree in journalism con-centrating in public relations. She has previously presented this research at the 2013 Eastern Communication Association's Undergraduate Scholar's Conference.

Austin Schatz is an undergraduate in organizational communication at SUNY New Paltz. He has previously presented his research at the 2013 Eastern Communication Association's Undergraduate Scholar's Conference.

Juliann Scholl (Ph.D., University of Oklahoma) is an associate professor of communication studies at Texas Tech University. Her research emphasizes health and crisis communication. Recent projects include the effects of humor in patient-provider interactions, crisis commu-nication within local communities, and patient- and family-centered care within palliative care. Dr. Scholl has published in such journals as *Health Communication, Journal of Applied Communication Research, Communication Quarterly, Communication Research Reports, Public Relations Review, International Electronic Journal of Health Education, Qualitative Health Research*, and *American Journal of Distance Education*. She serves on the editorial board of *Communication Research Reports* and is on the American Communication Associa-tion's board of directors. In addition to her research endeavors, Dr. Scholl teaches courses in communication, particularly health communication and small group, leadership, and orga-nizational communication.

Roy Schwartzman (Ph.D., University of Iowa) is Professor of Communication Studies, Lloyd International Honors College Fellow, and Faculty Affiliate with the Joint School for Nanosci-ence and Nanoengineering at the University of North Carolina at Greensboro. He is also a Shoah Foundation Institute Teaching Fellow and held a Holocaust Educational Foundation Fellowship. He is the author of more than 350 published poems, many scholarly articles and chapters, and the basic communication course textbook *Fundamentals of Oral Communi-cation* (Kendall Hunt). His research has won several honors, including the National Com-munication Association Outstanding Dissertation Award and the National Association of Communication Centers Joyce Ferguson Award.

Diana L. Tucker (Ph.D., Southern Illinois University Carbondale) is an academic coordinator and full-time faculty member in the College of Undergraduate Studies at Walden University. Dr. Tucker coordinates all the general education communication courses and supervises the 20 faculty who teach these courses. Her teaching specialization is in public relations and organizational communication with an emphasis in how sports organizations engage in either practice. However, she presently teaches a wide variety of general education communication courses. Research interests include gender and sport rhetorical criticism as well as critical communication pedagogical practices as well as public speaking theory and pedagogy.

Brett S. Vergara is a junior majoring in communication/journalism at St. John Fisher College who is also pursuing two minors, in digital cultures and technologies and visual and performing arts.

Thomas Wagner (Ph.D., Kent State University) is an associate professor in the Department of Communication Arts at Xavier University in Cincinnati, Ohio. Dr. Wagner teaches courses in interpersonal communication, organizational communication, persuasion, and research methods. His research interests include attitudes in communication and student veterans' communication. He holds a passion for advancing the understanding and practice of effective communication and is dedicated to helping students succeed.

Kristin Roeschenthaler Wolfe (Ph.D., Duquesne University) received her doctorate in rhetoric from Duquesne University. Previously, she worked for thirteen years in corporate communications and for various integrated marketing and dot com companies in the Pittsburgh and surrounding areas.

"Iris" Shuang Xia is a graduate student and teaching assistant in the Department of Communication Studies at Texas Tech University. Iris earned her bachelor's degree in administrative management from Hainan University, China. She currently teaches both business and professional communication and public speaking at Texas Tech. As a "Raiders Who Rock," she strives for the best of her students. Iris is also a council representative of the Graduate Student Advisory Council. She is active in department and university activities, as well as in the Chinese Students Association. Her research interests focus on interpersonal communication, especially on deception and relationship maintenance strategies for couples.

Cory L. Young (Ph.D., Bowling Green State University) is an associate professor of communication management and design in the Department of Strategic Communication at the Roy H. Park School of Communications, Ithaca College, New York. She is also the chair of the graduate program in communications. Her research expertise is in the area of crisis communication, public relations, and social media. She has been published in a wide range of peer-reviewed and trade publications, and has presented research papers at regional, national, and international conferences.

Paul Ziek (Ph.D., Rutgers University) is an assistant professor in the Department of Media, Communications, and Visual Arts at Pace University. His primary research interest is how the communication-information-media matrix shapes interaction and communication. Paul holds a B.A. from Rutgers, an M.A. from New York University, and a Ph.D. from Rutgers.

Appendix A

CASE STUDY WORKSHEET

Argument for including these criteria:

How you will measure?

Decision Criteria Ranking: Rate your decision criteria on a scale from 1 (not overly important) to 10 (very important).

Criterion 1:	Not Overly Important	1	2	3	4	5	6	7	8	9	10	Very Important
Criterion 2:	Not Overly Important	1	2	3	4	5	6	7	8	9	10	Very Important
Criterion 3:	Not Overly Important	1	2	3	4	5	6	7	8	9	10	Very Important

Now rank your criteria in the order of their importance, from 1 (most important) to 3 (least important).

1) Most Important Criteria:

2) Middle Important Criteria:

3) Least Important Criteria:

Justification: Please provide a justification for how you ranked the criteria in this section.

Decision Alternatives

Decision Alternatives: List a minimum of three possible alternatives the main character in the case should consider. Decision alternatives should be clear and concise.

Remember, all alternatives should be realistic and implementable given the confines of the case.

Alternative One:

Alternative Two:

Alternative Three:

Decision Alternative Analysis

Recommended Alternative: State the decision you are recommending and summarize the reasons for it. Also, provide evidence from the textbook or other course readings to help support your recommended decision. Be brief!

Decision:

Justification from Research/Theories: Apply any relevant organizational communication research or organizational communication theories you have used to help you make your decision.

_____
_____
_____
_____
_____
_____

Application of the Criteria: In this section, demonstrate how you see the three criteria clearly applying to this decision alternative. Please remember that all three of the criteria should clearly point to this decision alternative.

Justification using Criterion #1:

_____
_____
_____
_____

Justification using Criterion #2:

_____
_____
_____
_____

Justification using Criterion #3:

_____
_____
_____
_____

Risks Associated with the Recommended Alternative: What do you think are the major risks associated with the alternative you have chosen? How will you mitigate the likelihood of these risks turning into crises?

Risk	Mitigation

Decision Alternatives Not Selected Analysis

Non-Selected Alternatives: In this section, you are going to clearly explain why you opted not to choose the other two alternatives. First, you need to make your arguments using both relevant communication research and/or theories. Second, you need to make your argument using the three criteria that you have selected.

Decision Alternative Not Chosen #1:

Justification from Research/Theories: Apply any relevant organizational communication research or organizational communication theories you have used to help you make your decision.

Application of the Criteria: In this section, demonstrate how you see the three criteria clearly applying to this decision alternative. Please remember that all three of the criteria should clearly point to this decision alternative.

Justification using Criterion #1:

Justification using Criterion #2:

_____
_____
_____
_____
_____

Justification using Criterion #3:

_____
_____
_____
_____

Justification from Research/Theories: Apply any relevant organizational communication research or organizational communication theories you have used to help you make your decision.

_____
_____
_____
_____
_____
_____
_____

Application of the Criteria: In this section, demonstrate how you see the three criteria clearly applying to this decision alternative. Please remember that all three of the criteria should clearly point to this decision alternative.

Justification using Criterion #1:

_____
_____
_____
_____

Justification using Criterion #2:

Justification using Criterion #3:

Alternative Implementation

The implementation plan is where you describe how you will carry out your chosen decision alternative within the organization.

Goal(s): What are the basic goals or outcomes that you hope to achieve by implementing your decision alternative? Additionally, based on how you decided to measure your criteria, demonstrate how you will determine if your goals are being met.

Goal #1.

Evaluation of Goal:

Goal #2.

Evaluation of Goal:

Goal #3.

Evaluation of Goal:

Action Steps: Most implementation plans have clear short-term and long-term action steps that need to be taken. What short-term and long-term steps do you feel are necessary to implement completely your chosen decision alternative?

Short-Term Steps
1)
2)
3)
Long-Term Steps
1)
2)
3)

Based on your overall analysis, how confident are you that your chosen decision alternative and implementation plan will solve the communication problem you identified at the beginning of this worksheet?

Not Very Confident	1	2	3	4	5	6	7	8	9	10	Very Confident

Why?